WHOSE NEWS?

By the same author

IPI: THE UNDIVIDED WORD

THE EXPLODING CITIES
with Peter Wilsher

Rosemary Righter

WHOSE NEWS?

Politics, the Press and
the Third World

BURNETT BOOKS
in association with André Deutsch

First published 1978 by Burnett Books Limited
in association with André Deutsch Limited
105 Great Russell Street London WC1

Copyright © 1978 by The International Press Institute
All rights reserved

Printed in Great Britain by Lowe & Brydone Printers Ltd.
Thetford, Norfolk

British Library Cataloguing in Publication Data

Righter, Rosemary
Whose news
1. Title and underdeveloped areas
I. Title
301.15′43′0791812   PN4731

ISBN 0-233-97041-X

CONTENTS

Once, there was a tiger who was king in a great part of the jungle. He proclaimed that no other animals should live in his kingdom, and they all fled, except for one small mouse. For the mouse said to himself that life could be happy in the empty jungle. He would not have to fight other mice for food, and he could move in freedom. And as it proved to be the case, the mouse became more and more cocky, and he began to take walks through the jungle, and soon he was whistling as he walked.

And one day, he met the tiger. How dare you cross my path, and what are you doing in my jungle, asked the tiger, stretching out a menacing paw. Oh my king, said the mouse, let me stay in your jungle, and I will not walk in your way. I go as I please, said the tiger, and how will you know what is my way? But the mouse replied, be assured, oh my king, I will find how not to walk in it.

A few days passed, and the mouse met the tiger again. And the tiger grabbed him in his claws, and said, you are walking in my way, and I will kill you. But the mouse said, I will find a new path, oh king, if you will only spare me. And the tiger let him go. And then, a third time, the mouse met the tiger. And the tiger said, it is as I told you: you will always walk in my way. And the tiger ate the mouse.

Indonesian tale, told by Mochtar Lubis

This book is dedicated to those who live with the Tiger
and do not seek to bargain with him.

PREFACE AND ACKNOWLEDGEMENTS

'Facts are the shadows which statements cast on things', it has been said. Statements about the relationship of the press to the evolving world politics of the end of this century are likely to be shaped by the sensed shadow they cast, rather than on a repetition of 'bare' (unshadowed) facts. The nature of news is changing in two ways. One – which is important, and which the press everywhere faces with much uncertainty and some evasiveness – concerns the extent to which we are more and more concerned with understanding processes: events are increasingly intertwined, less and less possible to present as single and discrete 'facts'. The second is a matter of statement, of politics and ideology; and it casts a long shadow: this is the change of optic, in an increasing number of countries, where politicians pretend that news is what serves society's ends, as they conceive them.

Our picture of the world, in this view, becomes what *raison d'état* dictates that we should discern. This second mutation of the traditional meaning of news has brought the situation of the press – of freedom of expression – to the centre of the political stage. And this is the reason for attempting to give an account of the historical processes which are creating the mutation. We need to understand it, to know how our world will be interpreted to us in the coming decades.

I have used certain 'shorthand' words in this book. The one which most requires prefatory explanation is 'Third World'. I mean it to suggest, quite simply, those countries which do not belong either to the 'Western' grouping of industrialised civilisations which includes the United States and Western Europe, or to the grouping which is generally referred to as the Soviet bloc. The variety of cultures, economic and social systems, and wealth in the Third World needs no emphasis; but one of the curious accompaniments of the growth of political sensitivity in all these countries is the simultaneous assertion, by so many of their political leaders, both of 'Third World solidarity', and of arguments that the term 'Third World' is a pejorative coinage by the post-imperial powers.

I have concentrated principally on the written press. This is for the principal reason that the broadcast media are almost everywhere under governmental control, and the principles of independence therefore assume their full meaning generally only where the written press is involved. But I have also used the term 'press', often, to imply all the news media; just as in the mouths of politicians, government information and the press often merge their meaning, so journalists are often too touchy – the result of old rivalries – about the distinctions between the media which, within their different limitations, carry the news.

In writing a book of this kind there are many forms of obligation. I am particularly indebted to Peter Galliner, Director of the International Press Institute which has sponsored the study with the financial support of the Ford Foundation and the Fritt Ord Foundation of Norway. Peter Galliner and members of his staff have given valuable assistance throughout. The planning, organisation and content of the book are, of course, the author's responsibility. Any conclusions I have drawn are personal, based on the evidence I have accumulated. Any errors of judgement are mine.

I should also thank Harold Evans, Editor of *The Sunday Times*, for giving me leave of absence from the staff, and for his encouragement.

In the course of my research, I have been assisted by a large number of people, not all of whom would wish to be named, who have discussed particular events or issues, or who have indicated sources of material.

At Unesco, I have been grateful for the help of Julian Behrstock, Leon Davico, Asher Deleon, John Fobes, Hamdy Kandil, Makaminan Makagiansar, Pierre Navaux, Jean D'Ormesson, Dr Lakshmana Rao, and Lloyd Sommerlad.

Preface

Some of them have disagreed with my perception of Unesco's work in communications, but have nonetheless—and properly—made material available.

Discussions with members of the International Commission for the Study of Communication Problems – especially with its Chairman, Sean MacBride, but also with Elie Abel, Mochtar Lubis and Michio Nagai – have been extremely valuable.

And among many professional colleagues and academics, I am especially grateful to Stan Swinton and Mort Rosenblum of the AP, H. L. Stevenson and Julius Humi of UPI, Gerald Long and Michael Neale of Reuters, Claude Roussel of AFP; Abdelhakim Belkhiria, Amithaba Chowdhury, Jonathan Fenby, Guido Fernandez, Mohammad Gawad, George Githii, Sven Hamrell, Cushrow Irani, Clement Jones, Masaaki Kasagi, John A. Lent, Ranald MacDonald, Herbert Schiller, Jorgen Schliemann, Leonard Sussman and Mahmoud Triki. I also have a special debt to the late Lester Markel, whose unsentimental but passionate interest in the flow of news through the Third World was in some senses an important point of departure.

Paris, 1978

The News and the Politics

There is a group of words which comes easily – perhaps too easily – to the leader-writer's pen, especially when the subject is the press itself, its role, power, and importance. Words like freedom, independence; progress, individualism; truth, responsibility; identity, democracy; newly-fashionable old-timers like human rights. They may be a little over-used and under-practised, but they represent for most readers a shared and agreed set of values and ideals.

In a large and growing number of countries, where most of the population has neither the means nor the opportunity to read leading articles, governments are asserting that many of these values are not shared or agreed, and that many of the ideals are irreconcileable. The price of independence may be freedom; progress may require the sacrifice of individualism; the truth may appear irresponsible – and responsibility may require the evasion or suppression of truth. National identity may be achieved only by redefining democracy in terms of the 'general will'. And it may be that the leader-writer and his views should be subject to the censor's stamp. The model of society which he exists to defend must give way to a social system in which debate cedes pride of place to the national interest: in the process, truth becomes the 'truth' of a society. If the idea shocks those – in Third World societies and in the West – for whom the universality of these values has been an unquestioned assumption, the proponents of this argument imply that it may be because they find it easier to be horrified by a challenge to such accepted truths than by the unequal world order which, it is alleged, the propagation of those truths helps to perpetuate.

The common denominator of these words, according to those who challenge their place in the moral universe, is that they are cornerstones of an international structure created by the former imperial powers, and still operated in their interest. The words form a mantle of liberalism under which there is imposed on the developing world a pattern of political, economic and cultural dominance. The national institutions which promulgate such values within Third World countries are Western in origin, alien to the countries concerned and actually destructive of their social traditions. Just because institutions such as parliamentary democracy, an independent judiciary or a free press support individual rights and liberties against the powers of the State, this does not mean – say Third World leaders – that they are therefore universally desirable.

One paradox underlying the attack on 'Western' values, is that it is launched in the name of essentially 'Western' ideas – about the rights of states to sovereignty, about self-determination, and about the importance of national identity. All of these were developed in the context of a belief in the primary importance of individual human rights. But in attacking them, Third World leaders argue that human rights, when over three hundred million people still suffer from acute malnutrition and eight hundred million are illiterate, must be seen as essentially corporate and material. Again, they argue that it is more important for their post-colonial societies to find a national voice, than to encourage the assertion of individual identity and the freedoms of dissent.

Freedom, on this reading, is a suspect word. As an ideal for social organisation, it is derided: and Western insistence on the universality of a value developed in the long evolution of Western societies towards open democratic systems is seen as a form of cultural imperialism. Moreover, freedom – whether of the individual, of trade, of cultural exchanges or of the flow of information – is also rejected as a fraud. The concept, it is argued, has simply enabled the rich and powerful to impose their views and their market economies on vulnerable countries, to further the interests of their highly profitable multinational business enterprises, and to subject economic and social development to the requirements of a privileged, Western, minority. Choice, in this view, is merely the freedom of the many to take one of several brands of the wrong medicine. And the medicine must be 'wrong' because it is brewed in an alien culture. These arguments are as persuasive as they are circular.

This book is about an evolving international situation, in which the growth of what might be called the political consciousness of the Third World – for all the immense diversity of the countries which belong to it – has as a common factor a rejection of the ideals of individual opportunity and freedom of choice. One or two things should be clear from the start. The first is that the rejection comes from governments, most of them authoritarian. The second is that there is enough force behind the argument that Western values perpetuate, in practice, a destructively inegalitarian world system to demand serious scrutiny. It is as dangerous to reject out of hand the complaints about economic and cultural dominance as it is to adopt the 'liberal' fallacy of assuming that they have merit just because they come from the Third World. Arrogance distorts the debate, and so does guilt.

An absolutely primary element in this new growth of Third World consciousness is the recognition by the governments of developing countries that it is through the media that consciousness grows. There is a trend towards the collectivisation of human rights, and it focusses directly on the press. Seeking to break the chain of dependence on the developed world, through the creation of alternative economic and social models, policy-makers are making it a cornerstone of national policy to reform the press, to use it for the general good as they perceive it – as a tool which governments use for the task of nation building. In the past, national leaders have argued that their societies are too vulnerable to permit an independent press to operate in freedom. They still use this argument. But much more importantly, they now argue that the Western model of the press is undesirable in itself. Instead of championing the right of the public to make the fullest use of the mediating institutions between their individual rights and the constraints of power, the press should adopt a didactic, even ideological, role, explaining to the people their part in forging a new social order.

It is this new approach which, at national level, alters in a crucial sense the old debate, common to developed and developing countries alike, between government and the press. Essentially, governments now assert that debate itself is not valid; because the press exists to promote national goals. It must therefore support authority, instead of challenging it. At the international level, the new official view of the function of the media has brought home to politicians across the developing world the extent of their dependence on the international press both for the image of their societies which reaches the rest of the world, and for the foreign news circulated in their countries. This international press is dominated, technologically and in terms of manpower and skills, by the Soviet and, above all, the advanced Western countries.

Third World resistance to this domination focusses on the Western-based press – for the obvious reason that Soviet-style news services are widely perceived as a form of propaganda, subservient to political requirements and to a large extent predictable. There are valid complaints about the performance of the international news agencies and the accuracy of Western correspondents. And it is natural for any country to resent the fact that its news is presented to the world by foreigners – however knowledgeable or sympathetic they may be. But the battle for control of the news extends further than that: those who believe in a free press, as a universally applicable ideal, are increasingly aware that the 'remedies' proposed are the remedies of authoritarianism. They will create a model for the media which is fundamentally opposed to the principle of the right to be informed; a model which will harm, first and foremost, the citizens of Third World countries in whose name the 'Western' model is being rejected. If supporting the principle of the free flow of information is 'cultural imperialism', some argue, it is our duty to be 'imperialists'.

How irreconcileable are the two views of the function of the press in society? Disregarding the special pleading on both sides, and the failures of competence, comprehension or interest in the way the existing system works, it is worth sketching out the opposing models, to provide a framework for the political arguments.

The traditional, or 'Western', concept of a free press is based on the premise that an open, democratic society requires a freely-informed public to function effectively. In theory at least, accurate and rapid information is considered the vital hinge between government and governed. The press gathers and sifts the raw material of information which enables people to form their judgements. It informs, it monitors the performance of those in authority, and it 'reminds the powers that be, corrupt and venal as they always are, of the forces they have to control'.

Information is subject to a fairly simplistic definition, limitedly workable in the complexities of industrialised society: 'news' is something which actually happened, and which we learn about for the first time. A free press tells us the 'truth' about an event, representing it as closely as possible in the terms in which it actually happened. It may answer to our need to know about what directly affects us, or just our natural curiosity. To the extent that some events are less simple than the 'man falls from window – did he jump or was he pushed?' variety, the press is expected to report conflicting opinions on matters of common interest. It may also conduct campaigns to arouse public concern over major issues; but its broad task is to provide a world picture which presents the choices, interprets facts and alerts the public to current trends.

In the same spirit, the media monitor government policies, nationally and in their dealings with foreign countries. They may do so from an openly political standpoint, although the pressures to depoliticise the media in the interests of 'objectivity' have been a major feature of postwar journalism. In most countries broadcasting is expected to present a nonpartisan service. In the portentous phrases of a 1946 United Nations resolution, 'Freedom of information . . . requires as a basic discipline the obligation to seek the facts without prejudice and to spread knowledge without malicious intent.'

A free press also acts as 'an indispensable feedback system from governed to the governing, from consumers to producers, from the regions to the centre,' creating a two-way flow of information which reflects minority views as well as the broad sweep of that most elusive element, the 'state of public opinion'. The justification is that the media have the ability to do this better than any other social institution: 'Governments cannot govern well without reliable reporting and criticism. They do not have the knowledge.' That assumption of ability is based partly on their closeness to the ordinary citizen, whose rights they share without exceeding them or claiming a special position, and partly on the social and ethical responsibility placed on them to judge competently and report accurately.

For the essential myth is that these activities are value-neutral, even impersonal: the neutrality of 'the facts' guarantees objectivity, given only the skills to report them fairly and fully. But reality is also interpreted – and here objectivity is presumably ensured by the absence of 'malicious intent'. And reality is selected.

This is where 'objectivity' fits together with other features such as the public's desire for information. This desire can show itself randomly, in the spirit of enquiry of Dante's Ulysses (or Carrolls' Alice), or because the reader's interest has been stimulated by something in what he already knows which points directly towards what he doesn't (which made *The Washington Post* during Watergate the world's most quoted newspaper).

The symbiosis between public and press is shaped in the marketplace, where the press, guardian of the people's rights, competes through its credibility (and its ability to entertain) for the public's confidence (and purchasing power). And also through its sensitivity to public taste: 'what' and 'how much' are both regulatory factors. (So is the question of how much we are prepared to pay, and whether we have the right coin; but theory assumes means which experience may or may not provide.) The public chooses, even if its most evident power is negative – cancelling subscriptions, 'giving up the papers', pushing the off-button. And this emphasis on plurality of sources reflects an attitude to freedom of choice which is important, whatever the limitations on its expression, because the audience is respected by the press as is the voter by the candidate in a liberal democracy. And this informs the social, cultural, economic and educational foundations of the media: they represent a world of many voices, and one of the West's deepest values is that this is so.

A sketch of Third World news values must inevitably be still more blurred, partly because governments' recognition that information can be used as a national resource is recent, partly because there are profound differences between some journalists and their governments on the role of the press, even where both agree that some new and distinctive model is needed. Journalists have argued that a double standard is impossible, that there is no comfortable half-way between a free press and a press in the service of government – and that no government can claim a monopoly of judgement as to the meaning of 'constructive'. It is a measure of the politicisation of the debate that they have often been branded proxy Westerners and elitists.

But certain features are clear enough. The basic premise is that news is a national resource and must serve the development process through the mobilisation of public opinion. There is no such thing as a neutral fact. The least fragment of information conveyed has an intentional element – all news is from someone to someone. 'Information,' says a Third World leader, 'is a double-edged weapon: used well, it can only be beneficial, used badly it can spell catastrophe for the country.' Information thus becomes a property of the state: the link between governing and governed works from the top down.

It is not enough for the media simply to focus on subjects of immediate concern to developing societies – even positively, reporting that literacy is climbing or food production improving in a certain province. Education in its active, persuasive sense is the primary task of the media. This implies, naturally, that there must be adequate coverage of official speeches: the people must be fully and thoroughly informed of their government's views. This is as natural as it is necessary: 'the government is the guarantor of stability, and security; and it is also the main catalyst for development, the entrepreneur responsible for the vast proportion of investment. If one accepts that role, it must be given the fullest opportunity to muster community support through the media.'

In this new approach to communications, Third World leaders argue that the Western world's journalists are subject to the *déformation professionelle* implicit in a market system. News is selected in accordance with what will sell more of the *Daily Beast*, sensationalism abounds and reporting reflects the public taste for entertainment and the habit of the 'bad news syndrome'. They cannot therefore speak to the developing world in other than an alien voice – even if the international press were prepared to make the imaginative effort to try to do so. National self-reliance, and the retraining of Third World journalists to a new format, are therefore essential. Domestic policies along these lines should be combined with cooperation between developing countries to exchange news of their mutual achievements. News will thus be genuinely free – free of external domination, free of alien values, free to promote the interests of society as a whole.

To some extent, each of these sketches is a misleading fiction; and the lines between the two views of the role of the press are not quite so clearcut as they suggest. Western media do exert influence, and set an 'agenda for society'; in the era of crusading journalism, few editors wholly repudiate the missionary element, the educative function. But it is still true that 'something happened' and that to that extent reporting is value-free however much it may also be true that it was reported by someone for someone. On the other side, 'nation-building' journalism does not automatically mean a controlled press, though it in practice it operates in that context. And some of those – mostly journalists or professionals rather than politicians – who agree with the need to change the international system and to 'decolonise' information are still uneasy when they hear approving voices from the East describing the new policy as 'a solution oriented to national needs and real possibilities in the interest of building an anti-imperialist order.'

But traditionally, the Western 'liberal' approach is accepted as non-ideological, matter-of-fact. It has dominated the media for the last century; and it is held with great tenacity by Westerners to be a model for all free societies. The second is overtly ideological, shaped to a concept of society rather than arising out of accumulated practice. In its own terms, the model is evangelical, purposive. Whether governments own the media is probably secondary to the major issue: to whom does the right to information belong? Should developing societies be protected and guided, or should the public discern the truth through a multiplicity of voices and opinions? Which serves development best and strengthens cultural identity?

To many Third World politicians, even the posing of such questions reflects not only the failure of the Western imagination to understand their societies – thus making their case from the start – but the inability of the industrialised countries to accept that the revolution in communications is central to the shift in international politics implied by the call for a New International Economic Order. As the governments of the Non-Aligned movement expressed it at their Fifth Summit, at Colombo in August 1976, 'the emancipation and development of national communications media is an integral part of the overall struggle for political, economic and social independence for a vast majority of peoples of the world who should not be denied the right to inform and be informed objectively and correctly.'

This is where the two models clash: essentially different views of society produce largely irreconcilable concepts of the place of the media within it; 'objectively and correctly' mean different things. But the Third World is in search, internationally as well as nationally, of a distinctive voice: its governments insist that the superior power of the West to make itself heard must be challenged. And because the dominant Western media have stressed freedom of information as a primary value, that concept is being rejected along with the structure of the international press.

There is an urgent need to look at these issues coolly. Some of those who attack the existing system use valid arguments about its shortcomings, and about the imbalance in the international flow of information. Some who defend it – in the name of vitally important moral issues – are in reality too unimaginative to see beyond a narrow defence of a *status quo* of whose virtues not everybody is convinced. There are conflicts between the sympathies which many Third World complaints should arouse, and the natural wariness as to the implications for thought control contained in the model of journalism which has the declared purpose of supporting national unity and development. Unthinking rejection of the case against the West will be harmful, possibly accelerating cultural protectionism and reinforcing the barriers to information which are already in the making. Even where the arguments are shot through with logical contradictions, or being used as an excuse for tighter

Introduction

political control, it is important to recognise that they are being used to make policy, present and future. And that there is an organised campaign under way – through supra-national agencies like Unesco, in inter-governmental groupings, and in a number of academic and quasi-political institutions – to give the concept of a guided press international respectability.

The campaign takes much of its strength from the slow progress towards a more equitable international economic order. As the West drags its feet over the North–South 'dialogue', ideological bitterness mounts. Some experts believe that the ideological gap between South and North now threatens the prospects for negotiated change even more than the physical problems of economic disparities which gave rise to the dialogue in the first place. Frustrated Third World governments become increasingly united in their rejection of Western economic models. And with the search for alternative forms of development, and for self-reliance, goes a steadily more marked rejection of Western social and moral values. 'Interdependence' is giving way to emphasis on 'diversity'. And diversity often means the very opposite of pluralism – a cultural nationalism in which government-regulated 'national perspectives' have a monopoly. Ironically, these monopolies are being created in the name of a struggle against the monopoly of the international media. In the sense that communications are perceived in the Third World as an important means of realising new political and economic goals, the issue of the freedom and independence of the press – its freedom to protect essentially 'Western' values – is moving to the centre of the international political arena. In a real sense, the otherwise variegated and often mutually hostile governments of the Third World are united in putting the Western press on trial.

CHAPTER 1

The Challenge to the West

The Third World's attack on the established international media is based on three main arguments. The media are too powerful – they penetrate too widely and effectively. They represent an alien viewpoint, which they impress on nations trying to build an independent, modern identity. And they lack the attributes – of accuracy and objectivity, for example – on which they have based their claims to pre-eminence.

On all these grounds – and the emphasis varies with the politics of the challengers – the commitment to the freedom to transmit information regardless of frontiers is being dismissed as at best outdated (belonging, they said at Unesco's 1974 General Conference, 'to the nineteenth century') and at worst a fraud, a smokescreen for the continuing Western monopoly of the world's information networks. International understanding, and a new world order, require that this monopoly be broken. On the one hand, there must be co-ordinated efforts by Third World countries to counterbalance the volume of news flowing from the industrialised centres to the rest of the world. On the other, there must be radical changes in the criteria by which the content of the news is selected. In place of the established order, there is need for a 'balanced' flow of news – balanced to reflect national priorities in the countries to which two-thirds of humanity belongs. Freedom of expression, freedom to publish, may well be inscribed in the Charter of the United Nations and the Constitution of Unesco, and embodied in the Universal Declaration of Human Rights; but this, it is said, simply reflects post-war

Western hegemony. The linking of human rights to the free flow of information has in practice simply given *carte blanche* to those best supplied with the means to make themselves heard. Freedom of information must imply freedom for all; and human rights themselves should be placed in the context of an international order which rejects post-imperial dominance. In other words the Third World's case rests, ultimately, on a belief that the traditional definition of 'human rights' needs to be radically modified in the light of their national 'realities'.

Inevitably the accusations are filled with contradictions and paradoxes. Demands that the Western media improve their performance, particularly in their reporting of the Third World, are made in the same breath as demands that they should execute something of a withdrawal, making space for other viewpoints, other voices and other cultural perspectives, as expressed through the national news agencies of the developing countries. The international media are under attack both for their success in penetrating world markets, and for their failures to provide a truly international service. And the accusations are also heavy with political rhetoric; after all, Dr A. T. Ibrahimi, Algeria's Minister for Education and Culture, reminds us, 'the end of dependence in information is primarily a political act.'

Naturally, too, the fiercest critics are generally governments, some of whose members are using the language of cultural emancipation to increase state control and to silence both political opposition and awkward minority viewpoints. Many quite openly assert that they do not believe in the value of free speech. But none of these factors lessens the need to understand the nature of the dissatisfactions and the political and social forces behind the accusations. Support for a New Order for Information – the rather vague title which expresses for many Third World governments and their supporters the essence of their challenge to the existing structures and content of information – is growing, and it runs deeper than showcase politics. The call for change unites governments of strikingly different political persuasions. Above all, the accusations take their force from an element of truth.

They are principally directed at the four main news agencies of the Western world – the Associated Press and United Press

International in the US, Agence France Presse and the British agency, Reuters. Tass, the equally large Soviet agency, is seldom grouped with them, presumably because few even among the most radical of the Third World's leaders think of it as a 'news agency' in the same sense – if its aims are widely perceived to be persuasion rather than information, its influence is to that extent limited. (Tass, which has 325 foreign subscribers as against 13,000 in the USSR, formally describes the aim of its World Distribution Service in these terms – 'to systematically explain to foreign readers the peaceloving foreign policy of the CPSU and the Soviet Government . . . disseminate information about the achievements of real socialism in economy, science and culture, publicise the Soviet way of life, expose the concoctions and slander of bourgeois ideology . . .')

The 'Big Four', on the other hand claim to provide a world news service, guided only by the interests of their subscribers and limited by no purely 'national' viewpoints. And the emerging countries of the Third World, whatever their political leanings, are forced, for lack of alternatives, to rely on the 'Big Four' and on overseas radio services for world, regional and sometimes even national news.

Second in the line of fire are the international news magazines – *Time* and *Newsweek* above all – and the Western press. Pressures are also slowly building up against the exports by the industrialised countries of television programmes, largely because of fears about the difficulty of controlling their content which the prospect of direct broadcasting by satellite has aroused. But the arguments still centre on the written media, and particularly those which transmit news across international frontiers.

To send a cable from Lome to Accra, a mere one hundred and fifty miles away, takes around forty-eight hours while the message is routed through Paris to London and back to West Africa. The distance, a Ghanaian editor points out, could be covered faster by a runner. Throughout the world, it is easy to chart the old colonial patterns of influence by reference to the telecommunications grid and, although two satellites over Africa could solve most problems of the Lome–Accra variety, satellites are not only prohibitively costly but – to many countries –

raise fresh fears that the dominance of the industrialised countries will be still further increased by means of the new technology.

Past imperialism and present financial and technical power form, it is felt, a linked chain which shackles national independence in the impoverished Third World. And the international news agencies – whose daily budget exceeds the annual outlay on communications of many small countries – symbolise not only the imbalance in the flow of information, but the dominance in the economic, political and technical spheres of the industrialised powers. The agencies still provide effectively the only means for developing countries to be in touch with the rest of the world. Seen from the perspective of Third World politicians, the 'free flow' of the news is a system for perpetuating an already overwhelming advantage, whereby – as they noted at the 1976 New Delhi conference of the non-aligned countries on communications policy – 'the great majority of countries are reduced to being passive recipients of information which is disseminated from a few centres.'

The basic resentments, then, begin with the fact of dominance – the clear imbalance in the flow of information which so favours the North. An imbalance of resources which means, among other things, that in the non-aligned countries (who are not the biggest importers) 65 % of television and radio programmes come from abroad. In country after country, four fifths of world news in the national press is credited to one or more international agency. The *New York Times* features service is taken in around fifty countries; AFP reaches clients in 147 countries and uses four languages, Reuters has buyers in 153, and uses six languages; and AP and UPI, who between them provide the bulk of foreign news material in Latin America, have clients in 110 and 114 countries respectively. All four reach their customers with the help of the latest in video-editing and other new technologies, provide the basis for the news programme schedules of radio and television, and are in the vanguard of telecommunications research.

Seen from the Western angle, the fact that they are so widely used is both a tribute to the quality of their service – and to their reputation for neutrality and accuracy. Seen from the receiving end, it is a tribute to the persistence of neo-colonialist patterns of power. The agencies are believed to set 'the international political agenda'; and, with more truth, to define the international criteria for news. And their power to influence, to 'make the news', is widely considered to give them an unwarranted monopoly regardless of the content of the messages conveyed.

The simple fact of a 'hegemony founded on financial, industrial, cultural and technological power, maintaining most Third World countries in a state of chronic dependence', is intolerable to Mahmoud Triki, head of Tunisia's national agency Tunis-Afrique-Presse. Triki is a user of the big agencies' services, and professional in his recognition of the short-comings of Third World alternatives to date. A liberal among Third World spokesmen on the media, he seeks new forms of cooperation based on greater mutual respect. The existing system is still more intolerable to national leaders. And politicians used to controlling their own media find it inconceivable that these powers are not used, and used for the malign ends of superpower politics. A fine example of this kind of thinking is offered by a distinguished Argentinian editor, Raul Kraiselburd. After all the detailed reporting of the US agencies on the Watergate affair had circulated in Latin America, he records with a certain irony, 'many people here believed that the Pentagon had decided to dismiss Nixon and used *The Washington Post* for it.' It is a reminder of the assumptions in an increasing number of countries about the links between the press and national power structures.

From the fact of power to its uses, real and imaginary, is thus a short step. The international media are widely believed to buttress – intentionally – two aspects of Western dominance: its historical, political and economic influence, and the capitalist philosophy which buttresses it and which, to many, is symbolised by the multinational corporation. This is a conspiracy theory which works by analogy. Those who know how information is manufactured in their world, assume that this is how it works outside. The fact that the theorists so readily associate the press with political power-structures is not encouraging. The 'alternative' structure is likely to incorporate machinery to ensure that this is the way the national media work in future.

The wilder accusations assert that AFP is owned by the

French government (it is certainly heavily subsidised, but there is a distinction); that Reuters is covertly subsidised and influenced by the British government or – the alternative thesis – MI–6; and that AP and UPI are extensions of the State Department. Since the revelations of the CIA's use of American journalists overseas, the US agencies are liable also to be branded as a wing of intelligence.

A point-by-point refutation, even if accepted, would produce among many Third World politicians (and some academics) the argument that details are irrelevant. Just as the communications networks were built to serve colonial interests in the nineteenth century (largely but not wholly true), so 'most of the gigantic press and media agencies located in the advanced countries are the by-products of the political power these countries have exercised . . . [as] a basis for commercial and political exploitation.' This particular formulation comes from Mohammad Yunus, head of the government news agency Samachar during the Indian State of Emergency, and one of Mrs Gandhi's chief helpers in creating an 'orderly' press in India; but it could have come from politicians with more open and moderate views – who would still agree that the Western media were and are tools of the political process.

At this general level, it is possible to produce chapter and verse – particularly if you go back before World War II. Sir Roderick Jones, then Chairman of Reuters, addressed an audience of journalists in 1930 on Reuters' performance and purposes. 'In the Far East', he said, 'Reuters services have existed for the last sixty years . . . no other single factor . . . has contributed more in those sixty years to the maintenance of British prestige . . . I do not think there is any other factor that has been consistently working directly and indirectly throughout that period with such effect for the advancement of British influence.'

It is possible, of course, to reply that the BBC has also done much for British standing, simply by the reputation it has built, and largely deserved, for honest and full reporting. But Sir Roderick is explicit: 'working directly and indirectly . . . for the advancement of British influence', however you go about it, is a political activity. And the point is sharpened by reference to the American view, between the wars, of the cartels then formed between the principal European agencies, Reuters, Havas and Wolff. Today's critics of the agencies, from the US Marxist writer on communications, Professor Herbert Schiller, to some of the Unesco officials most closely concerned with communications policy, quote extensively from *Barriers Down*, the account by the AP's Kent Cooper of the struggle by his agency to break the European cartel. Although Schiller doesn't emphasise it, Cooper's autobiography burns with an almost embarrassingly evangelical zeal for the 'free flow of information'. But the nature of the complaints against the established agencies of the time otherwise parallel modern demands in many ways.

Reuters' position was made possible by British power and technology – notably in the British near-monopoly of the cable networks. Reuters used it, Cooper claimed, to denigrate the US in reporting American news to the world: 'It told the world about the Indians on the warpath in the West, lynchings in the South and bizarre crimes in the North . . . nothing creditable to America ever was sent' over the wires. The cartel, Reuters and Havas, governing the two Americas, also often ignored important news and played up the 'good news' reaching America from their own countries.

Cooper fought a long and determined battle to break the cartel, into which the AP had bound itself by an 1890's news exchange agreement with Reuters, so that world news might be freed of 'government influence': the truly independent standing of AP, he insisted, would ensure a genuinely free flow of information. A new agreement, based on a policy of free exchange of international news, was signed by AP and Reuters in 1934. And ten years later, as Schiller notes, the situation was reversed; he quotes the tart reaction of *The Economist*, in 1944, to Cooper's campaign: '(he) experiences a pecular moral glow in finding that his idea of freedom coincides with his commercial advantage. . . . Democracy does not necessarily mean making the whole world safe for the AP.' The article expressed the fear that the huge resources of which the US agencies now disposed would enable them to dominate the world. Thirty years later, criticism of the agencies' performance also emphasises the commercial links more than the political – a change from the inter-war period which is nonetheless not surprising, since much of the criticism comes from countries which assert that government ownership of the media need not affect the media's independence. But commerce is simply seen as the long, crooked arm of politics; the media are the servants of both. The 'free flow of information', as practised by the Western 'monopolies' is decried as a form of *laisser-faire* trading which enables the strong to assert their will; it is often compared to the 'Open Door' policies of post-war America. As such, information is both a commodity (which can be subject to the same protectionist measures as butter or bicycles), and a metaphor for the untrammelled exercise of the Western will to dominate.

Before the actual performance of the international media comes under attack, then, they attract increasing hostility because they are assumed to reflect by their very existence and omnipresence the political and commercial interests of the countries in which their headquarters are found. Paradoxically, the *better* they do their job, the smaller the room on stage for the rest of the cast, and the more open they are to accusations of this kind.

Aside from the resentments and suspicions which their size – their quantitative domination of the news-flow – arouses, they are under more sharply focussed attack where the actual content of the messages is concerned. Their selection of the news, the argument runs, is entirely shaped by their home markets or by 'the values, perspectives and personalities of the transnational culture'. This catches the agencies either way: they look too carefully inwards; or they project their 'transnational' values (and they are assumed to have a coherent set of them) onto the helpless world. They set the 'international agenda' according to markets, cultures and economies which are 'alien' to the Third World, in a *déformation structurelle* which seriously distorts our ability to see the world scene steadily and whole.

In measured language, which nonetheless casts the net as wide as possible, Amadou Mahtar M'Bow, Senegalese Director-General of Unesco, accuses the international media of so operating to protect the *status quo* that they damage cultural and economic life and impinge on the collective rights of nations to their sovereignty. In the 1976 book *Moving Towards Change*, which sets out Unesco's public stance on the New International Economic Order, he offers a modern version of Cooper's anti-monopoly crusade:

> Operating on a world-wide scale, some information agencies – most of which have their headquarters in the industrialised countries – have, by reason of their equipment and capital, acquired a position of strength which probably enables them to offer better services but also leads them to convey one-way information reflecting the point of view of those countries, and which, above all, allows them to dominate the information market to an extent which borders on cultural aggression. Only a few powerful countries and – what is more serious – a few transnational companies are in a position to control both the production of infrastructures and the transmission of programmes. This *de facto* monopoly is opposed to the establishment of a new international economic order.

There are several points worth making. The first is that M'Bow clearly intends us to understand that even if the agencies 'offer better services', their domination of the information market – the *news* market – amounts to *cultural* aggression. Not because what they say is not true (although he suggests that it can hardly be the whole truth) but because so few say it.

The second is that he firmly equates the international agencies with transnational companies – with the strong implication that the profit motive predominates over any other. The financial structures of the agencies will be discussed in the next chapter; but it is a curious irony that those who attack the agencies as subsidised tools of government and extensions of their political will (as M'Bow does not outrightly do, though he claims that they reflect the point of view of their 'home' countries), also accuse them of being uncontrolled, freebooting international profit-seekers, battening off the sorrows and disasters of the underdeveloped world. These two conspiracy theories, both fashionable, are difficult to reconcile with each other.

The final point is the incompatibility, in M'Bow's mind, of the continued pre-eminence of the agencies with the introduction of a New International Economic Order. In other words, they report the news in such a way as to further the interests of the Western consumer and industrialist. Their international news service is thus an extension of imperialism. Venezuela, an oil-producing country, will obtain information dealing with oil markets not merely from agencies based in consumer countries, but expressing those countries' interests.

M'Bow has said elsewhere that the news agencies use their 'virtual monopoly' to select news which 'systematically stresses the phenomena of tension or violence in the countries of the Third World ... those agencies keep silence on events of a positive nature ...' with the result that developing countries 'see their faces reflected from afar in mirrors that deform them'. Such distorted reporting risks 'seriously imperilling inter-national understanding' – and inhibits the efforts of Third World countries to act together 'for a new and more equitable order'.

These convictions are widely-shared, although the language differs. To begin with, the structure of the Western press is suspect: a free press is easily equated with a caricature of free-market capitalism. As another Unesco official puts it, 'in the West, communications is shaped in the hands of the giant transnationals and the journalist is part of the establishment. What comes across is what NBC finds acceptable and not what the journalist who gathered the story may actually believe.' The institution operates within a commercial framework which is assumed to be *de facto* subject to the pressures of powerful lobbies and political interests. The individual becomes sub-ordinated to the institution, and objective reporting in such circumstances is a mirage (or a cynical pretence). This does not prevent the individual foreign correspondent from being treated by Third World governments as though what appeared were his responsibility alone; but there is an assumption of *mauvaise foi* on the part of the agencies (and other international media) underlying the increasingly intolerant attitude to their representatives.

One of the most prevalent fictions is the 'nationalism' of the agencies. An Indian journalist, Narinder Aggarwala, claims that 'except for a few stringers and second-level reporters and sub-editors,' all the staff of the 'Big Four' agencies are either American, British or French. On the international side, he is mistaken; AP's 'few' stringers and reporters outnumber its American foreign staff eight to one and the proportion is six to one where fulltime correspondents are concerned. Of 559 on AP's journalistic staff abroad, 478 are non-Americans. UPI, in a formal report to Unesco in 1978, pointed out that the entire staff of its Latin American desk in New York was Latin American, as were one of the two top staff in every UPI bureau in that region. More than half the bureau managers in Asia were Asian, and in Europe they included eight nationalities. The chief editor of its International Desk was British – and most bureau staffs and stringers were 'nationals of the country in which they work'.

But this point is less interesting than Aggarwala's second claim: which is that however many 'foreigners' the agencies employed, it would make no difference because they would 'become conditioned to writing news with primarily a Western audience in mind.' The 'orientation' thus produced, Aggarwala insists, is what the developing countries' leaders object to in decrying the 'one-way' flow of news. 'They do not mean that the developed countries are not getting any news from the developing countries or vice versa ... Third World countries want to establish a counter-flow of world news with Third World perspective.'

In what would the difference consist? Aggarwala suggests that accusations that Western (or Western-employed) journalists have an 'alien' perspective which produces bias and distortion, do not imply that Third World leaders are generally 'questioning the factual accuracy of Western news agencies or the honesty of their correspondents.' The problem is apparently in the selection of news: it will correspond to the interest it may arouse in industrialised countries, rather than to the 'information needs' of the Third World.

How systematic is the selectivity process? Everol Hossein, Director of the Institute of Mass Communications of the University of the West Indies, points to the hostility aroused in the US by the support shown for Fidel Castro by Jamaica's Prime Minister, Michael Manley. What followed, he says, were 'negative' reports, or total neglect, by the American media – until a new day dawned with the announcement in 1977 by President Carter of a new Caribbean policy. Suddenly, both the volume and the approach of reporting changed. But Hossein does not suggest a conspiracy either of silence or of propaganda: what happened, he suggests, is that Jamaica was largely forgotten, until American policy awakened a fresh interest. And, he adds, the more balanced nature of the coverage could have something to do with the fact that, in the interim, the Jamaican government had started to activate its press office.

In reporting the Third World, claims one of its senior diplomats, 'it is the duty of the foreign correspondent to report news which seems important to us, his host country, whether or not that news assumes the same importance for him. He must take our news, as we see it; why otherwise should we accept and print the West's view of itself?' Threatening language, the language of isolationism. And also, too easily, the language of censorship. But in all sorts of minor ways, the 'Western perspective' can distort. A foreign correspondent may see, in the delapidated doors and shutters of an African country, the signs of economic chaos – whereas, if he knew that a country short of foreign exchange which does not manufacture paint had simply decided to spend its resources on something more urgent, he might have written a story about centralised economic planning. Even a highly-experienced journalist like David Bonavia, who had been the London *Times*' correspondent in Peking, could end an otherwise knowledgeable and perceptive description in *The Sunday Times* of China's eleventh Party Congress in 1977 by including, in a list of China's major social and economic problems, the lack of secondary education facilities. It does not take a sycophant to recognise that China's achievement in primary education is extraordinary; or a development specialist to point out that a marked expansion at this stage in secondary education could aggravate China's struggle against accelerating rural-urban migration. Secondary education is a measure of well-being in the developed countries; it is not necessarily one – certainly not in the same league as controlling population growth or developing health services – in the Third World.

But the gravest charge against the agencies' selection processes is linked to their neglect of whole geographical areas, or of issues which – like the financial crisis sharpened by the 1973 increase in oil prices – have been largely resolved in the industrialised countries yet remain acute, and insoluble, problems for the developing world. And part of the difficulty here is that many of the issues which most acutely concern the Third World are not readily perceived as 'news-worthy' by Western-trained journalists: they did not begin to matter yesterday, and there will be no solutions tomorrow. A cholera outbreak is news. It is more difficult for a correspondent to explain to his news editor why the world needs an article on endemic diseases such as river-blindness.

The 'Western perspective' produces other lacunae. When in the summer of 1973, the Watergate drama reached its climax, *Newsweek* feverishly cabled its bureaus round the world for 'reaction pieces'. Head office may have had better luck elsewhere, but the reporters and stringers trying to file from Asia had a dreadful time of it attempting to coax a reaction out of the region's elite who were either totally indifferent; or considered that, if the US were in the least efficiently run, no such revelations would have been permitted to surface; or were quite simply unable to see why Nixon's involvement in a bit of intelligence-gathering about his political opponents could be a cause for his resignation.

Perhaps, Raul Kraiselburd indicates – with a touch of irony – the fault lay with the agencies for failing to illuminate certain aspects as the story unfolded: 'it was never explained . . . why it was so grave that the President did not pay taxes when this happens to be a common practice in Latin America; or what was the crime of bugging a telephone when in many of our countries it is an everyday affair. Day after day we missed the explanations for events which might seem clear in New York, but were . . . comic or absurd in our countries. Nobody explained what the First Amendment of the Constitution of the United States says, or what is the reason for the belief that a newspaper will not be closed down or its editor killed. . . . They never understood that their story was not comprehensible, or seemed a work of fiction, in Latin American countries. . . . Cables arrived quickly and told the truth, but a deeper explanation was missing. . . .'

'If this [one-way flow] is neo-colonialism', observes Richard Hoggart, who was an Assistant Director-General of Unesco from 1970 to 1975, 'it is often of a kind which desperately sells short the coloniser ... as an open democracy the USA makes an exceptional practice of washing her dirty linen in public (a quality which some other countries find impossible to understand, and so take as a true picture of the pattern of American life)'.

Third World politicians who talk seriously about 'decolonising' information are also convinced that the news which reaches them from the West imposes values and creates demands which damage their societies – whether it is the number of cars per Scandinavian household published in a country where even a bicycle is a luxury, or a blow-by-blow account of a celebrity divorce circulating in a strict Islamic society. Acknowledging the grounds for their hostility to the Western model (although questioning the proposed remedies) the foreign editor of the *Journal de Genève*, Antoine Bosshard, wrote at the time of the 1976 New Delhi conference that 'the reproaches against the Western press ... are entirely natural. Made for and by Westerners, the news transmitted by the major international agencies invariably carries ideas, interests and prejudices to the poor countries which are exclusively Occidental.' Is it a problem of perspective, or deliberate distortion, which makes the Western media describe the rise in the price of one of the major exports of some Third World countries as a 'coffee crisis'? or fail to remind their readers and viewers, horrified by the 1973 decision on oil prices by the OPEC countries, that nasty as it all undoubtedly would be, the price had after all been static for a couple of decades?

The favoured example – it comes up in seminar after seminar from Third World speakers – also reaches back a few years, to a UPI dispatch of 27 February 1974. Datelined New York, it runs:

A meeting of a number of the main bauxite-producing countries, scheduled tentatively for March 5 in Conakri [Guinea], has caused understandable concern in Washington. Some experts feel that the conference could be the first step in the establishment of a series of international cartels for controlling raw materials essential to the industrialised nations, which could set the United States' economy back more than 40 years.

As Manuel Perez-Guerrero, the Venezuelan Minister of State who was co-Chairman of the Paris Conference on International Economic Cooperation, has pointed out, the assumptions behind such reporting have helped perpetuate a climate in which prices for the West's manufactures are fixed, and those for raw materials – which may constitute some countries' sole export earnings – are 'negotiable'.

There is a tendency, of course, on the part of the agencies' critics, to cling to certain clichés – to assert, for example, that a similar meeting of industrialised countries would be described by UPI as a meeting to reintroduce orderly marketing conditions. The Congressional Subcommittee looking into an uranium cartel formed by French, Canadian, South African, British and US companies was widely reported in the summer of 1977, and other examples could be found to balance the claim that the agencies adopt one language for the rich and another for the poor countries. But the bias of the 1974 UPI report is still unmistakeable. And the agencies' normal defence – that such items would be treated differently on the 'regional' wire and that the US file would naturally be directed to US interests – strengthens the Third World argument that they must be able to reach the industrialised world direct, with their own version, if 'distortions' are to be avoided.

To the sins of prejudice and cultural bias, the international media add the sin of neglect and indifference. The news from the industrialised countries forms the bulk of the total traffic. Mustapha Masmoudi, Tunisia's Secretary of State for Information who also coordinates the intergovernmental group of the non-aligned countries seeking to establish a new order for information, charges that only 10 % to 30 % of the international news-flow relates to the Third World.

This can only be an educated guess, drawn from samples of the 'world' services of the international agencies and those intended for Northern markets; it almost certainly fails to take regional services into account. And it is also characteristic of most such statistics that the news agencies are attacked for failing to carry material on the basis of what actually appears in the world's press – which only uses a fraction of the news items supplied. But in general terms, Masmoudi's complaint is fair enough; it *is* easier for a Pakistani to learn about events in London than in Tehran or Kabul; and the Western public remains appallingly under-informed about developing countries and their problems.

Targets can be ill-chosen. Masmoudi, again, indignantly told an audience of French officials in the summer of 1977 that 'at a time when they are moving heaven and earth to prevent the extermination of baby seals, it is revolting that there is not a word [in the media] about the fate of babies – human, this time – dying each day in Africa, Asia and elsewhere through malnutrition and other childhood illnesses.'

This is the kind of thinking that doesn't help. It is hardly fair to insist that every time the *Daily Mirror* writes about seals, it ought to check whether it is giving enough space to babies. And it also misses the point. There is a fair degree of public awareness in the West of the bare facts of starvation and malnutrition in the Third World. But there is much less understanding of the underlying social, economic and political ills which produce the situation. And one difficulty with reports which attempt to analyse the underlying causes is that if they touch on the domestic (as opposed to the international) causes of poverty or hunger, they are likely to be criticised as 'negative'. It is true, nonetheless, that too little is written for the public of the industrialised countries about the Third World's failures or successes in fighting hunger, poverty and illiteracy.

The agencies, inevitably but unfairly, take the brunt of the blame for the fact that worldwide, in the South as well as the North, limited space is allocated to foreign news - and the less space, the further away the country is. But the situation is aggravated, where the Third World is concerned, by a concentration - again worldwide - on the traditional centres of of power. By current criteria, a Libyan journalist told a Unesco meeting in Florence on the 'free and balanced flow of information', the developing countries must recognise that the rich world was simply more headline-worthy, and that 'the voice of our countries does not reach, and if it reaches, is not heard in the roar of progress of the developed world'. Countries fortunate enough to escape a *coup d'état*, a major natural disaster or a hijacking incident may vanish from the media of their neighbours and of the industrialised countries for months on end.

If the excuse for this failure to inform is that the people of industrialised countries are not interested, the Third World argument runs, it is inadequate. The job of the press is, put simply, to demonstrate to their public that international news is not remote, not foreign, but intimately concerns them and their immediate interests. The failure of the media is therefore a professional as well as a moral one. Developing countries' politicians are demanding both more coverage of their affairs by the international media, and – because even then they recognise that, whatever Mark Twain said about the AP, 'the agencies are not the sun and cannot cover the whole world' – access by their own media to the world market.

The urgency behind the complaints of neglect by the international media is directly related to the call for a New International Economic Order. Four years after the Sixth Special Session of the United Nations set out the principles for an order which, it was intended, would change a world in which a quarter of the population enjoyed more than two-thirds of the global income, negotiations to effect a redistribution of wealth and the creation of economic opportunity for the Third World had made little progress.

The message of the new order, the Commonwealth Secretary-General Sir Shridath Ramphal told a 1976 conference in Algiers which reviewed the Tinbergen report,* 'must reach the many ordinary citizens whose instinct of goodness tells them that the present system does not serve their own countries well and who are searching for the values of a just global society . . . and ways must be devised to ensure that [it] reaches them in terms they understand – using all the presentational and saturation techniques which the industrialised world has perfected, and which are now employed to propagate the old order and resist the new.'

This implies, of course, a demand not just for more reporting of the Third World, but for a special, committed kind of reporting which some Westerners would class as propaganda. The language in which coverage is described – the coverage that 'ought' to exist – often has heavy overtones of a purely political kind. But it is reasonable to suggest that reporting of the

* *Reshaping the International Order*, ed Jan Tinbergen, 1975

Third World, if it is ever to be independent and broad of vision, must include information about the struggle to realign the economic system, and the reasons for the struggle from a Third World perspective.

Part of the problem is that Western audiences start from a considerable degree of ignorance about existing circumstances and conditions of life in developing countries. Few who heard of the Lima Declaration of 1974 on industrialisation probably realised that, at that time, the Third World was responsible for only 8 % of the world's industrial production; fewer were well enough informed to be able to judge of the degree of realism (or of justice) in the demand that by the year 2000, the proportion should reach 25 %; fewer still to guess at the implications for their own jobs which such a revision of the international division of labour would involve, or for the economic situation of the Third World should such a target fail for any set of reasons to be reached.

Third World leaders appear remarkably convinced that, if only the public of the industrialised countries were properly and fully informed of the implications of a new economic order, they would rush to lobby their governments for its implementation. The thesis has yet to be tested; they might just as well take fright. But even to begin to undertake such a task, the international media would not only have to increase the quantity of Third World news in their total files, but to change – even without committing themselves to 'missionary journalism' – the criteria by which news is selected, and the assumptions they hold about their audiences. The Third World is demanding no less.

How do these goals square with what the Third World perceives as the present attitude of the mass media? Very ill, by all accounts. Where they do not ignore developing countries altogether, both the agencies and foreign correspondents of national media are accused of focussing only on coups and disasters. These accusations do not only come from governments. Peter Lim, Editor of the *New Nation* in Singapore, who went out of his way to insist at the 1977 Commonwealth Press Union Conference that the Western agencies still commanded considerable respect in Asia for 'the scope and the competence of their news coverage', added that therefore, the Western media has a special responsibility to inform not only the public of the developed countries, but readers and listeners in the Third World. 'It has a duty to respond positively – and also urgently – to calls for a greater understanding of developments in the Third World and for less prejudice based on preconceived notions, cultural values or a superiority complex. I say the situation is urgent, because there is a growing impatience . . . with the distortions, deliberate or otherwise . . . there is still much in the way stories are angled and in the nuances of words used that is objectionable from a purely professional point of view.'

Put, as it generally is, more harshly, the international media are accused of 'spot reporting' which is as inadequate and irrelevant as it is (often) objectionable in tone. At the same conference, a Kenyan journalist asserted that 'correspondents are sent to sniff failure and imaginary dissension . . . [they] should not misinform their readers by giving the impression that the developing countries are politically unstable and stagnant in national development.' There are particularly vivid resentments of the 'visiting fireman' approach by the Western media – even producing demands that nobody should be sent to Nigeria, for example, unless they had mastered *all* the national languages and dialects. The 'three-day expert' who zooms in on a country to cover what the West considers a major event, rarely has time to file additional copy on development trends and social customs in transition; and under existing habits of news selection, developing countries' spokesmen add, has little incentive to do so: the extra effort involved would result in a story which hit the news editor's spike.

Because news is a merchandise rather than a service, stories are selected for their impact, exoticism, ability to entertain. The Western journalist's penchant for trains which do not run on time may be all very well in his own country, where the public has plenty of other news to balance sensational reporting of failure or corruption. The same criteria, applied to the thinly covered developing country, where the news item is the first on that area likely to have appeared in the media in weeks, can be seriously damaging. Even if every word is true, in the absence of other stories an article can gravely distort the country's image abroad, and, when exported back to its national media by the agencies, create a sense of outrage.

But, beyond the failings which produce casual distortion, or a lack of professionalism, the international media are accused of deliberately malicious reporting, underhand campaigns and the determined manipulation of public opinion. Beyond the pre-occupation with trains which do not run on time, Third World critics detect an obsession with the much rarer train which is actually sabotaged; this obsession is alleged to be part of a conspiracy to keep the Third World in a state of subjection.

Addressing the New Delhi conference of non-aligned ministers in 1976, Mrs Indira Gandhi accused 'the media of the powerful countries' of wanting 'to depict the governments of their erstwhile colonies as inept and corrupt and their people as yearning for the good old days. This cannot be attributed entirely to the common human failing of nostalgia. To a large extent there is a deliberate purpose. Leaders, who uphold their national interests ... are denigrated and their image falsified in every conceivable way.' Mrs Gandhi was still smarting from the reporting in the international press of her declaration the year before of a State of Emergency, and the suspension of civil rights which went with it, including the right to publish freely. 'The Western media interpreted it as an onslaught on democracy ... which was not at all correct. Most, if not all, developing countries understood the position. Yet many were misled into believing the Western versions to be objective reporting.'

A free press in India is now once again able to set the record straight. But Mrs Gandhi's allegation that the international media deliberately aim to deride Third World countries finds many echoes. Politicians are strikingly lax in coming up with concrete examples, generally referring to the 'coverage' in general of, say, the oil crisis or a famine or other natural disaster in their respective countries. It is this clinging to general accusations which gives credence to suspicions that many of those who complain the loudest are unable, or unwilling, to make a distinction between 'fair' reporting and propaganda. In January 1977, however, a *Neue Zuercher Zeitung* leader and an article by David Lamb of the *Los Angeles Times*, appearing within two days of each other in the *Inter-*

national Herald Tribune, attracted a formal letter from the Zambian Ambassador in Paris which protested very much in these terms.

The Swiss newspaper's leader was dismissed as 'simply malicious'. What did it say? Commenting on the country's economic difficulties, it insisted that although it was customary in Lusaka 'to blame the situation on the colonial legacy', it was 'due to internal mismanagement' and the apathy and corruption of Zambian officials. It ended, after reporting by way of example that European consultants had recently found that half the truck fleet 'existed only on paper' and that nobody seemed worried about the losses, by saying 'No wonder Zambia's President Kaunda is now sometimes seen weeping in public.'

Half-leader, half-report, the article clearly sought to portray a desperate national situation, and to lay the blame squarely on internal factors rather than copper (or oil) prices. The alleged malice lay presumably in publishing this judgement – with the tone an added aggravation. The Ambassador's criticisms of the Lamb article, a 1,200-word feature, were not directed at Lamb's description of a country in crisis – but again at his concentration on the internal factors which had gone into its making. Lamb had quoted extensively from a recent speech by President Kenneth Kaunda; why had he not reported that Kaunda had placed 80% of the blame for the crisis on 'external factors over which Zambia has no control'? Lamb, said the Ambassador, had 'missed an opportunity to convey the sense' of the speech, and his article had therefore had 'the effect of transposing the problems'.

Lamb's article certainly quoted the standard cab driver, the foreign correspondent's best friend, saying just the sort of thing that puts Mrs Gandhi's back up: they should bring in the Americans to advise them on agriculture, said the cabby, adding, 'The land hasn't produced since the colonialists left.' Should Lamb have reported that ? Kaunda himself, a month before in his speech, had demanded how any Zambian could say such a thing – implying that they were doing so and that Lamb's cab driver was not an isolated case. And Lamb's article was attempting to trace the reasons for Zambia's poor economic record 'despite great mineral wealth, fertile farmland

and a moderate, benign government'. He did not forget to point out that copper prices were at a twenty-year low; but he criticised the government for having failed to diversify the economy when prices had been higher and liquidity therefore greater; quoted Kaunda on Zambians' 'lack of will to work'; and, although he described the effect on the economy of Zambia's war with Rhodesia, ended by quoting a Western businessman who said 'Kaunda is going to have to learn that he can't survive on ideology and bromides for ever.' The article, the Ambassador complained, had failed to include another part of Kaunda's speech – the 'three-pronged strategy for an economic take-off' which it included. There was more to the speech than ideology, or than the warnings of 'stringent economy measures' which Lamb had reported.

Since the strategy, as described by the Ambassador, relied heavily on encouraging foreign investment, the article's failure to spell it out may have seemed like a crucial misrepresentation, highly damaging to Zambia's future. And beyond these failings, Lamb's 'Western perspective' had led him to suggest that Kaunda had 'lost popularity'. This, the Ambassador pointed out, showed that he 'misunderstands self-criticism in Zambia'; Kaunda was 'as popular as ever'.

The anxiety of the Third World is directed not only to the possibility that articles like Lamb's (which to an outsider might well read like an impartial, and even sympathetic, represent-ation of the Zambian predicament) deter foreign investors; but that in general terms articles which concentrate on failures force the developing countries – because of their dependence on the international media – to form a negative image of those countries with which they should naturally have most in common. This in fact would be the theoretical force of Mrs Gandhi's statement, however unfortunate her example or mixed her motives.

Western correspondents, generally because of their un-familiarity with a country, sometimes 'deliberately', damage countries by failing to observe certain taboos: one such case appears to have been the February 1974 report by Arnold Zeitlin of the AP on the fighting in Mindanao in the Philippines between the government and rebel Moslem forces. It is an interesting case, because Zeitlin can have had no reason to suppose that the subject had become taboo – plenty of reporting on the civil war had already appeared in the international press.

But Zeitlin was accused by the Chairman of the Media Advisory Council, not only of getting the casualty figures wrong in his story, but of seeking to 'alienate the Philippine government and people from the Arab world.' Oil contracts were reportedly under negotiation at the time; and Libya's keen interest in events in Mindanao became evident when it moved later to mediate in the conflict. Zeitlin's hostile attitude must have continued to offend the Philippines government; on 3 November 1976 he was expelled.

Speaking to the Foreign Correspondent's Association, at their request, nine days after his expulsion, Public Information Secretary Francisco Tatad refused to discuss Zeitlin's case. But foreign correspondents were totally free, he said, the Zeitlin affair notwithstanding, even 'those who report only bad news or who write only adverse opinion. But every once in a while, we welcome being seen for what we are, rather than only for what others believe is the way in which we should see ourselves.' However, Tatad went on, the situation in the Philippines was not normal; correspondents in exercising their freedom should remember that martial law was in force, and had overwhelming support from the Filipino people. Martial law was a fact and the foreign correspondent was 'not expected to support or endorse it, but neither . . . to suppress or question it . . . he has to suspend both belief and disbelief in this respect . . . simply because . . . it is . . . the will of the Filipino people and their wisdom or intelligence that are called upon to validate the ordering of their own environment.'

To question martial law in the Philippines, in other words, would amount to a deliberate attempt to manipulate public opinion abroad, maliciously to interfere in the internal affairs of the Philippines and (if the report were circulated in the region or in the country itself) to create tensions and instabilities within the host society, and in its relations with its immediate neighbours.

A few cases make a bad basis for general law; but Tatad was sufficiently anxious to see that his views reached a wide audience that he had them distributed by A. Cristobal Cruz, his representative from the Ministry of Public Information, at the

April 1977 colloquium for journalists organised in Florence by Unesco.

The Western press is also accused of failing to accord a fair right of reply, on occasions where it has either reported events inaccurately or deliberately misrepresented an event in the view of the country concerned. The Editor of Tunisia's *La Presse* (the ruling party's daily paper in French) published an example on 21 September 1977. *Le Monde*, the article claimed, had quoted from the London *Financial Times* the news that Tunisia was floating a loan on the international market. The *Financial Times* had gone on to say that Tunisia's development record had been good since it had gained independence in 1956, and that the traditional reasons for confidence in the country remained well founded. *Le Monde* had omitted this aspect of the *Financial Times'* story, and suggested that there was a domestic crisis of confidence which had led to the withdrawal of important sums from the banks – and which had undoubtedly prompted Tunisia to float the loan. Worse still, reported *La Presse*, *Le Monde* had failed to print the reply sent to it by 'financial circles' in Tunis in its original form, but had altered it both to read 'official financial circles' and also stated that these 'circles' were happy to be able to quote the *Financial Times'* expression of confidence (whereas in fact they had complained that *Le Monde* had failed to quote that part of the original article).

From such acorns, great trees of mistrust develop; and not all of it can be dismissed as paranoia, or as the belief expressed at Florence by an Indian diplomat that all news should be 'true, pleasant and beneficial'.

Those who do not seek confrontation, but who are dissatisfied with the performance of the international media, insist that they are looking not for lower standards in reporting of the Third World, but higher ones: not for any sacrifice of objectivity and truth, but for closer adherence to the standards of knowledge and even-handedness applied on more familiar ground. And for some tact.

Mort Rosenblum, Director of the AP's Paris bureau, gives an example of what 'tact' might mean: 'One Western correspondent was expelled from Zaire (then the Congo) because he mentioned that President Mobutu was wearing Israeli paratroop wings. If such a detail is vital to the story, it must be included. If it is only a gratuitous irritant, it can be dropped. Sensibilities are . . . important.'

The difficulty for the agencies is summed up by Gerald Long, Managing Director of Reuters, who gave an interview to the IPI Report in October 1976. The Emergency was still in force in India. What, Long asked, was the greatest obstacle to giving a 'rounded report' of India for the world? 'From the criticisms, one might tend to think that it is that this reporting is in the hands of a group of people who have no sufficient knowledge or sympathy or have some distorted motives . . . that's quite untrue. The major difficulty in reporting India is India. It is a country of vast size, with an enormous population. Who knows in India what is happening in India? Not necessarily because things are being suppressed . . . but just because of the difficulty of knowing what's happening.'

If the agencies were being criticised, said Long, 'because they do not report the whole truth about India, they are being criticised for something which they have never claimed to do and never could do.'

The unreality of some of the demands, and the insubstantiality of some of the cases, do not divert from the strength of much of the argument. Nor should the governmental origin of many of the complaints blind the international press to the elements of truth in them. Cases will continue to be pressed, new cases and similar ones, in a process of accretion. The Third World challenge is backed by a collective determination among its leaders to force what they see as essential reforms on the world information system. One of the issues at stake is therefore whether the major agencies are willing – or able – to meet the core of the complaints with constructive change.

The second issue, in the light of the criticisms made, is what attitude developing countries' governments will take to the international media once their own means of information are strengthened. They may demand that only nationals of their own countries are used as correspondents; in many countries, these nationals will not be able to report fully and freely, except at unacceptable levels of personal risk. Regional news pools will be set up in the Third World – even if progress is slow, and even if regional animosities and governmental controls make them far from complete or credible sources of news. It is uncertain whether they will develop as additional media, or whether the desire to see that the 'Third World voice' gets across will tempt some governments to shut off access to the international media, thus ensuring that the pools and the output of their governmental news agencies form the only sources of information. It is often argued, almost in the same breath, that 'essential reforms' imply that the international media must do a better job of reporting on developing countries' affairs – *and* that they imply acceptance by the international media of reports circulated by national agencies. 'It is difficult' commented one news executive, 'to accept an invitation to come in and to leave at the same time'. The big agencies may accept a new role: UPI has offered its telecommunications channels as carrier for an Asian newspool, if and when it gets going, doubtless in the hope that its own freedom to gather and circulate news will in return be acknowledged. But there is a strong possibility that the demand that the 'criteria' for news selection must be changed, will, as interpreted by governments, result in a diminution, not an increase, in the flow of reliable information from the Third World.

CHAPTER 2

The 'Imperialists'

Daily across the globe, about 48,000 offices sift through the news services provided by one or more of the five major international agencies – The Associated Press, Reuters, United Press International, Agence France Presse and Tass. If each took the world service of all five and nothing else, it would be swamped by a daily 300,000 words – equivalent to more than fifty pages of a newspaper unrelieved by photographs or advertising. Some of these offices are governmental – embassies, information ministries, prime ministers' offices - and some are official news agencies which will filter the material before relaying it to national media; most are newspapers or broadcasting organisations.

The news may clatter in on noisy, worn-out teleprinters, or come through on the screens of video-terminals. It may reach the offices by the millions of miles of international cables and landlines leased by the agencies, or by microwave or radio teletype, or it may be 'bounced' from communications satellites. Although some countries are still atrociously served by the international networks, particularly for regional communications, the news travels fast in most circumstances; using a mixture of all three methods, a correspondent in Kuala Lumpur could reach his office in New York – via Singapore, Hong Kong, Manila, Tokyo, and San Francisco – in less than a minute; computer-edited, and translated into Spanish, the news item would be on the desk of a Buenos Aires sub-editor within the hour.

And the fifty newspaper-pages worth of the combined world

services are only the tip of the iceberg. Reuters, which operates thirty services in six languages, sends out 1.5 million words a day from its London headquarters; AFP issues more than double that, although their total includes extensive domestic coverage. The UPI computer operation in New York processes, according to its General Manager for Europe, Julius Humi, a daily fourteen million words through the company's recently-installed Information Storage and Retrieval System; eleven million of it is news-copy. Subscribers can choose from a large range of regional services, stock and commodity prices and specialised economic news, and supplement the diet with news photos and comic strips.

The combined turnover of the four Western agencies is no more than $300 million. But between them, estimates Stanley Swinton, AP's Director of World Services, they provide over 90% of the international news printed or broadcast around the world. Although Swinton is careful to emphasise that on a global average, three quarters of the total news printed or broadcast is devoted to local or national events (for which reliance on agency coverage is much lower, and may be virtually non-existent in some countries), he agrees with the agencies' critics on one point: 'What is carried by us, the major agencies, profoundly modifies human ideas and value judgements.' Through the 9,500 subscribers to the AP alone, nearly a third of the world's population has access to that agency's reporting, its daily output is seventeen million words.

The five world agencies do not operate in a vacuum – there are more than 120 regional and national agencies, including major ones such as the Deutsche Presse Agentur, Japan's Kyodo or China's Hsinhua which all have extensive international networks – but the big agencies dwarf them in terms of capitalisation, manpower, technology – and in the task they set themselves. Each of the five has correspondents in not less than sixty countries; they have clients in at least 80 countries (the number Tass claims to serve) and, in the case of the AFP, in 152. And the requirements of increasingly sophisticated means of processing and transmitting international news, in terms of financing and research, may in future increase the distance between them and their competitors. UPI's computer storage and retrieval system in New York cost $12 million, according to its General Manager, Bob Page. Heavy investment in new technology pushed Reuters' operating costs up to $74 million in 1976, against a total turnover in that year of $80 million. Round-the-clock satellite circuits link both US agencies with Latin America, and networks of computerised information retrieval systems are spreading between strategic points. It is expensive; and it puts the world agencies into a different technological age than the one in which national news organisatons live.

The dominating position of the agencies has been described as 'abnormal' by Unesco's Director-General, Amadou Mahtar M'Bow; but it has been the norm for a century – or at least since seventy years ago, when the UPI was founded. Their pre-eminence has been challenged with the founding of a multitude of would-be competitors at regional or national level. But the exponential growth in the volume of information carried world-wide makes them harder to beat: news editors prefer to sift through one or two news-files, rather than many.

'Conferences', complained Sergio Lepri of Italy's ANSA news agency, 'pose a false problem in speaking about the need to *increase* the flow of information. ANSA receives, on merely average equipment working only fifteen hours a day, 220,000 words from the socialist countries, 110,000 from the Third World and 250,000 from the international agencies. A third of our output is foreign news. It stands to reason that most of what we receive goes into the rubbish-bin, which ought to be the symbol of our discussions. Even Hsinhua sends me 35,000 words a day. Interesting background material, but mostly unuseable.'

ANSA is a highly professional, medium-sized agency with its own network of foreign correspondents and an established international standing. The countries of the Third World, many of which have extremely limited national news-gathering resources and no means of establishing an international network even for the purpose of verifying the reports of the world agencies on their immediate neighbours' affairs, resent not only the fact that much of the copy is, in their terms, unuseable, but the simple fact of being permanently on the receiving end. In an important article which argued passionately for the independence of the media, written at the time of the Nineteenth General Conference of Unesco in Nairobi, a leading Kenyan journalist, Hilary Ng'Weno, editor of the *Weekly Review*, expressed a common feeling of cultural claustrophobia and anxiety.

> Through the power of the Western news media, especially the major international agencies, . . . Third World people have come to feel a great sense of impotence over the cultural influences which permeate their relations with the western world through the mass media. It is an unrelenting one-way traffic of ideas and values from the western countries to the Third World with little opportunity given to Third World nations to examine the content of the materials which daily flood their own presses and other media from the West.

It is not an adequate response to say that no agency, however powerful, can force a client to take its services. For most developing countries, the choice is between isolation and choosing among the Big Four (and/or Tass). The lack of opportunity to examine the content, of which Ng'Weno complains, cannot be laid either at the door of the receiving countries – for all their lack of trained personnel – or of that of the agencies; it is part of the worldwide problem of the sheer volume of information. This fact, more than any other, puts a particular burden on the agencies to free themselves of national or 'Western' bias; and to tailor their news carefully to the known requirements of their subscribers.

The agencies claim to do both. Their dominance, they say, does not prevent them from providing an honest and impartial service; their resources positively assist them to regionalise and to be more receptive to their clients. How well do these claims stand up?

> *Nigerian editor:* There is an element of hypocrisy in the Western claim to be objective. We are being given the impression at international conferences like this that the Western press is out to be fair, yet we know better where we are with Tass.
>
> *American editor:* What hypocrisy?

Nigerian: The output shows that it is not the case.
American: What output?
Nigerian: What we have been discussing.

'It is,' sighed H. L. Stevenson, Editor in Chief of UPI, a few hours after this helpful exchange of views, 'like wrestling with a ton and a half of jello.' Most senior newsmen in the world agencies appear genuinely baffled by the ferocity of Third World attacks on their integrity and the quality of their services. Several are inclined to write it off to ideology and nationalism; a few, to say that covering certain parts of the world is nothing but an unrewarding expense anyway, and could be abandoned if the criticisms continue. All are irritated by the shortage of specific cases of distortion or manipulation provided as evidence by their discontented subscribers, and most agonise over such complaints as are made. A few, generally those closest to the news-gathering side, admit that in certain areas their service is disturbingly inadequate – but will point to the considerably difficulties placed in the way of their correspondents by governments which then loudly complain of the resulting coverage.

It stings many of them to find themselves cast in the 'imperialist' mould, partly because the whole conscious emphasis of their training has been international. And because they have prided themselves on meeting the most disparate needs and requests.

The unequal balance of coverage, as between North and South, is recognised by some agency men, fiercely contested by others. Roger Tatarian, a former Vice-President of UPI, speaking at the international conference organised in New York in May 1977 by the Murrow Center of Public Diplomacy, reported that not only was the flow basically from North to South, but that 'of the millions of words the agencies transmit every day, most by far deal with events in or of immediate interest primarily to more developed areas' – a pattern, he added, which simply reflected the global distribution of power. But Gerry Long of Reuters insists that his agency, at least, shapes coverage to a region's interests. In a 1976 interview, he gave Africa as an example: services to Africa were 'composed to give 65 % to 70 % of African-interest news. Now that would be news from other African countries, African activities outside Africa, at the United Nations, ministers travelling and news of other Third World countries that would interest them. The news of the rest of the world is there – we try to make it complete – but it's there in very short form.'

Long continued with a comment which goes near to the heart of the argument about content: 'We are not trying' he said 'to tell anybody what news they ought to want, what news they ought to have. We try to find out in every case what sort of news service they want. If we can, we try to supply it.'

The Third World leaders who most loudly object to their many and disparate countries being treated as a homogeneous mass by observers from the industrialised North are also quick to lump the agencies together. In terms of financing, the details of their operations and areas of particular strength, this is nonsense, as we shall see later. But there may exist what could be called an 'agency ethic' of reporting which has strong common elements.

And one of them is founded on commercial sense: if you don't make efforts to find out what your subscriber wants, he can switch to your competitor who tried harder. The 2,500 journalists working for the AP have at their elbow – in theory at least – a large looseleaf manual called *World Service Signposts*. It serves as portable credo – beginning 'you are part of the most extensive news and photo distribution network in the history of communications' – and as practical guide: to subscribers' interests, needs and even deadlines. Salesmanship, if you like; news as a commodity; but witness to the fact that agencies produce a basic diet in terms of what their subscribers want, as well as what they themselves think is important. Stan Swinton points out that one of the AP's difficulties in the Third World is that 'not only do our clients not complain, but we don't hear nearly enough from them in general; it's our repeated request to them.'

A typical complaint might go like this. A Fiji newspaper publisher, Philip Harkness, says that he pays the Australian Associated Press (AAP) about $33,000 a year for a 'tailored' service out of Sydney which is based on the combined news output of the AAP, the New Zealand Press Association, and the 'Big Four'. It would be worth it, he says, if the service were really tailored; what he objects to is the regularity with which his editors are snowed under with irrelevant material such as the British football results. Yes, indeed, he can use a call-up facility to request missing news items; but he has to pay the transmission costs, which come to around $2,000 a year, and he claims that he shouldn't need to tell the agency what he needs. In the nearly five years the *Fiji Sun* has been taking AAP services, he adds, the agency has paid the paper only one visit; and that was to talk about money, not the quality or suitability of the service.

He has two options: the first is to take a UPI service at half the cost; which he is reluctant to do because although UPI gives excellent coverage in his opinion of the Western Pacific, and the Philippines and Hong Kong beats, it cannot provide enough material on Australia and New Zealand. The second, which his staff is pressing him to adopt, would be to spend $1,000 on a receiver able to monitor the Voice of America, the BBC, and the Australian and New Zealand broadcasting services. The entire cost of the monitoring operation, he reckons, would be less than $7,000 a year. But it is not the cost-saving which is the greatest temptation, but frustration: 'From the copy we get', he says, 'I'd be surprised to learn that the AAP's duty editor in Sydney who selects our file knows the names of the Prime Minister, two other cabinet members and the leader of the opposition in Fiji. He *may*, of course, but it certainly doesn't show.'

Despite such problems, the effort to see that content reflects regional interests is generally made by all four Western agencies; but how tailored is it in other senses to local sensitivities and values? The news-file may differ, to reflect regional interest – but the *actual story* tends to be identical, wherever it is circulated. This shows up particularly in reporting of UN debates and international conferences, where subscribers want – and do not get – a news-lead telling them what their own country's representatives had to say.

In a perceptive paper for a Unesco meeting of experts in Colombo in December 1977 – a meeting which was discussing the development of news agencies in Asia – Pran Chopra discussed the problem of news values. The international agencies, he said, 'see Asia wholly through Western eyes and for Western audiences, and an overwhelming proportion of their traffic is of Western origin. . . . But there is hardly any point in blaming the Western agencies for that. They work for their customers, and their customers are largely the Western media, not Asian. . . . They call the tune.'

This would seem flatly to contradict the agencies' claims. But Chopra also said that 'the meagreness of Asian coverage in Asia' could not entirely be blamed on the Western agencies. Most, he said, 'give a great deal more of Asian news to their clients than the latter care to use. In fact quite a few of their Western clients carry some of their Asian coverage more extensively than their Asian clients do. . . . The explanation for this lies at least in part with the news values and selection criteria of the Asian media themselves, and very little of it lies with the lack of resources they sometimes plead.'

To the charge that the agencies are incapable of providing an objective service, harnessed as they are supposed to be to Western interests, the agencies reply, first, that objectivity is essential if news is to be acceptable to countries with governments of left or right, countries which hate each others' guts and have for centuries, countries with different legal and social traditions. One consequence, in fact, of their acute awareness of foreign sensitivities is that they stress 'hard news'. 'Our job', says Humi, 'is to inform without regard to impact or political influence. We are not concerned with being sympathetic or unsympathetic. We report the news – which has to be something which has happened and which people haven't heard about. And our emphasis is accuracy, speed and reliability.' The difficulty with this approach is that it provides limited tools with which to cover the gradual evolution of a society – an evolution which cannot be 'pegged' to particular events like the opening of a new steel mill except in the context of judgements. The steel mill could be an extravagant showpiece whose justification is basically political; or it could be the much-needed motor for a well worked-out strategy. And there might be no 'steel mill' at all: the correspondent might need to work more impressionistically to give a true picture. Humi is, of course, aware of this problem; but for him and many others the old criteria hold. Criteria unchanged since Lawrence Gobright, AP's Washington correspondent, said in

1856: 'My business is to communicate facts. My instructions do not allow me to make any comments upon the facts. My dispatches are sent to papers of all manner of politics. I therefore confine myself to what I consider legitimate news and try to be truthful and impartial.' The rub lies in the process of 'consideration'.

The intellectual basis (as opposed to the requirements of a world market) for this attitude is one shared in many newsrooms. It has much in common with Hayden White's description of the nineteenth century historian, for whom the 'historical method' –

> consisted of a willingness to go to the archives without any preconceptions whatever, to study the documents found there, and then to write a story about the events . . . in such a way as to make the story itself the explanation of 'what had happened'. . . . That different 'points of view' might be brought to bear on the past was not denied, but these . . . were regarded as biases to be suppressed rather than as poetic perspectives that might illuminate. The idea was to 'tell the story' about 'what had happened' without significant conceptual residue or ideological preformation. . . . If the story were rightly told, the explanation of what had happened would figure itself forth from the landscape, in the same way that the structure of the landscape would be figured by a properly drawn map.

Or, in the terser language of the AP: 'No adjectives'. The rules are dependability and accuracy, and reporters are trained not to make value judgements. 'We would prefer,' says a senior editor, 'the accusation of blandness to that of partisanship.'

The agencies insist that they report from *no* country's viewpoint; most of the complaints, they say, come from governments who simply want a better public relations job done for their country. Yet all judgements as to what is news must have some anchor. And the agencies must work both in and for societies which differ – at least officially – in their criteria. It is possible to play neutral, to say that 'we try to see countries and peoples as they see themselves.' But when it comes to filing the report, which audience, which set of cultural criteria ultimately influence the selection of the story and the way it is written? The agencies face two simultaneous dilemmas: they must be sensitive to local values, yet meet the requirements of a consistent style on which their international claim to objectivity is based. Their task is qualitatively different from that of a Western correspondent with one set of readers to answer to.

White's description of the historian-reporter's perceived task distinguishes between 'bias' and a 'conceptual residue or ideological preformation'. There may be no adjectives; there is almost bound to be a cultural shorthand. And one of the frequently-voiced complaints from the Third World is that East-West terminology is often applied by Western media to events and personalities in these countries in a simplistic and often misleading way. So-and-so is described as a 'Marxist' leader; the adjective 'right-wing' is heavily loaded with concepts of social polarisation common to Westerners and perhaps alien to Indonesia. Distinctively Asian or African situations may be described, for the sake of 'clarity' in terms which give them a Cold War image. And the habit of labelling, they say, can give a news story a racist or neo-colonial flavour.

Leonard Sussman, Director of the US institute Freedom House, reports the comment of a West African editor who, while sceptical about the quality of the 'alternative' coverage provided by African news agencies, insisted that 'new understandings' are needed: 'Stories coming to us over the wire services from South Africa and Rhodesia,' where agency correspondents are sometimes based for the simple reason that they cannot operate freely in other African countries, 'refer to "terrorists", yet we know them as "freedom fighters". So in every story we change one term for the other, and when we get a story about Ian Smith, instead of calling him prime minister we refer to him as "terrorist".'

There are also certain requirements, which differ from agency to agency. The correspondent for the UPI and AP, while he will be filing a lot of story-material which will interest the citizens of Dallas not a whit and will be intended purely for regional circulation, 'must cover anything meaningful to the US.' Short of total schizophrenia, he is likely to have an eye to the marketability of a local item at home as well as on the regional circuit. 'A man going overseas,' remarks one of the agencies' key gate-keepers, 'has to have international needs in mind; it is hoped that, while he will file some stories only used regionally, most will serve all markets.' There is a clear conflict of interest. The internationalism theoretically works against bias; but there is perhaps a double edge to the enthusiastic encomium of the press agency ethic, written of the UPI forty years ago by Stephen Vincent Benet: 'the world is a local assignment.' This is true not only in the sense that an agency is committed to the accurate coverage of all parts of the globe but—given the impossibility of this mission—also in the sense that covering the world risks being *treated like* a local assignment. The diversity is so great, that making order of it for the reader almost requires that it be explained in the relatively 'local' framework of a set of cultural and intellectual perceptions. And there is some truth in this, however many foreign journalists an agency hires, and however much material may even be a rewrite of the national press or news agency output of the host country. All human life can only be there if a process of 'interpretation' brings it into a common focus.

Yet how harmful is the existence of 'Western criteria'; how great a distortion does it imply - and how different in fact are 'news values'? The question can only be answered in terms of the many differing situations in individual developing countries, but it is worth noting one or two points at this stage. There are two basic complaints about the agencies' treatment of the news: first, that what reaches the Third World offends against national traditions and values; second, that what is sent from the South to the North is crudely and distortingly sensationalist.

The AP's Mort Rosenblum, whose article for the July 1977 issue of *Foreign Affairs* is one of the best (and most readable) accounts of how the agencies actually set about international reporting, insists that values are not so different or irreconcilable as governments pretend. For all the outcry, he says, readers in Asia actually *want* stories about whether Idi Amin ate his enemy's liver, rather than carefully balanced reports on school projects in Tanzania.

On a more serious note, Gunnar Naesselund, at the time Deputy Assistant Director General for Communications at Unesco, raised some doubts at the New York seminar about the heavily governmental news-content of the Non-Aligned

News Pool. 'I can accept and even defend the concern of non-aligned countries to obtain reports of ministers' speeches and so forth' he said. 'It may even be a more rapid substitute for ministry reports. But to what extent,' he asked the Pool's director, Pero Ivacic of Tanjug, 'do you believe the news values of Third World readers to be very different from other people's? Do they want to read Mrs Bandaranaike's every word? If you want to reach a critical and discerning public, how do you evaluate the Pool?' Ivacic's reply was that there *was* an effort to condense official speeches; but 'at least we report them where the main agencies don't, in the conviction that what their leaders say must be of interest to all the peoples of the non-aligned movement.'

Speeches of leaders - a distinctively Third World approach, perhaps. At a dinner on the eve of another conference, in Tunis, journalists from that country were attempting to convince a couple of Western colleagues that Third World journalism implied a responsible, because much more all-embracing, approach: the people must be told everything. As an example, one said that space had already been allocated in tomorrow's paper for the speech that Prime Minister Hedi Nouira would make the next morning in opening the conference.

This particular form of 'complete' information is not, at the sending end, limited of course to Third World countries; it is a common aspiration of governments everywhere. In Mozambique, under the careful eye of Salazar's Portugal, newspapers were required to print all the great man's speeches in prominent positions. The *Tribuna*, the leading opposition paper, managed to stay in print by observing this rule to the letter: it printed every word, with extravagant lay-out, in a special four page 'pull-out' section. Its readers happily did just that; and authority was powerless.

In one sense at least, an AP study in March 1971 of sixty-four papers in eighteen countries found, 'news judgements round the world tend to be very similar': averaging around the globe, all the papers surveyed devoted 72.8 % of coverage to local and national news – and the percentage between areas differed by not more than 3 %. In the limited space available for foreign coverage of any kind, news can only be sampled. The daily slot may accommodate only a dozen stories.

Third World leaders accuse the agencies of operating like typical multinational companies, in there only for profit, selecting and filtering the news with callous indifference to Third World needs and interests. They feed their home markets stories from the developing countries which encourage neo-colonial arrogance, just as multinationals milk them of their natural resources with only the rich world at heart. But in treating the agencies like any other conglomerate, they betray not just resentment but some ignorance of the nature of the agencies' financing and operations.

Nor, perhaps, do they always register the fact which the AP survey brings out: that there is only a limited interest, anywhere, in foreign parts. Rosenblum is not simply a victim of a typically 'Western' form of self-deception when he says that 'editors feel they must select what their audiences want'; and that however objective the reporting of a particular event may aim to be, in determining whether or not to report it at all 'news judgement rest on the potential impact and interest of stories rather than any sense of international fair play.' The agencies deal in markets; it is natural that they should be attacked by those whose ideas about the role of government, and the nature of the right to be informed, differ from those originating in societies which, in the final analysis, rest their political credo on the virtues of a free market in ideas.

The common characteristic of AP and UPI is that both – although the AP in particular – could pack their bags in the Third World and much of the rest of it, and survive comfortably at home. This does not mean that they are about to do so; they are as anxious as the other two Western agencies to maintain their access to as many countries as possible. But the fact that in each case, about three quarters of their income derives from the United States, adds fuel to the 'anti-imperialist' attack on their activities.

In other respects they are structurally very different. The AP, which claims to be the oldest agency dealing in general news for newspapers (as opposed to economic and financial news for business clients, which is where Reuters started), was founded by six New York publishers in 1848. It continues to be a cooperative, now including 1,320 US newspaper publishers.

A further 3,400 US broadcasters and some 5,000 foreign organisations are not members and have no voting rights, but buy the services. But the AP calls itself a non-profitmaking cooperative ('as little non-profitmaking as we can be'). To charges that it is part of a monopoly of few decision-makers, its executives reply that its gate-keepers are not merely within the organisation: 'We have 2,000 managing editors monitoring our coverage; it's our hair shirt, but it means we check and recheck our stories or find ourselves in trouble.'

The AP's network of over 2,500 journalists and photographers are spread over sixty-two foreign countries and 107 US cities, producing between them the more than seventeen million words which flow in different directions over the agency's communications system. Services have been somewhat regionalised; all Asian news, for example, goes to Tokyo where it is 'cleaned up' and sorted. Some is sent back to Asia on the regional service, major items also go to New York for the world services. But computerisation has brought much more intimate linkage between the various parts of the system, and now that all copy can be coded for regional or world distribution, AP expects to swing back to a more centralised system.

The fact that copy goes to New York is one of the standard Third World complaints. It is alleged that stories originating in developing countries, even if honestly and fairly written, go through editing in New York which twists them according to US private or governmental interests before sending them bouncing back to the country of origin. An extreme statement of this view was quoted by Unesco, in a background paper for the international meeting of journalists it assembled in Florence in April 1977.

It charged that 'the control of news flow into the Latin American region is dominated by United States wire services that systematically distort through selection and manipulation the image of the world outside presented to the Latin Americans through their papers. The distortion by the wire services also extends to the coverage of specific Latin American items . . . the images of Latin America in the US media are sensationalistic and untrue, with a special bias against situations of directed social change and revolution.'

For both AP and UPI, Latin America is the part of the Third

World over which, ironically, nationals have most control. In addition, computer-editing and satellite connections have minimised editing, and enabled New York headquarters to go straight to the reporter with any queries.

Much copy, in any case, does not go to AP's headquarters but is processed regionally. For the world services, however, all agencies inevitably are highly centralised. And privately, UPI and AP staff members will admit that – though they absolutely reject any accusations of wilful distortion – the Latin American services each provides are scattershot, if only because the agencies' networks cover only major centres.

AP is seeking to remedy this sparseness of coverage, a general problem in its Third World network which is much more serious in Asia and Africa than in Latin America, by 'building up area pools of experts whose brief is to cover groups of countries, supplemented by specialist reporters to cover particular topics worldwide.' But for all the AP's emphasis on its cooperative status, it has to stay in business; the books must balance.

The agency makes a small profit on the two 'selling' aspects of its news distribution activities: the service to broadcasters, and to foreign subscribers. The financial and economic news service which it runs with Dow Jones, and the news-photo services, are assuming an increasingly large role. But in the Third World, where the subscriber market is relatively small and operating costs high, Swinton says that the AP 'derives less than 1 % of its total income – and spends five times that sum in covering events there. We are far from profiting.' This may well be true – since all the agencies (with the partial exception of UPI) refuse to provide full and adequate statistics, it remains a question of faith – or, more noticeably, suspicion – for those in the Third World who consider themselves neglected. The difference between the world news agencies and transnational companies is that the profitability of operations in a certain area cannot be a decisive factor. They cannot simply withdraw. But they do tend to put their chief efforts into parts of the world where markets exist for their products and from where (not always the same thing – Moscow is an example) the demand for news is greatest. Africa misses out on both counts.

UPI, formed by E. W. Scripps in June 1907, exists to make a profit by selling its services to all-comers. It makes a point of emphasising that its strength is that it is not dominated by any one group of newspapers; and it has traditionally sought foreign markets and access to foreign news stories. It has, according to its 1978 report, 7,043 direct subscribers (ie not counting those who get their services indirectly, via a ministry of information or national news agency). In the US, 1,131 newspapers and 3,650 broadcasters buy its services. Its operating budget is over $75 million · still $25 million less than the AP's, but in the same bracket. Spread over seventy-eight cities in the US, it has bureaus or correspondents in ninety-eight other countries and sells to ninety-two.

Starting later than the other major Western agencies, UPI retains the strongly competitive instinct which marked its struggle for international recognition. Speaking of relations with the Third World, one senior executive recently insisted: 'Access is what worries us; not what they do with our copy. We're used to selling to governments and controlled channels. But access is our life-blood. If we couldn't reach these countries, sooner or later our standing and credibility as a world agency would be affected in the home markets where we do make money; then we'd be fatally pinched.' Whereas AP makes an overall profit on its foreign services, the UPI breakdown is different. In an average week in 1977, the US provided 75% of income and absorbed only 67% of operating costs. Europe (which in the UPI organisational system includes Africa and the Middle East) yielded 12% of income and accounted for 18% of worldwide costs; Latin America almost breaks even, with 4% and 5% respectively; and Asian costs exceed revenue, 4% comes in, for an outlay of 7%.

There are limits, UPI people say, to the extent to which US profits can subsidise world coverage. In Africa, the UPI (like the AP) is barely represented; and it has also had to withdraw its services from several African clients because they didn't pay their bills. But the agency makes a point of insisting that it cooperates happily with national agencies – beginning with its assistance to Tass in the 1920's. In addition, like most of the agencies, it is using more area correspondents and providing regional services. Some of these are highly developed, and run by nationals of the countries concerned. From New York, UPI sends out about 250 items a day on the main Spanish wire, of which Latin American newspapers will carry around 10 %; the company insists that more than 50 % of all the UPI news circulating in Latin America originates there; that virtually all the copy received is used, and that it is only lightly edited. In addition, UPI's Stevenson says, the international news Latin Americans receive provides more European than US material: 'the US is just another country; we try to de-emphasise it and act as an international rather than a US agency.'

To the charge that, as a profit-making organisation with its main market in the US, the UPI must represent the interests of the US capitalist machine, the agency replies with Benet's credo: that UPI 'must never be obligated to any financial, business, governmental or political interest . . . (and) must be international in point of view.' And that its credentials, as it built itself up, were essentially its strength in foreign reporting.

If UPI is suspect because of the high percentage of its revenue which originates in the US, Reuters ought to be the least suspect, to Third World eyes, of the Big Four. Less than 20 % of its revenue originates in the UK and, uniquely, Reuters is an international news agency only: the national agency network in the UK is the Press Association, which is responsible for domestic news. Not only must this proud claim be tempered however by recognition that 46 % of its 1976 turnover of $80 million came from Europe, and only 18 % from the countries of the Third World; but Reuters is also most vulnerable to accusations of being intimately linked with, and sensitive to the requirements of, international corporate enterprises.

Reuters says it does not break down its accounts, on a regional basis, between its economic services and its news services. But 82 % of its total turnover stems from transmitting specialised business information to the world's financial and business community. And it is this service which has retained Reuters among the Big Four: twenty-five years ago, its total sales came to half its 1976 profit. Turnover has tripled in the last five years alone.

Economic intelligence was in fact what was carried by Reuters' famous pigeons 120 years ago, before the future Baron

Julius de Reuter had moved to London. The pigeons beat the mail train from Brussels to Aachen by seven hours; Reuters' first service was to get the market quotations from Paris and Brussels onto the Aachen–Berlin telegraph just opened by the Prussian government well ahead of any possible competition. After Reuter moved to London in 1851, stockbrokers kept him in business for seven years before the press were persuaded that his telegraph network could provide a general news service. But it was not until Reuters used computers in the mid-1960's to hook investment brokers into stock market prices that economic services – which now include a vast range of services on commodities, investment and money, and instant retrieval systems for stock market information and prices from 38 exchanges – again became the essential cushion for its news-gathering and distribution. Ten years later, Reuters moved into North America with an ambitious new economic retrieval service transmitted over coaxial cables at six million words a minute.

The cushion is essential because Reuters has neither a vast home market to fall back on, nor any form of subsidy. It is a limited company, jointly owned by the Newspaper Publishers Association (the Fleet Street press), the Press Association, which represents the British and Irish provincial press, and the equivalent organisations in Australia and New Zealand. Particularly strong in Africa, and with 529 full-time journalists abroad and over 800 stringers round the world, Reuters would almost inevitably lose money overall if it were not for domination of information services connected with the international foreign exchange market through its Monitor system, which by September 1977 numbered 1,547 subscribers after only four years' operation. 'None of the international news services', asserts Reuters' Media Development Manager, Michael Neale, 'makes a profit from news distribution to overseas media when revenue is set against total costs of worldwide reporting and communications.' But there are spin-offs; the news collection network can feed into the profit-making business file. Reuters got the news that the Paris Peace Talks over Indochina were to be set up, an hour before anyone else: those with that information were able to profit from the rise on Wall Street when the news became general knowledge. It is still true that the cash flow generated by business services has not only enabled Reuters to computerise its news production, but to reach 153 countries – more than any other agency – with a combination of thirty services in six languages. In the days of increasingly vocal opposition to neo-colonialism – the phrase is creeping into an ever-increasing number of UN resolutions, and is explicitly connected with the international media in Unesco documents and declarations – the great financial tail behind Reuters' news service is accused in some developing countries of wagging the dog: the animal as a whole, the accusations run, is the obedient servant of monopoly capitalism and the old economic order.

These suspicions do not emerge in the form of specific objections, it should be noted; Gerry Long, to whom all complaints are brought, comments that there are few from developing countries 'either about the news we put out about them or the news we send to them.' And Reuters has succeeded, to a remarkable extent, in shedding its image as the vehicle for the extension of British diplomacy by other means, acquired during the period of the Empire.

Partly because of the subsidy voted it annually by the French parliament, which amounted to over 70 % of its 1976 budget of $43 million, the Agence France Presse has retained a good deal of its flag-carrying image. The subsidy is not direct; AFP's budget shortfall is made up by payment of official subscriptions to its services by government offices and embassies. Officially autonomous, the AFP needs its government subsidy to maintain uneconomic bureaus and to provide its services at low cost in the Third World. Its network of foreign correspondents – 171 people – is backed by 1,200 stringers abroad plus a corps of Paris-based roving reporters. And it has people in 167 countries, operating 108 bureaus – more than either the AP or UPI. In Africa, the network is particularly dense, and made possible because AFP receives more than $12 million for subscriptions from French governmental agencies, according to Professor Robert Bishop's study in the Winter 1975 issue of *Journalism Quarterly*. World-wide, directly and through national news agencies, AFP reckons to reach 12,000 newspapers; the 'formal' list of clients is about 1,200, including sixty-nine national news agencies.

The benefits to African newspapers of this support are considerable; but both in the Third World and in Europe, some editors prefer to rely on other agencies for stories in cases when France's national interests are at stake. AFP considers itself totally independent; and has surely a stronger claim to be so than most Third World news agencies. Like Reuters, it maintains a strong network in Africa, where it has twenty bureaus manned by 'head office' correspondents and another twelve staffed by nationals.

Developing countries claim that their own government-owned agencies can be objective, yet they tend to develop a special (even, in the circumstances, hypocritical) scepticism when colonial or ex-colonial governments are involved, even at arm's length, in some form of financial support. And AFP is also highly centralised; the Paris base, computerised since 1976, will on completion of the change-over to the new technology use seventy-two video-terminals.

Centralisation, with the adoption of video-editing, could provide all agencies with some opportunites. 'Before video-editing came in', explains a former agency editor, 'the correspondent's story went into the computer; the easiest thing for an editor to do was to send it straight out again by touching the various routing codes. If he wanted to change even a comma, the story had to come out of the computer – and be repunched manually. This took, above all, *time*: but with video-editing it isn't necessary to repunch. The question is whether we will take the opportunity to edit stories so that – at least – they lead off with something likely to interest a particular country or region.'

No attempt has been made here to describe the functioning of any of the agencies in detail, or to discuss a multiplicity of special services which back up the basic distribution of news (and, in the case of the US agencies, a highly sophisticated photo service). The curious fact, however, is the level of ignorance even of the basics of news agency organisation betrayed by most of those who are most vociferous in attacking them. This ignorance is not merely, or even principally, revealed by politicians; the increasingly large army of radical 'communications experts' marshalling behind the New Order for Information is filled with writers and intellectuals who have very little idea of how stories get processed – and none at all, judging by their pictures of carefully rewoven and distorted reporting, of the speed at which processing takes place. An agency reporter, lunching with one of Unesco's key figures in charge of its communications policy, was astonished to receive a confidential, conspiratorial request over the coffee for his agency's secret '*dossier noir*' of 'managed' copy.

The agencies have reacted defensively and with some bewilderment to the majority of the accusations against them, but to none more perplexedly than those of deliberate manipulation. They all admit that mistakes occur; but find it quite simply illogical that they, who serve several thousand clients of many hues the same basic menu, could be thought to find it possible to cook the ingredients by any means other than a straight boil.

Outside the atmosphere of international conferences and the confrontations they produce, the agencies concede two basic problems. One is the difficulty in covering all areas adequately: 'we fail,' says Stevenson, 'to cover South Illinois for North Illinois. So what are we to do about Zaire?' The other is the extent to which their emphasis on 'hard news' lends itself to the 'coups and disasters' coverage of which the Third World complains.

A rough estimate of the annual cost of maintaining one Western correspondent abroad – salary, expenses and communications – is around $100,000. The last item accounts for about a third of the bill and sometimes more; with costs rising the more economically backward the region and the weaker the communications links between a particular developing country and headquarters. Unesco, to give a comparison, prides itself on being able to furnish advisers and technical experts at around $104,000; and they are not filing expensive daily dispatches. All the agencies, aside from their technological investments, report that coverage costs abroad are escalating sharply.

The result is of course a tendency to cluster reporting strength, and fill in the gaps with roving missions and stringers. In many countries, national stringers are very closely watched; they may even be nominated by the government (in severa cases, stringers have been suggested to agencies who accept, and then discover that the person concerned works in the ministry of information). They are vulnerable to reprisals. And quite often, they have never worked as journalists. 'What is commonly referred to as the world flow of information,' writes Rosenblum, 'is more a series of trickles and spurts. News is moved across borders by surprisingly thin networks of correspondents. ... The smaller countries are squeezed into rapid trips during lulls between major stories in the larger countries.' And he quotes a Latin American scholar's ironic amazement that 'news always breaks in South America along the direct lines of the Braniff route.' Chance, Rosenblum adds, produces a form of distortion; because riots in Jamaica coincided with the 1975 meeting there of the International Monetary Fund, they were reported 'in chilling detail'. Had the reporters not been there, 'the local Jamaican stringers might not have seen fit to write, and the disturbance might have been a tree falling unheard in a distant forest.'

Any journalist working in Asia during the Indochina war was likely to be asked by colleagues in other parts of the world how much time they spent in Vietnam/Cambodia/Laos. If they replied that they were covering 'the rest' of Asia, the automatic response was a look of polite bafflement; whole groups of countries can be forgotten when the regional centre of news gravity is obvious and dramatic.

Computerisation to some extent increases the pressures for news of general, worldwide interest. Language difficulties – and an inadequate grounding in the history of an area – both complicate and distort. Correspondents for news agencies, even more than for newspapers, are required to be all-rounders, covering sports news, development issues, politics and macroeconomics. And their sense of isolation can be considerable, leading them either to cluster with the diplomatic corps, or to immerse themselves in local tensions, political or social. Stan Swinton comments that one of the things the AP watches closely is any tendency for correspondents to become too absorbed in internal conflicts: yet the balance between superficial coverage and too committed an immersion in the life of a country is extremely difficult to maintain. Third World leaders also accuse foreign correspondents of staying in the capital city and forming their judgements on that artificial basis. Most correspondents travel as much, if not more, within countries than the journalists of the countries' national press who are based in the capital; but not all are equipped to understand what they find – and some governments make such trips extremely difficult.

In singling out the agencies for their principal attacks, governments are in fact tackling correspondents whose duty is to try to report for an international audience, and who therefore in fact cast their net wider than newspaper correspondents who must meet the narrower perceived demands of their domestic readership. Agency reporters file more, on more subjects; and the chances of their achieving a balance are thereby the greater. But common to all correspondents is the requirement that their copy be 'useable' – five thousand words on the visit by a foreign minister from a neighbouring country, or even the contents of the new five-year plan, will simply not fall into that category. A problem with many of the complaints made against the agencies is that those who make them forget that news of any kind only exists if it is read by somebody. Evelyn Waugh's *Scoop* gives a parodic but salutary definition: 'News is what a chap who doesn't care much about anything wants to read.'

Even the effort to refrain from subjective judgements, to report the 'facts', militates against the rounded picture. Between the twin pressures of the market and the concept of 'neutral' news, there is a strong tendency to give priority to major events with clearly defined aspects. Stories on development trends, social change, evolutions which cannot be easily 'pegged' to a particular happening, tend to get fitted in when there is time. The criticisms are to this extent valid, although not the implication of deliberate neglect or distortion which accompanies them.

Gerald Long of Reuters has commented on the 'frustrations which are felt, very understandably, by these countries about the way in which they see themselves represented'. He agrees that 'the prevalent school of journalism throughout the world is a journalism of exception. In other words, you don't report that everything is fine today in Pakistan. You report that there has been an air crash. Now, this whole attitude towards events can be criticised. I'm not too happy about it myself. We in Reuters do try very hard ... not to concentrate on disaster, the negative, on the criticisms and the troubles ... because we're aware there is this danger.'

But the 'bad news syndrome' includes, for many Third World critics, what they call deliberately divisive journalism, often meaning stories about the political opposition. Does the international press exaggerate the importance of dissent, because it operates in terms of 'alien' standards? Long, again: 'If a government says that, I believe no government on that subject. ... Enlightened governments tolerate a great deal of information which isn't favourable to them. But all governments like most of all only to have that information disseminated which reflects their view of life. That's in the nature of governments.' But there is a persistent belief in the Third World either that Western correspondents, in reporting opposition views, seek to destabilise the existing government; or they are ignorant of the genuine dangers to a developing society's stability which such reports might represent. These can be real; they are almost always a convenient pretext. The question which divides the West from its critics is, who is to judge?

Experience and understanding are vital. Raw reporters are rarely sent by the agencies to the Third World – although they will generally be young. More comfortable – and prestigious – Western postings still go to the senior journalists. The AP selection process, as described by Stan Swinton, runs as follows: the agency hires people generally after they have had two years experience, 'on a member newspaper'. They will then have a couple of years in a small US bureau, move to a larger one and – if they want to go into the foreign service – are tested on their knowledge of particular areas, their languages (with tests to establish the degree of fluency) and their overseas experience. If they pass these tests, they are brought to New York to handle the foreign stories for domestic consumption, or the world service which distributes both foreign and domestic news internationally. They may have been eight years with the AP before their first foreign posting. Non-American correspondents are generally brought to New York for training.

All of this may indeed mean that the AP correspondent is steeped in the news-values and the market requirements of the

agency – which may, as they are said to do, colour his judgements. But he is not inexperienced. And he will have been told
to provide a rounded picture. 'A year's file', says a senior
editor in New York, 'should ideally give us an across-the-board
feel for a country.' He will also be under increasing pressure to
offer much more social and economic reporting.

Part of the reason for this new emphasis is the agencies'
sensitivity to the criticisms by the Third World. An internal
UPI memo of April 1977, from H. L. Stevenson to Frank
Tremaine, Senior Vice-President, reflects these concerns.
UPI's coverage, reported Stevenson, 'is comprehensive and
reflects progress being made . . . as well as frustrations and
failures. Our critics say we concern ourselves only with violence
or bloodshed and that we look only for "negative" news. This is
far from the case. . . .' Stevenson's confidence was based on a
sampling of thirty to forty stories, picked 'at random' over
nine months and covering about thirty countries. Only three
were concerned with war and disease: they reported political
violence in Argentina, defence preparations in Mozambique,
and a malaria outbreak in India.

Such lists mean little, whoever compiles them; but the UPI
snap survey also brought out something else. The world is
largely agreed on the definition of 'bad news'; good news is
quite another matter. Indonesia's progress in the post-Sukarno
years was measured by UPI's correspondent in terms of the
skyscrapers in Jakarta, improved communications, paved
streets and 'highways bustling with traffic'; the same description could equally figure in an article discussing the inappropri-
ateness of Indonesia's patterns of investment to its overall
needs, and the gap between the status symbols of affluence in
the capital and continuing poverty in the countryside. Would
it then have entered the 'bad news' category? In either version,
judgement and 'values' enter in.

But the survey also suggested a considerable emphasis on
social themes, the problems of development and relations
between different countries of the Third World. Journalists in
all four Western agencies report a growing interest in background features and 'people' stories which give a picture of
living conditions and development efforts in the Third World.
And editors are trying to encourage reporters to 'illuminate

the spot event' – to describe how restrictions on certain imports by the West affect the producing country's economy, or the impact of modernisation on the Gulf States. By contrast, they point to a diminishing interest in traditional foreign reporting – coverage of political speeches and diplomacy. 'We still cover the fall of the sparrow,' said one editor, 'but what gets printed are the circumstances surrounding its death.'

If these trends are genuine, they could alter the balance of agency reporting in a way that to some extent meets Third World complaints. One editor also expressed the conviction that 'the focus of interest in news is shifting to the Third World. That's one reason why the technique and content of stories from these areas has changed, to emphasise in-depth coverage. These are going to be the news centres – just speaking professionally, and not because of any pressures coming from these countries. How could we not seek to describe a world in ferment?'

Do such changes in the hearts of the agencies' gate-keepers, the people who govern news priorities, affect the political debate? They could produce more reflective coverage, less sensationalism – but will this divert the challenge to 'free market imperialism'? Third World countries want not only more comprehensive (and sympathetic) reporting of their affairs by the Western press; they want access to the international market for their own views of themselves, an alteration and balancing of the one-way flow of information. While some Third World spokesmen clearly mean by this an increase in the lateral flow of information between their countries, complementing the existing structure, many more look to 'structural' changes – and mean by that a controlled flow of information. Amithaba Chowdhury, a highly experienced journalist who was Assistant Editor of *Jugantar* in Calcutta before becoming the first Director of the Press Foundation of Asia, warned in a speech in the US in 1977 that 'for some countries in the Third World, I believe, control of exportable news is a political necessity.' He meant that news, for those governments, has become a form of international diplomacy.

By coincidence, perhaps, the call for a more balanced flow of information has coincided with the growth of restrictions on the media in developing countries which runs the gamut from

President Samora of Mozambique's plans for 're-educating' journalists and bringing the media under 'popular control', to the refusal of visas to agency journalists seeking to cover an anti-apartheid conference in Nigeria in 1977. If the agencies' public stances have been largely defensive, it is because many of their senior editors fear that no matter how they seek to improve the quality of their coverage, frontiers and sources of information are closing, and for reasons which have little to do with professional criteria.

CHAPTER 3

Realities of the Marketplace

To the supporters of the liberal traditions of a free and independent press, the diversity of voices makes possible the intelligent choices essential to a democracy. Respect for the citizen is imposed on the media by the fact of his power to choose a paper or programme. A little irresponsibility, certainly, is built into the resulting product; but it is a small price for liberty.

To its detractors, this freedom is a fraud: choice is only apparent because diversity masks the machinery of power – not, perhaps, always the power of governments, but the more insidious powers of big business. In the structure of the Western press, money is king and advertising is queen. The so-called freedom of information is in practice the freedom for a small elite of the rich and powerful to impose their views on the many: the mass media are 'both the expression of a system of domination and a means of reinforcing it.'

Insofar as independence and the reader's judgement are cornerstones of sound journalism in liberal eyes, both have developed some rough edges. Government subsidies have become a fact of life in most European countries, even if the United States (as in so many industries, assisted by the huge size of its home market) is still free of the need for them. The implications for the continued independence of the press differ in each case, but the trend is unmistakeable. And even with subsidies, there is increasing concentration in ownership, itself partly due to the requirements of advertisers for larger circulations. And the advertisers cannot be ignored, because the tradition that a newspaper costs markedly less than the cost of producing it is firmly entrenched; advertising makes up most of the difference. Again, the consequences are limited in most countries, but not all. The marketplace does not destroy the possibility of telling the truth; but it compromises it in certain ways. Nor is the 'free' press free in other ways. From Equatorial Guinea and Czechoslovakia to the United States, there are only gradations between the restrictive and the permissive. The battle between the media and the State will always be unequal, if only because the State makes the laws. Libel, contempt of court, privacy, obscenity, official secrets, and various forms of *lèse-majesté* hedge truth about with varying degrees of justification or absurdity. Few of these apply with any vigour to the United States; yet in 1977 a US Reporters' Committee identified ninety-eight Bills which it asserted would affect press freedom.

'Freedom' at best means that the journalist shall not exercise his profession in conditions more restrictive than those which apply to the ordinary citizen. Yet the citizen himself applies tests, the tests of the marketplace which are the least visible but most effective influence – most effective in the sense that no editor can fight it off or urge that the conditions be liberalised. He cannot separate himself from the citizen. This is a strength of sorts, but it also imposes limits, as a British journalist, John Whale of *The Sunday Times*, pointed out in a recent book: 'The speed at which most [newspapers'] contents are written, and judged, means that they reflect certain human reactions with an undissembled accuracy. Their content cannot exceed the capacity of their writers, clearly; but, even more limitingly, it cannot go beyond the range of their readers. It is therefore the readers, in the end, who are the figures of power.'

Marxists would dismiss this as a feeble fiction: the readers, they would argue, have been so conditioned that they exercise their supposed power in so marginal sense as to be irrelevant to the debate. The media still dictate the narrow boundaries of choice, so effectively that the consumer's influence is meaningless.

The core of the debate, insofar as it concerns the international scene, centres on the real power of the media, and the responsibility (in the strict sense of the word) with which they exercise it in a free market system.

Two men went to the United States, within ten years of each other, in the first half of the nineteenth century. They were Charles Dickens and Alexis de Tocqueville. To Dickens, the no-holds-barred press that he found there was a 'mortal poison . . . a frightful engine'. Unlike the dignified press of Europe, discussing the high issues or the day in the language of diplomats, here was a disrespectful mass enterprise whose power was to be feared, and 'while that Press has its evil eye in every house, and its black hand in every appointment in the state, . . . while, with ribald slander for its only stock in trade, it is the standard literature of an enormous class . . . so long must its odium be on the country's head, and so long must the evil it works, be plainly visible.'

Tocqueville's observations, by contrast, grasped the essence of the function of a pluralistic press; and the effect of the already advanced commercialisation which had occurred. No-one, he remarked with amazement, 'dared to suggest restricting the freedom of the press'; three-quarters of these fat newspapers would be filled with advertising; and the number of them, he wrote, 'surpasses all belief'. They might be filled with political news, anecdote, or scandal; the journalist, he found 'disregards principles to seize on people, following them into their private lives and laying bare their weaknesses and vices.' Unlike Dickens, however, he recognised that diversity actually weakened the powers of newspapers to impose their views, and the aggressive style produced 'the result . . . that the personal views expressed by journalists carry, so to speak, no weight with the readers. What they look for in a newspaper is knowledge of facts, and it is only by distorting those facts that the journalist can gain some influence for his views.'

With extraordinary percipience, he went on to describe the function of such a press in much the terms it might be described today: 'It makes political life circulate in every corner of that vast land. Its eyes are never shut, and it lays bare the secret shifts of politics, forcing public figures in turn to appear before the tribunal of opinion. . . . Through the press the parties, without actually meeting, listen and argue with one another . . . . Each individual American newspaper has little power, but after the people, the press is nonetheless the first of the powers.'

If this plurality created a freedom, the principle danger of which was the mean level of the common denominator – and Tocqueville's great work on America is shot through with his awareness of the price of egalitarianism – the essential distinction which he clearly conveys is between a press which sees itself as councillor, purveying considered opinions on high policy based on sound knowledge, and serving the public good through its balancing of experience; and the rude press of a popular democracy, whose value resides not in the assumption of any moral mission, but in the mass dissemination of the raw material which enables others to choose and to participate themselves in public life. A distinction, too, between 'public interest' and 'what interests the public' which, he perceived, did not mean that the latter might not be the most effective servant of the former.

The American press, despite closures which have led to serious studies of the dangers of the concentration of ownership, and which have created a monopoly for a single newspaper in many towns and some cities, has by world standards prospered in the 140 years since Tocqueville observed it. In 1975, the US was consuming over three times its annual newsprint production of three million metric tons, to circulate around sixty-four million newspapers a day. For all the concern about low readership figures in the younger age-groups, most surveys have still shown that the considerable majority of Americans take their news basically from newspapers rather than television. With over 1,150 daily newspapers in circulation, the vital ingredient of diversity would seem to have been preserved.

But this apparent richness masks a much greater concentration where international news is concerned. Here, a much smaller number of organisations set the agenda. Only a tiny proportion of newspapers or broadcasting stations have correspondents abroad. Foreign news reaches the US through few gateways. The AP and UPI, the *New York Times*, the three television networks, the *Washington Post* and *Los Angeles Times*, the news magazines and a handful of newspaper chains and individual publications have correspondents abroad or send out roving reporters. A smaller number still sells its reports to the rest. The number of foreign correspondents, never very large, has been shrinking – the Overseas Press Club register of Americans working abroad for the media had dropped from 563 in 1969 to 429 in 1975. Fulltime employees of other nationalities, working as journalists abroad for American media, had fallen from 366 to 247. And more than half the total was based in Europe. Thousands of stringers notwithstanding, the happy few must wield, in Tocqueville's terms, great power in shaping the image of the world for Americans.

In Europe, applying the same criteria, the foundations of diversity look weaker still. Between 1965 and 1976, out of ten British national papers, a Royal Commission found that only three had increased their network of foreign reporters; only one of those three had not cut back in the lean years since 1974. In just over a decade, *The Times* had cut from twenty-five to eighteen, *The Daily Telegraph* from thirty to thirteen and the only major paper to make a serious effort to increase its foreign reporting capacity was *The Financial Times*. Financial pressures, in Britain and in the rest of Western Europe during this period, affected not only the outlay on foreign correspondents but ownership patterns and the principle of financial independence. There is also a tendency during financial and political crisis to concentrate on domestic problems. While no figures are available, there is widespread awareness in the trade of an increased tendency to look inward in most of the Western press.

Blanket criticisms of the 'free market' approach to information necessarily do not concern themselves with the widely differing patterns of ownership, and the degree of influence ownership may confer. Thomson Newspapers executives involved in the non-news aspects of the business find that the ownership of news media is 'a mild public-relations disadvantage', reports Whale; there is a tendency in many newspapers or commercial broadcasting companies not to mention an owner's other business concerns at all, for fear of bias (or the accusation of bias). In France, journalists report that the government or big business do seek to influence the press by withholding advertisements from papers which publish certain articles, or take an editorial line, of which they disapprove; the problem is particularly acute in economic and financial reporting. West Germany's chief problem is the concentration of press ownership, and the steady drop in sales. In both France and Italy, owners are in many cases people – journalists or industrialists – who want to influence opinion; the question remains whether the concentration of private ownership, or the political commitment of some owners, threatens pluralism so much as heavy state intervention.

In Europe, however, even state intervention has been explicitly directed at preserving diversity where the written press is concerned. Broadcast media are another matter, as the battles over 'pirate' radio stations challenging public monopolies have demonstrated in Britain, Italy or France. The Swedish subsidies pattern, which in a complex series of policies includes production subsidies for low circulation papers, is an example. Subsidies are both universal, in one form or another, and widely accepted as necessary to prevent further closures; France has less than half the number of daily papers it had at the end of World War II. Throughout Europe, the arrival of television – either commercial, or 'state' television part-supported by advertising – has drawn on a total of advertising revenue which has not increased proportionately and which in some countries has shrunk during the recession of the 1970's.

All of these concerns – increased competitiveness in the bid for advertising revenue, steeply rising production and newsprint costs (the latter sharply affected by the rise in oil prices), industrial problems often connected in the newspaper industry with the attempt to leave the age of Gutenberg for cost-cutting but capital-absorbing offset lithography and computer typesetting systems – have put high circulations at a special premium.

The temptation, for these reasons, to cut back on news which has little popular appeal has not prevented the growth of new reporting techniques – much greater concentration on investigative reporting and in-depth team studies of major issues. Financial crisis has even assisted the emergence of serious economic reporting for a general public. But in times of crisis, independence can also be vulnerable to restrictions in the name of the national interest. As Sir William Haley – a former editor of *The Times* and also a Director-General of the BBC – warned in chairing the 1974 Granada Guildhall lectures, 'the open pressures on [journalists'] freedom may be great.

The hidden pressures will be even greater. The graver the situation becomes, the more persuasively will they be told that to reveal the whole truth would be dangerous, that the outlook is too precarious for *complete* candour.'

The press of the marketplace, in other words, was in the 1970's beset by many of the strains that Third World leaders are apt to consider peculiar to developing societies. The resources with which they can attempt to meet the strains are of course incomparably greater; and the social fabric, the markets and the traditions of free argument support their efforts. But by sad irony, the Third World's call for better and more complete coverage of their affairs in the West has coincided with economic and political circumstances which have encouraged editors and producers to look homeward rather than towards the so much more precariously placed developing world.

At least some of the criticisms levelled against the Western media and its values are applied equally to the written and broadcast press; they attack not the particular case of prejudice, the specific policies relating to foreign or domestic coverage, or the shifting balance between news coverage and journalism of opinion, but what are seen as the structural defects of the marketplace, in good times as in bad: the 'institutional circumscriptions, stereotyped approaches, conventional procedures and traditional codes ... tantamount to built-in mechanisms of censorship and control.' These, as much as sensationalism and the 'journalism of exception', are said to contribute to what are seen as actual barriers to informing the citizen. The marketplace fails by its own criteria.

The phrasing comes from Professor James Halloran, a British communications researcher who also happens to believe that the role of the media is far too important an issue to be left to journalists. But it is a fair enough summary of the claims advanced by theorists and politicians, many of whom conceive (as Halloran says he does not) of state journalism as the alternative. But whatever there may be in the accusation that 'the way the mass media deal with social issues impairs understanding, makes intelligent decision- and policy-making impossible, and precludes the existence of an adequately informed participatory democracy,' the market system with all its imperfections has a good claim to coming nearest to doing the job.

The most acute area of concern has been, on both sides of the Atlantic, television news. Common to journalism in all the media, as a Western journalist expressed it at the United Nations World Information Day seminar in Tunis in October 1977, are 'the institutional pressures, the received ideas and reflexes as to what constitutes news, transmitted to the new recruit and called training . . . and lastly, the professional cynicism which is both our defence and our limitation.' But to these common difficulties, television news adds a special dimension – that of space. A background paper for the meeting in October 1977 of broadcasters from non-aligned countries calculated that an averagely educated man could read 24,000 words an hour; but he could listen to only 6,000. A thirty-minute TV programme would come to about one and a half newspaper columns. This estimate may exaggerate the reading speed of *l'homme moyen lettré*, but a disproportion undoubtedly exists.

Writing in *Intermedia*, the International Broadcast Institute's journal, in December 1975, two of the most respected current affairs programme journalists in the UK, John Birt and Peter Jay, claimed that there is a built-in 'bias against understanding' in television journalism. News programmes might cover twenty items in half an hour, obviously allowing no time to put the news item in context; viewers, said Birt and Jay, were likely to be left 'confused and uneasy'. Features, they alleged, were liable to produce a diverting profile of an aspect of a particular problem without illuminating the problem or to 'link, say, one unemployed man and the real causes of un-employment'.

The small percentage of what they termed 'issue'programmes – attempts to analyse all aspects of a subject – which succeeded in doing what they intended then faced a further obstacle: boring the viewer. 'A well-made report on a famine will be more watchable than a report on the world food problem.' While, paradoxically, the writers finished up by calling for more 'journalistic' criteria for television journalism, they also found the system unequal to the task in general terms: 'reality is a seamless garment of interacting and developing processes while journalism is organised to collect innumerable nuggets of self-contained fact to report an atomised world of a million tiny tales.' The implied remedy was larger pieces of the garment, somehow to be tailored so that the audience would stay watching long enough to inspect the whole.

This, ITN retorted, 'would mean the end of the kind of television news programmes that have established themselves with many audiences, and the dissipation of those audiences;' the picture must come first, or interest could not be sustained. And variety must continue to be the spice of televised news; the only cure was more space for both news and analysis. The argument had progressed little since a 1960 Committee on Broadcasting had lamented that 'subjects billed as controversial sometimes avoided the controversy, and so served rather to reinforce than to disturb prejudice and complacency. . . . Our own conclusion is that triviality is a natural vice of television, and that where it prevails it operates to lower general standards of enjoyment and understanding.'

Concern about the structural problems of television news-programmes is compounded in the US by the conflict between news and entertainment – which there takes such an acute form that the resolution has edged towards making news *into* enter-tainment – and by the rivalry between the three huge corpor-ations, CBS, NBC and ABC, who between them bring the news each evening to some 26 million viewers. There is anxiety that respect for the viewer's interests has gone through the looking glass and transformed itself into subservience to the tyranny of the ratings (a modern version of Tocqueville's 'tyranny of the majority'); and fears have been voiced that the responsibility with which the networks exercise their franchise is beyond vetting by any independent body.

The networks vehemently repudiate the notion that any such vetting is necessary or appropriate; professional ethics and institutional ground-rules are enough, they say, to ensure that the news simply mirrors a part of national and inter-national events, selected on the well-tried and constantly monitored basis of the public interest and concern. If the mirror's image disquiets, the argument runs, the fault lies with society and not the medium.

There are two obvious problems with such statements.

Edward J. Epstein, in his book *News from Nowhere*, provides some telling illustrations of television's version of the 'neutral news' myth. He describes how ABC, in March 1969, decided to move from combat footage of the Vietnam war to inter-pretative pieces. Its executive producer, Av Westin, telexed Saigon correspondents that the focus should shift 'to themes and stories under the general heading: We Are On Our Way Out Of Vietnam' and went on to suggest some story ideas: the line for a blackmarket piece was 'Find us that Oriental Sydney Greenstreet, the export-import entrepreneur'; for medical care for civilians, it was 'Does the grand-daughter sleep under the old man's hospital bed, scrounge food for him etc.' The correspondents, faced with a radical change in their type of work, may have needed guidance; the story 'title suggestions' however suggest fairly specific prompting: to reveal the Vietnam which Americans were to leave behind as incurably corrupt, incompetent to the point where it was hardly worth supporting. No doubt ABC did not intend this to be the exclusive slant; a correspondent in receipt of that telex could have been pardoned for failing to realise that a rounded picture was called for.

Another problem is the obsession with the 'selling' of the news. This is the dark side of the economic logic behind the US mass media's legendary concern with the ratings. Not only do extra news programmes tend to be run by pre-empting time from entertainment (they must therefore be slotted in where they do least harm), but when it comes to news features, subjects must often be pre-sold to sponsors. The fickleness of audiences, the ratings show, turns to positive infidelity when controversial subjects are screened; a large proportion regularly switch off. Epstein quotes an NBC producer's comment: 'This does not mean that the networks won't do programmes that can't be sold on subjects that are not popular. It means the network won't do *many* such programmes.'

The commercial dependence on audiences, and the uncer-tainties as to their tolerance levels for serious programmes, is not limited to television or radio. But they face the added difficulty that whereas articles of interest only to a small proportion of readers can be published – because the page can always be turned – each item on broadcast news must be judged on its ability to interest the greatest possible number, as well as on its intrinsic worth. The conflict between excellence of objective and the uncertainty of the market place is particularly acute, for both media, when it comes to foreign news.

Do commercial pressures lead to inadequate reporting, particularly of developing countries? International reporting becomes steadily more expensive, and Western organisations are easily discouraged when governments of countries which they wish to cover – but which are not vital ingredients in the news schedule (as the Soviet Union, for example, continues to be) – block access to information and make the exercise virtually impossible in other ways. The fact that so many Western correspondents based in Africa operate from South Africa or Rhodesia (where half Reuters' Africa bureau chiefs, for example, are to be found) reflects no love for apartheid or for Ian Smith, but the *relative* freedom to report, and the better telecommunications facilities, to be had there. Having resident correspondents thrown out of a country is expensive and frustrating, even if it makes a good on-off story at the time. Institutional prejudices are also at work, among them the preference for the dramatic. And for all publics, where they are given a choice, the subs' rule of 'Afghanistanism' operates to some extent – the further away a country, the less interest there is likely to be, at least in its daily life. Disasters are different; they are truly international. Foreign correspondents develop habits based on their knowledge of what gets printed or broadcast; the 'spike' is a great censor.

Conflicts between editors and proprietors, journalists and editors, industrial disputes, all dramatise the tensions in the market place. At the same time, the structure of the free press is coming under more intensive scrutiny, partly because the industry is poised on the threshold of a technological revolution which could in theory alter the process of news-gathering and dissemination more radically than the invention of the telegraph. It is expected that the capacity of the Western media to reach (and persuade) people will be enormously enhanced before the end of the next decade. Simultaneously, they are under the microscope because their economic difficulties are making government involvement in the market place a growing reality. A French journalist, asserting to an international conference that the Western press might be free, but was certainly not democratic, added that government action was probably the only way to ensure the media's democratisation. Most Western journalists see any governmental moves to form policies for the media as the first step towards the establishment of a press which would have to justify its existence by demonstrating 'responsibility' – the first criterion of which would be a proper respect for the men in power.

An instructive example of what 'responsibility' can mean was provided by the French state-run television service just before the final round of voting in the French elections of 1978. Two programmes had been prepared: one on the schisms within the parties of the left, the other on the quarrels between Gaullists and Giscardians on the right. The first was screened; the second, in spite of bitter public complaints from the journalists, was not. It was found not to be sufficiently 'objective'. The fact that there is no independent commercial broadcasting in France is a major cause for the mushrooming, which occurs before every election, of new newspapers; the public turns to print to balance the images on the country's screens.

The triumphant example of the service a free press can perform in refusing to display that sense of 'responsibility' is Watergate. But despite the euphoria which that victory created, it was tempered by the knowledge that the service was not greeted with unmixed praise by the American public; surveys have indicated that some of the opprobrium of the affair has transferred itself in the public mind to the journalists who uncovered the unpleasant. The press is under pressure to demonstrate its concern for the public interest, not least because investigative reporting has heightened and made more visible the selective element in news-gathering.

The Watergate affair, and the role of the press in it, also gave the public a possibly exaggerated notion of the power of the press. Assertions that the news is 'value-free' fit ill with openly combative journalism, however laudable the motives for the combat and however great the public benefit. Watergate also demonstrated the ability of at least the leading newspapers to cling to a particular campaign or line of investigation because the subject seems of paramount importance, and not because it has established itself (at least in the important early stages) as something in which the public is particularly interested. The approach may produce dividends, in terms of circulation and prestige; but these considerations are not a primary factor.

Why should not such perseverence, and such power to persuade, be applied to the most important of all campaigns – the establishment of a more equitable international order? The question is being posed by Third World leaders; and Western editors can no longer reply in purely market terms. But such a campaign would necessarily be of a totally different order from investigations into Watergate or the marketing of thalidomide: insofar as it would involve uncovering injustice, it would still concern itself with what is wrong in the *normal*, as opposed to the exceptional, way of conducting affairs, with the customary rather than the illegal. It would also imply demands on Western publics to accept the consequences of an interdependent world – consequences which would hit their living standards. And there would be no tangible target for such a campaign – no 'guilty men' whose exposure and disgrace would produce the desired solution. Last but not least, it would demand a kind of reporting which exposed incremental and complex shifts in the world balance of power and the affairs of developing nations: explaining the international pressures for change, as they must affect the audience, without the help of being able to present the dénouement at the end of each story.

As the challenge is being posed by Third World politicians, the Western media are also being required to do more than to alert their public opinion to the changing economic and political situation: what is demanded from many quarters is a missionary approach to the moulding of that opinion, which is sharply at variance with most Western editors' ideas of their proper role. They make a distinction between the campaign which uncovers 'the facts' at all costs, and the acceptance of a policy-forming role in society. To many leaders in developing countries, this distinction looks like a hypocritical evasion.

'We do not understand why the mass media – radio, TV, press – have failed to grasp . . . the vital need for both developed and developing countries to ensure that public opinion is properly informed, and, indeed, formed and mobilised in the service of the aims which the non-aligned countries, the Third World, feel should be those of the international community as a whole.' The political case, in a nutshell, from Algeria's then Trade Minister Layachi Yaker. The place, an international meeting of journalists and politicians convened in Nice to discuss North–South economic relations and the role of the mass media; the time, October 1975 – just after the Seventh Special Session of the United Nations met to consider the New International Economic Order, just before the Paris talks on economic cooperation which were to last eighteen months and become known as the North–South dialogue. The organisers of the meeting was the Centre International pour le Développement, strongly backed by Mexico's then President, Luis Echeverria. And the evangelical purposes in convening it were quite specific: 'perfecting one of the most essential instruments in changing societies and in human and inter-state relations: *public information* . . . The transformation and improvement of the mass media is inseparable from the changes that are sought in the Order of regulating international relations.'

What did this mean? More self-reliance among the Third World's largely controlled media; or more Western involvement in getting the developing world's viewpoint across to their own publics? The politicians were clear: as Echeverria's represent-ative, Juan José Bremer, put it, the Western press must do a better job of presenting 'the tragic and shocking fact that more than three-quarters of the world's population was living outside modern society altogether, and the fact that these problems could not be postponed or dismissed lightly.' But Western journalists persuaded by such arguments also faced, from academic quarters, charges that the international media were 'servants of the structure of economic domination' and threats that they would not be allowed to continue their 'ideo-logical penetration' of underdeveloped countries. They would be controlled if not actually ejected by these countries as undesirable transnational systems in much the same way that a multinational corporation might be. Structurally, they were incapable of doing a disinterested job.

The contradictions between these arguments have become familiar since 1975. But there is a common denominator: the assumption that the press exists to create the climate in which politicians work without hindrance. Germán Carnero, later to become Unesco's regional coordinator for information in Latin America, argued straightforwardly that 'since it was agreed that the positions taken by the Third World were just and equitable, it was necessary for journalists to show a certain militancy in favour of those attitudes.' Yet there were eloquent arguments behind the pleas made to the Western press: to get rid of its prejudices and stereotypes when reporting developing countries' affairs, to give a true picture of their 'situation, viewpoints and arguments', and to explain to the people of the industrialised world that the eradication of mass poverty, far from being marginal to their interests, directly affected their longterm wellbeing.

The Western response, at that meeting, was sceptical. In the first place, an American journalist pointed out, making something as all-embracing as the New Economic Order intelligible to more than a tiny handful of readers would require not only new techniques of reporting, but more accurate spelling out by developing countries: 'We have heard many statements of principle, need, desires – on which we all agree. But the time has come to be much more specific about what the developing countries are proposing. . . .' Secondly, Gordon Tether of the *Financial Times* commented, the Third World case had failed to impress itself on developed countries' publics 'partly because constructive measures to resolve those problems had not been properly formulated' while at the same time, governmental aid to the South had a poor image because 'it was felt that it had failed.'

But the most pointed response to the 'mobilisation' thesis was made by Colin Legum of *The Observer*, who said that since changes would be required of the people of both developed and developing countries and that the problems of adjustment could not be glossed over, 'criticism of the shortcomings in the industrial and Third World countries must be well-intentioned and well-informed . . . if you want to persuade someone to make a change that will be difficult for him, the best way to do so is by enlisting his cooperation.' Obstacles to this, he said, were the hostility of Third World spokesmen; the clouding with myths – sovereignty, raw materials cartels, self-reliance in the Third World – of what must be a process of 'collective bargaining'. What was needed was not political mobilisation, but to establish 'a convincing list of arguments . . . which can be used in equal honesty in both developed and developing countries.'

How closely do the complaints about the Western media relate to their performance? The North–South Dialogue provided a test case of sorts.

Lasting for eighteen months, grouping eight industrialised countries and nineteen representatives of the Third World nominated by the Group of 77, and conducted with all the periodic secrecy which is the stock-in-trade of international conferences, the Conference on International Economic Co-operation presented classic problems for press coverage.

It is always difficult to hold the reader's interest in processes and discussions which evolve in important but not headline-making ways, and conferences of the Paris variety have long periods when sessions are secret and briefings off-the-record and short on concrete information. There was also virtually unlimited scope for bias in reporting the negotiations, because the main purpose of the meeting – as it rapidly became clear – was differently conceived by each side. Initiated by President Giscard d'Estaing, largely with the aim of keeping open a dialogue on energy supplies and prices, the conference began and ended with energy high on the agenda. But for the countries of the 'South', the whole point of meeting was to force a serious debate – using their one real bargaining tool, the energy question – on the structural changes required in the international economic order to bring about more equitable participation by the poorer nations.

As a further complication for the reporter, this general aim did not imply generally applicable solutions. The enormous disparities in wealth, economic interests, natural resources and degree of industrial development between, say, Zaire and Venezuela, naturally implied that a 'package' which would work for one might not benefit the other. If the industrialised countries were sharply divided among themselves, with some governments pressing for a generous response to the demands of the nineteen and others adopting almost wholly defensive postures, attempts to arrive at particular agreements exposed sharply diverging interests among the developing countries as well.

One case was the debate on the rescheduling or cancelling of debts accumulated by the non-oil developing countries. For a government anxious to maintain a high rate of economic development, following policies which it expected to create the liquidity required to service its foreign debt, and with good export prospects, rescheduling presented more dangers than benefits. For it threatens to make industrialised countries and major international banks more reluctant to lend to Third World countries. For those hardest hit by the oil price rise and the global recession, for whom key development programmes had been forced to a standstill, and whose economies were further hamstrung by the fact that investment funds were almost entirely eaten up by debt servicing and repayment, rescheduling was a matter of economic life and death. Yet many reports attempting to describe the inevitable differences of viewpoint, and their basis in economic circumstance, were sharply criticised by Third World governments as 'divisive' – even as deliberate attempts to sabotage Third World unity.

The conference achieved two major successes: it did not break up; and it succeeded in focussing public attention on the issues. The Western press coverage, while not constant, still filled four fat OECD library files, and there was a serious attempt to guide the reader through the development of the debates, even if lapses of press interest meant that the changes in the political and economic climate between the opening of the talks in 1975 and their end in June 1977 were inadequately analysed in terms of their implications for the conference. One consequence of the amount of press coverage was to bring out the intractability of the problems – and the extreme difficulty of putting across the overall Third World position *without* resort to stereotypes.

Predictably, French coverage was the most extensive: French prestige was affected by the outcome of the conference. But it was also serious: *Le Monde*, in particular, analysed the issues at regular intervals in sensitive if sometimes sceptical articles; and at the end firmly laid the blame for what it saw as the bitterness with which the conference concluded on the rich countries' concentration on the energy dialogue. Coverage of the final sessions was marked by the efforts to assess Third World aims (and differences); and by the extent to which their representatives were lobbied and quoted. As the final communique revealed agreement on twenty points – and disagreement on twenty-one – *The Guardian* in London began an emotive leader, 'They asked for bread and we gave them a stone' – but in a long news analysis also pinpointed a difficulty which affected both the outcome of the conference and the job of reporting it: 'the apparent inability of the poor countries to move beyond dogmatic and generalised ideals, and to spell out specific, detailed, workable proposals for the kind of help they wanted.'

The overall tone of Western reporting was that the North had failed to be sufficiently imaginative, the South to be sufficiently realistic. Headlines emphasised the 'Western perspective' – the energy question; the articles under them did not. Assessing the areas of agreement, several Western papers made the point that the $1,000 million special fund offered by the eight to assist the poorest Third World countries amounted to less than a year's debt-servicing for the worst-hit nations. In two long articles in the *International Herald Tribune*, James Goldborough discussed the meagreness – and vagueness – of the areas of agreement, but pointed to the difficulties of a negotiating process in which one side presented a list 'which excluded little and was meant to lay the groundwork for the new world economic order' to a group of countries 'worried about stagnation, recession, inflation, energy shortages and, in many cases, losing the next election'. Some of the disagreements, he suggested, were over measures 'probably not in anyone's power to grant'.

The Western media's performance fell far short of a campaign to persuade their readers and viewers that an international system which they were accustomed to regard as natural must undergo radical change. They did not explore the nature of the short-term sacrifices for (vaguer) longterm goals which meeting the whole basket of Third World demands must entail for the industrialised countries. But they did warn of the pressures on the system, and do so in a reasonably even-handed manner.

Perhaps accurately, they reported Third World diplomats in Paris as disappointed, but convinced that some small progress had been made towards better mutual understanding. But *Le Monde*, in a follow-up article, described the reactions at the United Nations in New York. It brought out not only the fairly predictable information that most Third World delegates there considered the conference a total failure; but the bitterness with which the West was castigated for its concentration on the energy question. It quoted a well-informed (unidentified) African diplomat who concluded that 'the attempt by the rich countries to divide the Third World has failed' – a perspective echoing the Soviet view of the whole exercise. Views of this kind did not enter the bulk of the coverage. One reason was probably that the actual participants did not express themselves in this way; another, that the near-disaster situation in which the conference both began and ended may have been felt by correspondents to need no emphasising. But the failure to put Third World disappointments in the strongest terms has been interpreted by some Third World leaders as evidence of Western bias, or at least a Western perspective.

A few months later, the United Nations World Information Day was celebrated, in Tunis, with a conference on public attitudes in the West towards the New International Economic Order. Referring directly back to the coverage of the North–South Dialogue, speakers told Western journalists that – since Western governments in Paris had suggested that there was much more on which North and South might agree were it not that governments must reflect their public opinion – the press had evidently failed in its duty to inform and mobilise that opinion.

The media were thus directly to blame for the failure to establish the bases for a more equitable international order. It was the duty of the Western press, said Tunisia's Prime Minister Hedi Nouira in opening the conference, to persuade their readers that their 'real interest lies in a reasoned, altruistic approach' to Third World problems 'rather than hiding behind an inviolable egotism . . . to date most Western information media have either been unable tor have not known how to make the necessary adaptation.' The solution, he suggested, lay not with reform by the West but 'just as, at the national level, it is the State's duty to distribute information to all sections of the population, so the developing countries, at the international level, should be able to enjoy wide access to ... information.' The freedom of the press dear to the West, he said, was 'synonymous with injustice ... when ... the weaker party ... is unable to make its voice heard.' Formulated in these terms, the solutions to the Western media's shortcomings would be opening Western columns to government propaganda.

But the arguments centred on the claim that for more than a generation, the Third World had played the game of international cooperation, only to see the poverty gap widen – and to see the Western press focus on inequality, polarisation and unemployment in their countries without giving due prominence to the extent to which these were the social consequences of the inequitable patterns of international trade and the division of labour. 'Was it right,' asked Manuel Perez-Guerrero of Venezuela, one of the two co-chairmen of the North–South conference, 'that the economic boom of the 1960's widened the incomes gap? We must stop the transfers from the South to the North, through more equitable terms of trade. The role of the press is to put the issues in these terms and thus make them more palatable.' Another political leader accused the Western press of making Western publics believe that the economic crisis was rooted in the higher price of oil – an underhand and systematic campaign, he said, which distorted the fact that all the ingredients for crisis were already present before 1973. Campaigns against cheap textiles imports put people out of work in the Third World. Readers were being encouraged to build up prejudices rather than to develop a broader vision.

The press must reform, therefore; editors must commit themselves to the task of persuasion. They must swing their publics behind the new economic order. They must explain that the Third World demands are self-evidently fair. They had better do so, first because change is inevitable and it might as well be orderly; second, because the existing disorder is the result of inconsistencies – still reflected in Western policies on aid, trade and financing – which the press has a duty to expose; and, finally, because a stable world is in the West's longterm interest.

But, as Jean Schwoebel of *Le Monde* countered, 'the Third World must help us to project their point of view. What is needed is perfect frankness; hypocrisy is not a Western monopoly – and sometimes we do not dare to tell you the truth as we find it.' And Keith Richardson of *The Sunday Times* of London argued that it must be understood that public opinion was not a homogeneous entity in the industrialised world: 'We do not have your sense of unity, even domestically. I don't think it's my job to mould public opinion – and I couldn't, if I wished, push them in any direction they don't wish to follow. Nor could I be sure that, if I informed them fully of the sacrifices required of them, that the reaction would favour the Third World's case. Remember, too, that people in the West believe that there is a link between their fairly recent prosperity and hard work: they are hostile to being told that it's all exploitation. The best I can do is warn them about trends, dangers and opportunities, and to give a fuller and clearer account of the pressures from the Third World, and what is likely to happen if they do not go along with them.'

The arguments at Tunis had progressed from those advanced at Nice two years earlier in one important respect: there was greater mutual understanding that the introduction of a new economic order involved genuine conflicts of interest between the ordinary publics of both North and South, and that in the circumstances, there were limits to the media's ability to mobilise opinion for fundamental change. But they also emphasised the extent to which those who were demanding a qualitatively different kind of coverage by the West, were also those who – at the political level – were developing a distinctively *étatiste* concept of the role of the news media. What was largely obscured was the impossibility of presenting any sort of comprehensive picture of the entire world; however feeble the excuses for the parochial viewpoint of the Western media, there cannot be any equivalent of 'community news' – the filling out of the public sense of their society which balances the critical journalism in Western countries – to put the situation of developing countries in context. The news explosion increases the need for selectivity – and as Hubert Beuve-Méry, founder-editor of *Le Monde*, has put it, '*qui dit choix dit contestable*'.

The problem of the lack of context fosters grievances. At Tunis, a *dossier noir* on the distortions in Western reporting of the Cairo Arab–African summit of March 1977 was available. This conference resulted in the establishment of a £1,500 million fund by the OPEC countries to assist African countries. In the face of this 'colossal effort' by the Arab countries, the *dossier* claimed, Western press reactions had been 'sceptical and misleading'. Some of the coverage had been gratuitous – several articles underlined the role of the West in developing the Arabs' petrol reserves; a couple of them referred in the context of the meeting to the Arab–African slave trade. But the *dossier* was equally bitter about mention of the links between Arab money and the anti-Israeli stance encouraged among beneficiaries. And one article, from the *Journal de Genève*, could serve as an example of the misunderstandings about the media which have arisen.

The article was 'sceptical', certainly; and its headline was provocative: 'Petrol but no ideas'. It was an opinion piece, by Claude Monnier, of 8 March: and it began by saying that the logic behind the meeting was perfectly convincing: the African countries had been particularly hard-hit by the rise in the oil prices: cooperation to help them was 'if not indispensable, at least equitable'. It continued by outlining, fairly straight-forwardly, the problems in the Cairo negotiations for an aid package.

One could hardly, Monnier continued, expect the Arab countries 'to give away billions without getting any political advantage out of it.' But the article caused deep offence because of what followed: the rub, Monnier said, was that 'the Arabs have petrol and money, but barely any ideas. Neither ideas nor a political framework. Or rather, yes – fragments of an incoherent policy' – pressure on Israel. The Arabs were, he said, obsessed and blinded to the longterm aims of a common policy by their conflict with Israel. Without a 'general strategy', they retreated to the formulation of abstract goals like 'people's liberation, anti-imperialism, the struggle against exploitation, non-alignment, etc.'

Obviously, material for offence: but the problem is not there. It lies with the difficulty many Third World leaders have in distinguishing between an opinion piece and a news article – and understanding that these will be read in a totally different way by a Western public. Nor do critics of the Western press appear to understand that Western newspapers do not hesitate to publish similar attacks on their own or other Western governments. The press may well accuse them of having no policy, of making action a substitute for a proper strategy, or of being blinded by a particular set of prejudices. The essence of journalism, as it has developed in the West, is the suspicion of grand designs and particularly those of politicians. The governments are always the Greeks, especially feared when bringing gifts. To the extent that this is a 'news-value', Third World governments reject it; and their rejection of such a role for the press is at the back of the pressures for an independent, distinctive news network of their own. Its hallmark will, where governments have their way in modelling it, be respect, constructiveness, and caution about the offence which can be inflicted on those who govern what they insist are vulnerable societies with other priorities. The resulting paradox is that the Western press is being called on to show more concern for Third World problems – quite justifiably – by adopting a type of reporting which is contrary to the ethics of Western-style journalism and Western societies – a demand which cannot be justified. There is a demand for Western support, coupled with a rejection of Western values, and the likely consequence is increased, and mutual, misunderstanding.

CHAPTER 4

The Voices of the New Order

Most of those who attack the existing structure insist that they do not seek to block the free flow of information. On the contrary, they seek to make it genuinely free – free of domination by the powerful few, free of Western 'ethnocentric prejudices', free 'to defend the interests of society as a whole, and the rights of entire peoples to make known ... their preoccupations, their difficulties and their aspirations for a better life'. Free of the distortions of the market and thus able to 'respond to the real development needs of Third World countries.'

These definitions of freedom imply concepts which are highly political. The demand for what is called a 'New World Order for Information' is most often expressed in the language of global class struggle and revolution, rather than in the measured hypocrisies of *realpolitik*. It is important to sort out the language and the substance of what is intended. How do we assess the seriousness and the scope of the demands for change? We need to consider not just the urgency and frequency with which the existing system is attacked, but the ultimate aims. If the New Order for Information were installed tomorrow, what would it look like – where is the thinking behind it likely to lead?

'The widening of the capacity to inform must be viewed as an essential component of attempts to create a new international economic order,' says the Tinbergen report on *Reshaping the International Order*; 'as such, the monopolistic and discriminatory practices inherent in current international

99

information dissemination must be deemed as one of the worst, through subtle, characteristics of the present system. . . . That there is a need for reform is obvious.'

For 'reform', read 'radical split'. While any widening of the capacity to inform must obviously be welcome, the *RIO Report*, as it is known, drawn up in association with the Club of Rome in 1975 and edited by the distinguished economist Jan Tinbergen, lends itself to a conspiracy theory about the media whereby the international news organisations are supposed to operate a deliberate policy to repress 'alternative' sources of information. By placing 'reform' squarely in the context of creating a new international economic order, the *Report* makes the criterion for a new system its political efficacy in furthering Third World goals, rather than the professional quality of the information conveyed. Underlying much of this kind of talk is an assumption that reform must mean curbing the powers of the existing media, rather than supplementing the present information-flow.

The voices of the New Order do not speak in chorus. But there are certain themes which are constant – and which upset any comforting belief in the West that what the leaders of the Third World want is access to the existing club, merely an extension of the membership. True, that *is* demanded, as a right: but beyond that, the most forceful voices are calling for a break with the entire structure and *raison d'être* of the club – not reform, but a radical alternative. There is almost a kind of reverse *apartheid* operating here, in the insistence on a kind of separate development working according to new rules.

Some governments, including several in the non-aligned movement, certainly talk about the need for Western cooperation to develop their media and to accelerate the transfer of technology to the Third World on generous terms. But their views as to the proper content of the message and the overall role of the media are still radically different from Western thinking, and incompatible with most of the traditional tenets of journalism. Journalists in developing countries often hold different views; but policies are made not in newspapers but in government offices. And when governments say, as they did in 1976 at Colombo, that the New Order for Information is a precondition for a new economic order, they do not mean

The Voices of the New Order

merely that the developing countries must get their views across if there is to be any progress in the North–South economic bargaining process; but that it is part and parcel of a revolutionary vision. What is sought is a distinct identity for the developing countries, forged through a common rejection of the models – economic, political, cultural – of the industrialised world.

What concerns us is the shape that identity – allowing for all the shadings of cultural diversity which the New Order promises so insistently to respect – will assume. How it will differ from the Western model, to what extent it will co-exist with it, and what words like balance, responsibility or even freedom will mean in its terms. There is plenty of guidance. At the inter-governmental level, the non-aligned movement has published an outline of the New Order's goals. Unesco's communications policies, national and international, provide indications of the effects a New Order will have on Third World social structures. Influencing both is a network of private (or semi-independent) institutions, concerned with drawing up 'a new conceptual framework'. Not all of these institutions are in the Third World. Some of the main influences come, in fact, from the US, France and Scandinavia as well as Eastern Europe. Mexico is an active but late addition, with three interlocking institutions now working on the problems. Already at the level of individual governments, the concepts of a new kind of information are becoming political reality.

Common to all theorizing is the emphasis that communications must be seen as a totality: both when diagnosing the evils of the present system, and when prescribing a cure. A totality in the sense that government information, news, education, folksongs, satellites and the daily chat of a village are all fodder for communications policies; and also in the sense that the entire communications structure is central both to development and to the shaping of independent economic structures. A New Order for Information, therefore, is explicitly intended to be the lynchpin of the social system adopted. It is also seen as a common response to a continuing condition of economic and cultural 'colonisation'. As Leonard Sussman, Director of the US organisation Freedom House, has commented, this approach paradoxically arises out of the diversity of the different developing countries: 'their one point of agreement is the belief that they are dominated and exploited by the industrial countries. The radical states attribute to the developed nations a conscious ideological hostility. The more moderate believe the developed countries may *unwittingly* support a system that perpetuates social and economic injustice.' The New Order for Information has extremely widespread support in the Third World because it is seen as a means of distancing societies from what they perceive as domination.

The political centre behind the New Order for Information, as well as the New International Economic Order and other Third World demands, lies in the group of more than eighty countries which form the Non-Aligned Movement. The political history of the movement stretches back to the 1950's, and among the principal early actors were Chou En-lai, Josip Broz Tito, U Nu, Gamal Abdel Nasser, Haille Selassie, Kwame Nkrumah and Ahmed Sukarno. A meeting in Bandung, in April 1955, of some of these leaders was the first official manifestation of a Third World presence vis-a-vis the great powers. The concept of 'positive neutralism' which they invented created the basis for a Third World alternative to bipolarism and Cold War politics. Five years later, at the UN, these leaders joined to call for Soviet–US negotiations to reduce Cold War tensions, and in 1961, the Non-Aligned Movement was formally inaugurated in Belgrade by twenty-five countries.

From the first, it was regarded by its sponsors as the vehicle for an alternative world order which would assert Third World independence. The war in the Belgian Congo had encouraged greater radicalism in Third World thinking, largely because of the questions it had raised about US use of the UN peacekeeping machinery. But, in contrast to the Organisation of African Unity, which included communications on its agenda from the moment of its foundation in 1963 with a resolution (admittedly unimplemented twenty-five years later) calling for a Pan–African News Agency, the Non-Aligned Movement remained for the first two decades of its existence a primarily political organisation. As a vehicle for an alternative order, its usefulness at times seemed limited, even illusory. The language in which it expressed the goals of self-determination, its opposition to colonialism, neo-colonialism and imperialism, even its calls for total disarmament, echoed at times in the stilted vocabulary of international summitry, the old-fashioned phraseology of the Anti-Imperialist League, founded in Moscow in 1924, or of the Comintern's Congress of Oppressed Nationalities held in Brussels three years later. One consequence of what was largely a coincidental use of Marxist and Soviet terminology was to give both Western and Eastern observers an exaggerated notion of the 'solidarity' linking the Movement with the socialist industrialised countries.

At the beginning of the 1970's, the Non-Aligned Movement found a more distinctive voice, and a new lease of life, in turning to economic and social cooperation. By the Third Summit in Lusaka in 1970, which issued a declaration on economic development, fifty-four countries had become members; three years later, it had grown to seventy-five. This decade has seen the evolution of the movement from a sort of governmental pressure group to an established force in international politics. Two factors were vital in this transformation. The first was the increased use by the Third World of the changed majority at the United Nations. This had in fact developed during the sixties: even by the end of the 1950's, the US had ceased to be able to control the UN through a block of acquiescent Latin American dictatorships (and had in consequence ceased to refer to it as 'the moral conscience of mankind'). But it was only with the introduction of the second factor that Third World groups – the Group of 77 and the non-aligned – sought to use their political muscle to force structural change.

This factor was the realisation that although the gross product, worldwide, had nearly trebled since World War II while the population had increased by about two-thirds, hopes that increased prosperity would trickle through to the developing countries with the help of aid and sound development strategies had not materialised. The widening of the poverty gap aroused widespread scepticism about the validity of development models, the altruism of aid programmes, and the worth of cooperation. Self-reliance and independence increasingly became economic rather than purely political themes.

The impetus behind the Non-Aligned Movement, and the cooperation within the UN system which articulated the demand for a New International Economic Order, were thus broadened to embrace a much wider field of policy formulation. And, at the Fourth Summit of the non-aligned in Algiers in September 1973, a Yugoslav initiative established a link between economic coordination and international information structures. In a formal statement, the seventy-five heads of government at Algiers found it to be 'an established fact that the activities of imperialism are not confined solely to the political and economic fields, but also cover the cultural and sociological fields, thus imposing an alien ideological domination over the peoples of the developing world.' To meet 'the cultural alienation and imported civilization imposed by colonialism and imperialism', the non-aligned governments resolved to effect a 'repersonalization by constant and determined recourse to the people's own social and cultural values which define it as a sovereign people.' The search for an alternative model had begun.

But at this stage, agreement was simply reached in principle to reorganise the communications channels 'inherited from the colonial past' so as to exchange information more directly and rapidly; and to strengthen national media as part and parcel of a strategy of self-reliance which would 'eliminate the harmful consequences of the colonial era.' From this modest beginning, integrated as it was into the conference's Programme of Action for Economic Cooperation, evolved a qualitative change in Third World governments' attitudes to the role of information. At the next Summit, in Colombo in August 1976, a formal declaration asserted that 'A new international order in matters of information and the mass media is as important as a new international economic order.'

Attempts had been made to improve Third World communications, in terms of training, technology and cooperation, during the sixties. There had been little progress. There was little political muscle behind them, and less money. The first attempt by governments to force world attention to the imbalance in the global flow of information had been made by a group of countries led by India, using the forum of Unesco's

1970 General Conference. (And it was India, senior Unesco officials recall, which introduced the concept of 'balance' – meaning by it, they claim, some compromise position between the unimpeded flow of information and censorship.) The debate focussed on 'the rights of less privileged nations to pressure their own cultures'. But the transition from protest to concerted action was made outside Unesco, within the Non-Aligned Movement itself.

From Algiers in 1973, and with the active encouragement of Yugoslavia, Mexico, Algeria, Tunisia and, later, India, the components of a New Order for Information rapidly evolved. They fall roughly under three headings. The first is the development of domestic media as a 'social asset, in the service of the integral development of nations'. The second calls for steps to exchange news between developing countries on a basis which respects 'sovereign independence' and which focusses on the socially relevant, together with plans to co-ordinate a Third World approach to the dissemination of its 'reality' in the industrialised world. Finally, there is the rejection of the dominant position of the Western media – not only as a structure whose existence is contrary to the spirit of independence, but as the purveyors of information which 'is a blow to . . . authentic cultural values, and in the final analysis subjugates [Third World] interests to those of imperialism.'

The initial Western response to the non-aligned countries' strategy combined misunderstanding, unjustified panic and justified scepticism. The immediately visible outcome was the creation of a news pool of national news agencies, conceived and coordinated by Tanjug, the Yugoslav agency, and dedi-cated – as the Algiers Programme made clear – to 'exchange and circulate information on . . . mutual achievements.' The actual scope of the pool, which will be discussed in a later chapter, is limited; but the rhetoric attending its birth sug-gested both that it would replace, rather than complement, international reporting; and that it would in time become the sole source of news from the developing countries. Leaving aside the more strident public utterances (which were pre-dominantly Indian) at the July 1976 New Delhi conference of information ministers which established an official framework for the Pool, the final action plan expressed the need for 'a determined collective political will' to escape from the 'cultural dependence' produced by the existing 'communications net-work . . . created by and in the interests of the colonial powers.' It also noted the important role of the media in safeguarding developing countries against colonialism and in establishing a more equitable international order. The proposals which fol-lowed were essentially practical ones for strengthening the Third World's media – although the implication that the job was essentially governmental was certainly present. More ambitiously, they sought to evolve a 'common approach' to the right to information and the right to communicate; on 'the functioning of the transnational press and other agencies,' and on satellite communications. But the establishment of 'broad and free circulation' of news between each other, and (in theory at least) the provision of 'authentic information' about the non-aligned countries to the rest of the world, was a logical response to long-felt frustrations.

More reliable, because more extensive, sources exist as to the ultimate intentions of the non-aligned in calling for a New Order for Information. One is the findings of an international symposium, organised by Tunisia as the elected coordinator of non-aligned policies on information, held in Tunis in March 1976. The results were presented to the New Delhi meeting and to the Fifth Summit of the non-aligned in Colombo that August, and influenced the formulation of the statements issued then on the New Order. The Tunis symposium brought together thirty-eight member countries, another seven as observers, and half a dozen international organisations includ-ing Unesco. Finland was represented by the President of the Prague-based International Organisation of Journalists, Kaarle Nordenstreng, Peru by Germán Camero Roque – an activist in the field who was later to represent Unesco in Latin America – and Unesco by Gunnar Naesselund.

The tone of the symposium was unambiguous. Tunisia itself has traditionally exercised a moderating influence of sorts; but the overwhelming impression which came out of that meeting was one of confrontation. The notions of inter-dependence and internationalism were suspect for many delegates; typical is the view of the Indians (then speaking for a country which under the Emergency had indeed taken steps to sever its links with the West and to control information). The allies of the 'one-sided and loaded' system, they said, were to be found among the 'elitist section of the people in almost every country' who viewed 'any interference in this unequal flow . . . as an interference with its freedom.' To attack the 'elitist neocolonialist linkup' was part of the struggle against the dominating powers. Reform of information structures was thus placed in its political context, and by representatives of a government pursuing an anti-elitist policy: 'only' 253 journalists were jailed during the Emergency – less than ten per cent of all those in the profession; and the government's attack on the press focussed on half a dozen leading publications.

It was at Tunis that it first became clear that for many of its supporters, a New Order for Information means firm national (governmental) control of the information system, and classes it as one of the bases for the exercise of national sovereignty.

The meeting divided into three working committees. The first and most important, with Carnero as its rapporteur, dealt with the 'emancipation' of the non-aligned media. It based its findings on two working papers from Mexico: one from one of the country's three news agencies, Notimex; the second from the Latin-American Institute of Transnational Studies (ILET). Not surprisingly, they reflect the ILET thesis (which will be analysed later) that:

- 'domination in information' restricts independent development, blights 'authentic cultural values' and subjugates Third World interests to those of imperialism; that the 'big press transnationals' perpetuate dependence, by 'systematically distorting the facts about non-aligned countries by the use of the press for retaliation and political penetration;' and that their behaviour 'responds to the laws of the market imposed by their dominant position.' Because news is a commodity, 'the criteria used in selection are always contrary to the interests of sovereign independence'; the agencies are therefore 'a fundamental cog in the great wheel of domination.'
- that the 'free flow' doctrine is 'intended to justify the actions of the big information transnationals in developing their pernicious activity without any international supervision.

- that the antidote is information as a social good, in the service of development.

Gratefully acknowledging the ILET analysis of the problem, the committee proceeded to set out the principles for the emancipation of information. The crucial paragraph reads: 'Every developing country has the right to exercise full sovereignty over information, both that concerning its day-to-day realities and that diffused to its people. It also has the right to be informed objectively about outside events and the right to publicise widely its national reality.' The three results, if such a principle were to be implemented, would be: a controlled press at national level; screening of the foreign media circulated in the country; and a demand that national news, written expressly to further the national interest as conceived by those responsible for information policy, be circulated in the international media.

The second committee was chaired by Elebe Ma-Ekonzo, Director-General of the Agence Zaire Presse and convinced supporter of his government's view, quoted by Leonard Sussman, that 'the role of journalists is to help educate the masses and rally support for the government'. It dealt with the role of information in consolidating economic and social co-operation. Aside from the role of the press in 'the liquidation of imperialist domination over the economies of our countries and the asserting of the importance of our share in the world economy,' the commission urged special efforts 'to offset the harmful influence of the foreign news media which are hostile' to Third World aspirations: from now on, public opinion 'must be formed by means of nationalist information media which are capable of correctly directing and forming such public opinion.' Ma-Ekonzo is a member of the Unesco International Commission on Communications, set up in 1977 to consider the future of communications worldwide.

The Tunis symposium also laid the basis for future co-operation between the non-aligned countries, focussing on mutual self-help in building up communications facilities, training, the development of national news agencies, the common acquisition of satellites (and the drafting of rules governing their use), and first steps towards exchanges of broadcast news and features. Many of these proposals are necessary and most practicable in the short to medium term. Was the rest simply rhetoric?

A partial answer to this question is provided by the admirably clear book, *The New World Order for Information*, published by Tunisia under the direction of Mustapha Masmoudi, Tunisia's Secretary for Information, the coordinator of the non-aligned committee on information – and, again, a member of the Unesco Commission. The book is a concise statement of the non-aligned position. It traces the evolution of the concept, from the Algiers Summit to Colombo and the nineteenth Unesco General Assembly. It gives prominence to the series of intergovernmental meetings between 1973 and 1976. But it also makes clear the influence of an ILET seminar of May 1976; emphasises the central place of the Tunis symposium; and stresses the role of the Dag Hammarskjöld Foundation (the Foundation, based in Uppsala, Sweden, was one of the earliest institutions to single out information as a key instrument for creating an 'alternative' way of economic and social development – and to press the concept in publications and international forums). The resolutions the Tunisian book picks out from the Tunis symposium are the political ones, rather than the proposals for implementation and practical cooperation.

Tunisian policy lays stress on collaboration with the developed countries: for Bourguiba himself, information should 'have its place in the vast dialogue which seems to be getting under way between north and south in the hope of setting up a more equitable world economic order.' The development of information is also seen as a *sine qua non* of political and economic sovereignty. Making the valid point that the underdevelopment of the media in the Third World has created 'an obstacle between man's right to be informed and the exercise of that right,' Masmoudi says that non-aligned efforts to strengthen their media serve 'the free and balanced circulation of news' between their countries and the outside world.

He then comes to Western objections, from news organisations 'which seem to be very troubled by the "control" of the state on information structures. This "control",' he comments, 'has not happened by chance nor is it the sign of a desire to restrict the freedom of news services and still less is it the result of a wish for propaganda, but it is quite simply the natural consequence of the situation in developing countries.' Information is a weapon, and a means for inculcating the will for change: and, important as it is to respect the individual's right to information, 'from now on . . . one cannot contest the right of states and groups of people to speak nor refuse them the use of every means of communication.'

Masmoudi puts the point not only with conviction but with much greater restraint than other spokesmen use: but if the central point he makes – that control is the 'natural conse-quence' of the developing countries' situation, and that 'states' must have the right to speak – appears to echo Marxist thinking, this is not entirely concidence. The obsession among Third World political leaders with cultural 'dependence', and with the need to break away from the customs and values symbolised by the international press, have been fed by certain extremely influential Marxist analyses – influential even in countries where the Marxist political model has not taken root. They have been shaped and publicised in a number of centres, from the University of Tampere in Finland to the Unesco-backed CIESPAL institute for Communications Studies in Latin America. Longest in the field of the politics of communications is the International Organisation of Journalists (IoJ), founded in 1946 and – after a split between communist and non-communist members in 1947 – based in Prague. It now claims over 150,000 'progressive, democratic' members in 109 coun-tries, and runs two major training centres in East Berlin and Budapest in which over 500 journalists from the Third World have completed courses. It has a permanent staff larger than that of many Western newspapers and circulates five well-produced magazines to its members, together with an impressive list of full-length publications and occasional pamphlets. Even for a non-member, its glossy monthly magazine, which runs to twenty-four pages or more, costs only $4 a year.

Among the principles which the IoJ is pledged to defend are the protection of the press 'against the influence of monopolist and financial groups', and 'the struggle . . . against every form of journalistic activity in the service of individuals or particular groups of society whose interests are contrary to the working masses.' Its basic credo is perfectly clear: as its director, a Czech called Oldřich Bureš has emphasised at international meetings, the only free press is the press owned by the people. In the Third World, it has strongly supported the development of state-owned media, 'fighting so that developing states may have a free and truthful national press which will guard them against neo-colonialist plots.' Working from this standpoint, it has cooperated closely with Unesco on a wide range of issues, from training in developing countries, to the drawing up of a journalistic code of ethics binding journalists to 'influencing the public for peace and security' (a code which is still with Unesco and likely to be substantially modified, but which encouraged the organisation to keep the establishment of a code firmly on its agenda). Training focusses on the 'education of democratic, anti-imperialist and anti-colonialist journalists', and the IoJ received at its 1977 Presidium session in Paris Vietnam's Order of Friendship for helping 'the fight against American agression, for national regeneration and for the construction of socialism.'

The IoJ's President, a communications professor at Finland's University of Tampere called Kaarle Nordenstreng, is a former member of Finland's National Commission for Unesco, and has been closely associated with its formulation of communications strategies since the early 70's. He was one of the drafters, at the initial stage and again in 1977, of the Soviet-inspired Draft Declaration on the use of the media to combat war propaganda, racialism and apartheid (which will be discussed in the next chapter, but which was intended to give international respectability to the principle of state control over the media); through Nordenstreng's involvement, the IoJ has been closely consulted throughout redraftings of the document. At the final drafting in December 1977, it was one of the two organisations – the other was the International Federation of Journalists – to be invited to Paris for a special private consultative session.

The IoJ has used the call for a New Order for Information to highlight ideological schisms between the western media and the approach of some Third World governments. Prefacing the IoJ's pamphlet on the subject in 1977, Nordenstreng viewed the attack on the concept of the free flow of information 'as a reflection of the growing influence of the anti-imperialist forces on the world arena': the issue, he said had thus logically become 'a focal point in the current ideological struggle around the new information order,' as the international media sought to defend their 'ideological hegemony'. The pressures for a new order came from 'a front of the developing and socialist countries' to which the West had no alternative but to 'yield'.

And yielding, in IoJ terms, must imply the acceptance of different criteria for news, new structures and a new role for the press. Nordenstreng attacked 'western interests' for recognising at Nairobi the need to strengthen the Third World's media, while refusing to go beyond an acceptance that approaches to the role of the media were likely to differ. Cooperation and assistance - which most western journalists believe is their most useful contribution to a two-way flow of information – comes under attack from Marxist polemicists as 'repressive tolerance'. The West had refused, said Nordenstreng, 'to make normative references to the contents of the mass media. This would hit the real issues and would be a more direct risk to the "free flow" doctrine and the existing information structures'. Precisely. The New Order concerns content – quality not quantity. The latter may well in consequence be reduced rather than increased.

There is some uneasiness in Moscow about the New Order for Information. Leonid Zamiatin, until March 1978 Director General of Tass (and considered to be the chief Soviet ideological spokesman, after Suslov), insists that he has never heard of it, and that, as far as he is concerned, the phrase is meaningless. But as outlined by the IoJ and a group of institutes with an increasingly large audience among developing countries' leaders, a New Order would echo the Soviet theory of the role of information in important respects.

Domestically, ownership of the press would be vested in the 'people': collectives of workers, unions, the political party and other extensions of State organisation. (The Third World leaders who insist that they reject both Western and Soviet models of information - such as Libya - are installing 'the people' in the system in very much the Soviet way, while claiming that the Soviet media are governmental and theirs are not.) The media would have a didactic role – inculcating social virtues and criticising 'selfish individualism, proprietary instincts and so on', while mobilising the masses for their daily tasks.

The main reason that this can be presented as a model for a 'New' Order, rather than just the old Soviet model, is that Third World conditions change the nature of the task of mobilisation, or at the least, modify it. News in the service of development is not necessarily identical with building socialism. But the distinction is a fine one. In many developing countries, little editing would be required to adapt the following basic principles set out by Tass: 'information must serve the interests of the entire people . . . [it] plays an important role in the communist education of working people, in the forming of public opinion, in the correct orientation of people in questions of domestic and foreign policy of the Party and the State, in the struggle against hostile ideology.' Uncertainties as to how a 'New Order' might evolve, however, cloud the view from Moscow of the oft-proclaimed solidarity between socialist countries and their Third World brethren. One of the reasons for the pronounced efforts on the cultural and information fronts made by Soviet-supported organisations like the IoJ is the determination to see that the development of concepts, as yet not fully formed, underpinning the New Order for Information does not carry with it a firm rejection of Soviet as well as Western influence.

Rejection may be in name only; the Soviet model, with local variants, is likely to be attractive to governments – whether Marxixt or not. At least, the New World Order for Information objectively echoes aspects of the Soviet approach. The central point is that in practice, information integrated into national development programmes is likely to be closely directed by governments, many of whom will echo Lenin's views of the place of information in society incorporated in his famous speech of 1920. 'Why', he asked, 'should freedom of speech and freedom of the press be allowed? Why should a government which is doing what it believes to be right allow itself to be criticised? It would not allow opposition by lethal weapons. Ideas are most more fatal than guns.' Information, when it supports 'freedom for the working masses', is all too likely to become (in the words of a former Tass Director, M. Poulgounov) 'agitational writing, aided by facts'.

At the international level, Soviet insistence on 'non-interference' in the internal affairs of states, and the primacy of sovereignty over the 'free flow' of information, has distinct attractions for the governments of under developed countries; it is easily associated with arguments which employ the language of class struggle and anti-imperialism – and to this extent, the Third World's complaints about the existing system of information flows can be used to discredit the West. And, although the Soviet Union's leaders are uneasily aware that Tass, too, operates internationally and on a major scale – and could be tarred with the same brush – Soviet writers have continued, through the IoJ's magazines in particular, to stress the dangers of *commercially* motivated internationalism and to imply that the 'free flow' doctrine is simply part of the imperialist conspiracy.

The IoJ output, quantitatively formidable though it is and backed by expensive assistance and training schemes, is however often clumsily ideological. The pages of its journals are dominated by Soviet or Eastern European propagandists and party theorists, making for a certain heaviness which is not wholly compensated for by the presence, too, of articles by sympathetic Western writers – and senior Unesco officials. While its influence is greater than many Westerners are aware - if only because the scale of its efforts has been little appreciated outside the circles of the faithful – in many ways it is the least skilful of the advocates of a Marxist structure for the New Order. This has not prevented it from becoming closely associated with Unesco – at least according to its own claims. Some Unesco officials insist that there has never been any combined programme with the IoJ, or any sponsorship of its activities by Unesco. At governments' requests, they say, Unesco has provided financial assistance towards seminars, or placed recipients of fellowships in IoJ schools. But a conference in Baghdad, in November 1977, on 'decolonisation of information and the role of the mass media in the development and establishment of a new international economic order' appeared to several participants to be jointly sponsored by the IoJ,

Unesco and the Union of Iraqi Journalists. Appearances are important, particularly when a conference organised by the IoJ is liable – as this one did – to come up with resolutions blaming Third World problems on the 'manipulation of news by big corporations', and 'systematic aggression by certain mass media against the Third World'. And the impression of close liaison is also increased by the fact that the IoJ's book on the New Order for Information contains, as its key article, a contribution by Gunnar Naesselund, at the time head of Unesco's communications division.

One weapon in the IoJ's arsenal is the use it makes of the 'class struggle' metaphor in arguing for a New Order for Information. This not only unites Third World countries against the information media of the industrialised West, but helps – not only in the India of the Emergency, but in many developing countries – to discredit those who continue to insist on the importance of the independence and freedom of the press. These journalists and intellectuals are also, of course, often a regime's most persistent critics; and the journalists among them rely heavily on the international news agencies' services. The language of class struggle enables advocates of a controlled press to isolate them as 'stooges of imperialism', 'repressive elites' or – pityingly – as 'prisoners of an alien information model that bears no relationship to . . . information needs and indeed contributes to the persistence of dependence.'

The IoJ is not alone in employing this imagery. One of the most influential writers to do so is an American, Professor Herbert Schiller.

A conscious manipulator of the world of conferences and resolutions, Schiller revels in his battle – conducted from one of the spin-off colleges of the University of California – with the US media. It is fashionable in the media establishment to dismiss him as 'intellectually disreputable'; most editors would not, they say, give him the time of day. They may be missing the point: which is the extent to which his thesis – an extremely destructive one – feeds Third World frustrations and aspirations.

Essentially, Schiller starts from the argument that (principally American) multinational companies organise the world economy, and that their position of dominance compels them to seek to influence the entire range of cultural and 'informational' life in order to perpetuate 'transnational values' in the countries where they operate. As American prestige diminished in the wake of Vietnam and global economic crisis, 'deliberate management of the sphere of consciousness' became vital to the survival of the US business machine; but from the end of World War II, the 'free flow' doctrine had been advanced by business circles, in collusion with the US government, as an indispensable element in overseas economic expansion.

In *Communications and Cultural Domination*, Schiller claims not only that the 'cultural take-over' of entire societies – planned by the US communications industry initially for profit – is now being coordinated 'at the highest governmental levels' as part of a cultural policy aimed at promoting the values and structures which assure American dominance; but that there is inevitably a total continuity between the industrial/military conglomerate and the mass media; each feeds on the other. The international media simply control, and exploit by modern means, the countries on the 'periphery' of the world economy. Instead of military muscle, techniques of persuasion ensure continuing US hegemony. The media are weapons, creating the 'cultural imperialism' through which 'a society is brought into the modern world system ... its dominating stratum is attracted, pressured, forced, and sometimes bribed into shaping social institutions' in line with 'transnational values'.

To make this thesis work at all, communications as a category naturally has to include the entire apparatus of persuasion – advertising companies, mass entertainment and all; 'much more than the messages and the recognisable circuits through which the messages flow' and reaching into every aspect of 'social reality'. The failure of the victims to feel their chains (until now) is therefore a further 'measure of the effectiveness of the control processes'.

The principal devices of this all-smothering system have been, Schiller argues, the doctrine of the free flow of information, and technology. The first is a con-trick, serving 'to strengthen the already-powerful and weaken further the already-frail.' The second, 'conceived, developed and saturated with the interest and specifications of monopoly capitalism,' deepens Third World dependence. There is at work in this argument a conviction that the media are the totally malleable accomplices of political and industrial power – a conviction which conveniently surmounts the fact that none of us would know about the CIA's activities in Chile, or the secret bombing of Cambodia, if it were not for these 'accomplices'. But Schiller is not interested in the pressures which led to the US Freedom of Information Act, or the doctrine of the citizen's 'right to know': both are shams, lending respectability to the techniques of cultural repression. Again, for him, the proof of the role of technology in perpetuating the dominance of the 'centre' over the world's 'periphery' (terms used by many of Schiller's Third World followers) is the emphasis placed by US institutions on research into communications technology, and US offers to make technology available to developing countries in order to redress the balance in international communications.

By this reasoning, cooperation would sink the Third World even deeper in dependence: the US offer to help them improve communications facilities may tempt developing countries – but it is a 'technological and quantitative' trap which actually impedes the evolution of a New Order. At the national level, new technology would be 'employed either by local elites, or multinational corporations, or both, for economic penetration and political surveillance and control.' By emphasising *facilities* the US hopes at the international level to see that 'the larger and fundamental issue of *total systemic dependence*, including the *quality of the information produced and provided*, remains unaddressed and out of sight.' (Schiller's emphasis.) Aid is not only not neutral, but imports both ideology and a whole range of technical support systems which perpetuate the great chain of dependence.

For Schiller, therefore, the first priority is to break the hold of the American machine: 'to overcome the existing pattern of world information flows, an integrated, comprehensive reform of the entire dependency relationship . . . is required. Fundamental changes in media ownership, state responsibilities for new communication policies, critical criteria for cultural-information material serving public needs and sharp scrutiny of technological processes that have been developed under

capitalism' will be needed. While Schiller has to admit that
strengthened communications systems in the Third World
would 'cut into the market shares of the transnational media',
he asserts that Western 'cultural hegemony' would still be
saved because if the New Order were powered by Western
technology, and used Western organisational and administrative standards, it would conform to the rules of the market,
and disseminate information 'for profit, not for social use'. For
this reason, Schiller warns that even President Carter's bland
statement of 23 May 1977 that the US would 'cooperate more
closely with the newly influential countries in Latin America,
Africa and Asia', to win their 'friendship as the structure of
world power changes', should be viewed by the Third World
as a threat.

The antidote is self-reliance, Schiller suggests. What would
such a policy amount to? In outline, it would include the
almost total elimination of capitalism, the installation of some
basic features of socialism and 'highest priority' for 'central
planning and strict controls over economic life'. Not only
economic: strict import controls would embrace 'the level and
nature of personal consumption (including the consumption of
information), and, not least, the control and limitation of
tourism and similar activities that distort the structure and
behaviour of the economy and the people.' In a September
1977 interview, Schiller said that he did not necessarily imply
by this package government control, 'except in a broad-brush
strategic sense'. It is hard to see what else he could be implying.

In a paper on the 'decolonization of information' prepared
for the winter 1978 issue of *Latin American Perspectives*,
Schiller's views on government control had in fact become
clearer. 'One lesson learned at great cost to poor and weak
countries' in their struggle for political and now economic
liberation, he writes, 'is the vital need to make the terms of the
conflict understandable to the people engaged in the battle . . .
[and] to explain and justify the struggle to world public
opinion in the hope of securing support, or at least to avoid
suffering destabilisation. . . .' In this confrontation, he reasons,
'the ability to identify and to present the national version of
events' is as basic as controlling the national currency and the
armed forces. The openness to abuse of these powers (which

he admits) 'in no way weakens the necessity for such control. Political independence can scarcely be maintained and economic self-determination is unthinkable without firm national control of the information system.'

This will extend in the first instance to 'what comes in and what goes out'. But once the international news-flow is thus determined, 'if national news agencies are established' for the purpose, then the 'class relations' of national news structures must be put under the microscope, to determine what will be socially useful.

National communications policies are treated by Schiller as 'a new arena for social struggle', the explicit extension of class conflict into the cultural sphere. Policies should not only be directed, on the international plane, against the former colonial powers and the new 'imperialists', but, domestically, against the 'ruling domestic stratum' and in favour of 'indigenous mass needs'. The revolutionary message addressed to the Third World is that self-reliance clears the field – and clears it for a purpose. 'The objective of a cultural policy is not merely to exclude material: it is to assist the process of shaping consciousness. In its very essence it is opposed to established, traditional authority.' This is of course no barrier to authoritarianism, but an apologia for it. As Schiller added in the 1978 paper, national communications policies must be 'bound up with the characters structure and direction of the nation's development' and would therefore determine what the content of communication, should be, and in whose interest. As he concludes, correctly in terms of his line of argument, we are dealing with 'the ultimate issue of societal control, a question by no means settled in most parts of the world.' Third World countries had yet to settle internally the basic social issues; but at least, most were agreed in 'preferring national control to external domination.'

But Schiller recognises that, even here, total exclusion of the outside world is not possible. Some degree of economic interdependence is an inescapable fact and (in a phrase which suggests that the masses might be tempted by external pleasures after all) complete control is impossible in an age of 'powerful electronic instrumentation that transmits globally.'

The Cubans have an antidote, Schiller suggests, to living

with imperfect segregation; he quotes from a report to a 1971 cultural congress in Havana:

> The rising technological advance of the mass media and its infinite prospects oblige our revolutionary society to fight against the contamination of the air by imperialist ideology through the creation of ideological antibodies to neutralise its lethal effects. The only alternative reality permits is struggle, not asepsis . . . [preparing] the masses to face critically every form of expression of bourgeois ideology.

Secondly, strength may be found in the conscious membership of a new club, and in this sense communications policies are 'profoundly international', concerned with 'human solidarity against domination everywhere'. How is this to be effected? By policies in which 'the *definition of news* . . . may constitute one practical yardstick of the degree to which authentic internationalism motivates the news effort;' and the adoption of news formats which promote 'identification with worldwide liberation movements and the struggle against imperialism'.

The kind of dismissal of Schiller which would follow from any academic examination of his work – *Communications and Cultural Domination* must be one of the worst written and worst argued books on almost any intellectual subject – would miss the mark in two ways. The first is that it is not part of a world of logic, evidence and clarity, but of obsession and the passions of activist politics. Passions which are not dismissable on grounds of the feebleness of their intellectual presentation. Secondly, there is an overarching schematism in Schiller's work: he does not evade the consequences of the connections which he seeks to establish and the remedies he proposes.

While insisting that the New Order for Information must be seen as a dynamic process, in which aims would shift with expectations, he was clear in the 1977 interview that it 'necessarily implies structural changes, nationally and internationally. And there's no point in pretending that the New Order is going to be brought about by consensus, as some people suggest, or that it implies gradual and congenial change. In some countries, it will be nasty and brutal, without doubt. And the flow of news will be sharply diminished, in the sense in which it's currently conceived by Westerners, as changes take place. I don't see anything so tragic about that, it's inevitable. To alter the structure of information inevitably suggests shaking up, destroying, existing patterns.'

This has at least the merit of straightforwardness. Nor is it an isolated view. In a long article devoted to the New Order for Information, a new magazine published in Hong Kong called *Asiaweek* (whose claim is to present Asia to Asians by Asians) commented on the meeting of non-aligned information ministers at New Delhi, in July 1976. This was the meeting which formulated the official non-aligned attitude to the New Order, and at the same time endorsed the creation of the non-aligned news pool. The pool has been consistently presented, particularly after its creation was greeted by an exaggeratedly defensive outcry in the West, as a parallel and complementary channel for news. This was not how it was seen, as *Asiaweek* shows, by many of its defenders. Recognising the problem which setting up the pool would present, the magazine predicted:

> A long twilight between the introduction of restrictions on Western news agencies and the realisation of a substitute non-Western network; during that twilight, the standard of news-gathering may deteriorate to the point where established channels like the press and the radio are ignored by the public, and rumour will hold sway. But such considerations seem unlikely to reverse the trend ... the Third World appears set on achieving its new goal: 'Decolonisation of the mass media'.

The same article quoted extensively from two members of the ILET team set up in Mexico in 1975: Juan Somavia, the director, and Fernando Reyes Matta, the 'coordinator of activities on information and dependence'. Both assert, in contrast to director, and Fernando Reyes Matta, the 'coordinator of activities on information and dependence'. Both assert, in contrast to Schiller, that the structural changes, which they agree are fundamental to the creation of a New Order, will mean an increase, not a diminution, in the free flow of information. Both also insist that their organisation and its large circle of Latin American advisers does not favour government control of the media. The fact remains that Schiller's diagnosis, and most of his broad prescriptive strategies, have markedly influenced ILET's work.

Juan Somavia is a Chilean economist whose involvement with the theoretical framework for a new information order is rooted in Latin American efforts to assert economic independence through regional cooperation. Still in his mid-thirties when he took over the Latin American Institute for Transnational Studies (ILET), Somavia was economic adviser to Chile's minister of foreign affairs by the age of twenty-seven, and chaired the Andean Development Commission between 1971 and the fall of Allende in 1973. In the two following years, he served as *rapporteur* to the United Nations 'group of eminent persons' investigating the multinational corporations; and co-authored two documents to appear at that period which demanded a fundamentally different approach to economic development: the Dag Hammarskjöld 1975 Report, *What Now: Another Development*; and Tinbergen's *RIO Report*. ILET, founded in 1975, has the backing which Somavia's previous activities would suggest: the Centre International pour le Développement (CID) in Paris, which is headed by a distinguished Chilean exile, Hernán Santa Cruz; the Dag Hammarskjöld Foundation and, through its influence, the Swedish government; and the Dutch Ministry for Overseas Development, which until the end of 1977 was headed by a radical and energetic minister, Johannes Pronk, and which had also encouraged the production of the *RIO Report*. (Both the CID and ILET have the continued and close support of the former President of Mexico, Luis Echeverria.) Its specific goal is 'to promote national and collective self-reliance in Third World countries,' and its research field covers, in this context, the 'transnational' corporations; the international politics of technology; alternative strategies for development; and 'information and dependence'.

Somavia's basic approach to a New Order for Information first appeared in *Another Development* - a book which is in many other respects attractively imaginative as a ginger-group document, given that it starts from the 'necessary perspectives' of 'the world as a macro-economic system and as a stage for class struggle.' The outline diagnosis on the information front is that, together with education, it is 'monopolised by the power structure, which manipulates public opinion to its own ends and tends to perpetuate preconceived ideas, ignorance and alienation.'

The cure is first, the creation of a global communications system which would recognise people's 'cultural, political, social and economic diversity. The image of the Other should reach each of us, stripped of the prevailing ethnocentric prejudices.' It is all very laudable; the Orwelliana creeps in with the description of the *aims* of this system – a total one which embraces information and education 'in the broadest sense': it is the ' "conscientisation" of citizens'. The old order is rejected, as 'a basic element of the present hierarchical pattern of centre ideological and cultural domination' (the phrasing echoes Schiller): breaking the monopoly is a priority, even if Third World exchanges of news present a real 'danger that material provided may be incomplete or biased. ... The key element is the realisation that knowledge is power.'

Like Schiller, whom he frequently quotes and who works closely with ILET, Somavia is obsessed by the military/industrial complex of Western might, whose international expression is the 'transnational' company. In his first major paper as ILET"s Director – the base document for its May 1976 seminar on 'the role of information in the New International Order', which was also adopted as the report of the meeting – he dealt with the apparently inconsistent fact that the international news agencies have budgets hardly commensurate with the transnational image:

> Their role within the transnational system may be compared to that of the headlights on an automobile: to light up the road, pick out the danger signals and changes in the route, inform those steering the system about everything that concerns their interests ... without their valuable information the system loses operativeness and runs the risk of crashing into unforeseen obstacles.

Aside from the natural instinct to cry 'block that metaphor', the passage is a testimony of sorts to the reliability of the information the agencies provide: headlights must reveal the whole road, potholes and all, to be any use. Yet Somavia does not admit this. He accuses the agencies first, of transmitting 'their particular view of events according to the political and economic determinants of the transnational system of which they form part' and, in another twist of the argument, of catering to 'a sort of "entertainment" model by which people are distracted, but not informed'. Stretching his own logic, he then attempts to square this circle by saying that all these elements, far from being contradictory, emanate from the from the consumerist pressures of the transnational ethic.

What some would call conspiracy theory, and Somavia terms the structural approach, tends to obscure the validity of many of his more specific criticisms of the Western performance. There is a lot of truth in his assertion that the selection of news is often arbitrary, in particular where the Third World is the subject; that much coverage of developing countries weaves the anecdotal and irrelevant, or the partial truth, into what is then presented as a 'significant' story; that labels and clichés are used in a discriminatory way; and that countries or even whole areas have a way, like Rosenblum's tree in the forest, of dropping totally out of the news profile. But to imply that the reporting of facts is manipulated with the purpose of ensuring that 'the implicit conclusions to be drawn from them are favourable to the interests of the transnational system' suggests some ignorance of how news agencies operate, and an almost total incomprehension of the way journalists set about their work.

There are two dimensions to Somavia's proposals for charging the power-loaded and centralised structure. At the level of the international press, he advocates drawing up, between the international media and Third World governments, a legal 'framework of social responsibility' which, while defining the agencies' rights, would cover their 'obligations and the means to make them effective'. Among these obligations would be respect for cultural sovereignty, diligence in conveying the national 'context' when reporting for the outside world, and the recognition by the international press as a whole (and especially the agencies) that their rights 'ought to be exercised with responsibility and be subject to questioning and evaluation by the community in which they operate . . . of the manner in which they exercise the social function of information.'

And if the evaluation is unfavourable? Then the international press – which should further the causes of peace and understanding among peoples, being actors *de facto* on the global stage – could legitimately face sanctions. For Somavia compares the situation of the international media in any particular country to those of the diplomatic corps in one respect: they have rights insofar as governments believe their presence 'to be of value to the country and to international understanding.' The new framework would 'make it possible to eliminate or redress' the agencies' harmful conduct. They would be held fully responsible for their performance – however limited their power to influence the conditions governing that performance.

It all seems quite clear: but here Somavia wheels in his central paradox: the New Order for Information does not, he says, 'mean fostering government-controlled international information. Neither do we believe that the preponderant influence of private economic and commercial interests over present flows can ensure adequate information.' Between the state and the market, if neither is to be trusted, what is there? This ambiguity runs through the entire set of ILET proposals; at the national level, it leaves a strong flavour of the corporate state, and internationally, the search for an institutional form to express 'the people's will'.

In order to give the required teeth to what is in effect a revolutionary attack on the concept of news itself, Somavia and his advisers at ILET press for an international code of conduct for journalists; and, because they argue that codes can be ignored by the strong, for international legislation governing the agencies' conduct (and extendable to other international media). Again, Somavia insists that ILET opposes not the principle of the free flow of information but its practice. Yet he deliberately introduces the question of content. For his proposals are directed, not so much towards increasing the two-way or multilateral flow of information, but towards creating, through legal instruments, 'an equilibrated free flow of responsible information" Who judges (thus controlling) the responsibility which is a requirement of 'true freedom'? Somavia betrays his lack of commitment to a 'flow' of any unfettered kind by making it clear that, for him and for ILET, the central issue is the protection of 'the cultural identity of societies'.

The conflict between government control and the market is resolved for Somavia by his insistence that information must undergo a structural revolution in which it ceases to be a commodity, and becomes a 'social good'. Under whatever system of ownership may be adopted, the public will be exposed to what they need to learn. 'A social and legal framework of responsibility' must be evolved 'which reflects the social consensus of each society'. Since 'the instruments of communication are only a reflection and expression of the rights of others,' it is natural to conclude that 'their rights as enterprises exist to the extent that they perform adequately their social function.' It is easy - but not irrelevant - to recall that in Nazi Germany, the 'social consensus' required that the existence of the concentration camps was not reported in the media.

Who decides what is 'adequate'? Or, indeed, the nature of the 'social function'? Not journalists; Somavia is convinced that, although information is power, 'and every society should be organised so that those holding power are socially responsible for its use', its 'exercise should not be left to the exclusive judgement of those involved in the activity in question.'

So the 'community' decides on a legal framework: in practice, enter the State as legislator. And, since like Schiller and also like those responsible at Unesco for charting communications policies, Somavia believes that information embraces 'news agencies, advertising enterprises and data banks . . . information retrieval systems, radio and television programmes, movies, radio-photos, magazines, books and comics', the 'cultural identity' of a society can be fairly precisely moulded through the establishment of a 'consensus' on communications.

Provided, of course, that the influence exercised by the international media can be controlled equally comprehensively. Somavia gives this task priority, in fact, because - lumping together entertainment programmes, advertisements and news services - he finds that they stimulate desires to copy the 'social organisation and lifestyles' of the industrialised world - desires which can only be met in Third World countries, Somavia asserts, 'on the basis of a high and growing concentration of income in a few hands and unacceptable social inequalities.' He may have a case where advertising is concerned. But the essence of his approach is its paternalistic contempt for the intelligence of the 'masses'. He comes close to the Victorian idea that the servants' ideas should be kept within their station – and applies it to entire societies. If Somavia accuses the West of confusing the principle of the free flow of information with the defence of commercial objectives, he is at least equally liable to confuse Coke ads with news bulletins – for do they not emanate from the same source? The popularity of the corrupting model he ascribes, as do an increasing number of Third World spokesmen, to collusion between the Third World elites, whose own interests are well served by the 'transnational culture', and the international agencies which perpetuate it.

This collusion is made possible by the commercialisation of the media within the Third World; the existing structure must therefore be destroyed. If structural change cannot be forced on the international media, they can at least be made to learn respect for host societies' cultures, and to adjust their commercial lenses to the perspectives of public service as conceived by those societies' leaders. Domestically, more ambitious programmes are possible.

Echoing the Dag Hammarskjöld Foundation formula for 'another development', Somavia calls for 'another information' – based on the social good (and thus free of market criteria) and rejecting the 'transnational' model for one which emphasises self-reliance and national standard-setting. The media are to be treated as 'a basic agent of social influence', for which 'a new conceptual framework' will accordingly be required.

Part of the intention behind this obscure, and obscurely-formulated, concept is reasonable enough: it is important for journalists to explain 'the problems of development and the conflicts inherent to (sic) societies aspiring for change.' But the 'explicit framework of social responsibility' gives information a more centrally educative role than that of mere explanation. Again no real distinction is made between education and information: both are purposive.

The more fundamental obscurities creep into the ILET thesis through its insistence on cultural diversity, which leads to the notion that each national society will determine the relationship between producers and structure of production.

Because there are no criteria for distinguishing between one set of national formulae and another, the attempt to be pluralistic destroys the basic argument for structural reform. For in saying that 'each society ... must define the characteristics and concrete form in which the social function of informing is to be organised ... from private enterprise monopoly to exclusive State control, with intermediate forms ...', the implication is that it is *not* the structure that matters, but who agrees it, and who controls it. Information is the way of making the people's will known to the people; provided that the people happen not to will a transnational model. There's the rub; and the reason that international controls are a central part of domestic planning. These are ideas which are totally incompatible with pluralism (unless there is *dirigiste* pluralism), but which are put forward in a pluralist mode.

Who is 'society'? The 'principles of access and participation as fundamental components' of the new information structure are heavily emphasised. Access and participation for whom? For 'the organised public' who reflect the 'social consensus'. It is interesting to quote, in this context, the carefully-prepared article written for the April 1977 special issue of the Unesco *Courrier*, giving the Soviet viewpoint on the role of the media in society, by Yassen Zasursky, Dean of the Faculty of Journalism at Moscow University, and Yuri Kashlev of the Institute for International Relations, who had been part of the Soviet delegation at Unesco's 1976 General Conference in Nairobi. Because the Soviet press, they write, is 'produced by organisations of the Communist Party, trade unions, women and young people, and by artists' societies, collectives formed by academic institutions, factories and state farms ... we have ... a press which serves the workers and we can therefore say that the mass information media are at the service of the entire people.' Neither Somavia nor Reyes Matta, on whose 'model' for 'communication with active social participation' ILET heavily relies, satisfactorily meet the difficulty central to any thesis which bases itself on the 'social consensus': who is to prevent the government interfering with information in the name of the people, either directly, or by organising the 'organised public'?

In September 1977, ILET organised a conference in Amsterdam, with major financial backing from the Dutch government. The explicit aim was to carry Unesco resolutions, and initiatives by the non-aligned movement, into the arena of international legislation. The original theme of this seminar, set out at length in a draft agenda paper, was the establishment of principles for a juridical framework for the media. In this draft paper, it was pointed out that the changed majority in the United Nations presented an opportunity: 'the contemporary debate on the rights to information and communication necessarily will have another character, enriched by the experiences of cultural and informational dependence that the new nations now represented can contribute.' Little uneasiness, here, about the involvement of governments in communications strategies. The same document discussed the role at the international level of the 'alternative' information structure: Third World media must be 'committed to the will for liberation of dominated countries': identity, after all, is solidarity. The central reason for the overhaul of the organisational structure is to free it from the old Adam of transnationalism so that it can find a voice with which to rally the forces of liberation.

The Amsterdam conference ran into trouble with the Netherlands press. The draft agenda included plans to develop a framework for international legislation governing communications, including their 'function and role . . . in the relations among individuals and states', the 'changes required' to adapt the principle of the free flow of information to the imperatives of a new world order, and 'the norms of an harmonic relationship between the states and the international media'. Angry journalists demanded why Development Minister Jan Pronk was using taxpayers' money to support a conference whose agenda questioned the principles central to their society. On 5 September, an outwardly unruffled Pronk opened the conference; but the title had been changed to 'International communications and Third World participation: a conceptual and practical framework'. The original agenda disappeared, replaced by a two-page programme which only after the conference had begun was extended to include 'the obligations of states with regard to the internal and external flow of information'.

The emphasis on international legislation, and on the *content* of information, had alienated potential sympathisers. Somavia's paper for the conference recognised that many Western journalists and organisations accept the legitimacy of the Third World's questioning of existing structures; he also accurately judged that accepting the 'reasons for change as valid' left most with 'doubts or hesitation concerning the methods or instruments required' for greater Third World participation; but fundamentally the conference made little progress in debating the extent to which the ILET view of the 'requirements' was necessarily valid, or would achieve a more balanced exchange of information.

Essentially, the ILET conference assembled Latin American 'communications experts', united in their resentment of US domination of their countries' media (and most persuasive when discussing the 'cultural alienation' created by the overwhelming presence of foreign entertainment programmes on TV); and clearer in expressing their allegiance to the concept of information as a social good than on the means of implementing it. The meeting was a dialogue of the already convinced; the handful of Western journalists and academics were either, like Schiller or Nordenstreng, honorary members of the club; or invited because they were thought to be sympathetic to the Third World case. A few were present but not welcome: one Western journalist was angrily put down by the chairman of a session with the words, 'I see that you do not agree with us; there can therefore be no dialogue.' The debate combined naivety – 'there is a conflict between freedom of expression and national sovereignty which makes it advisable to draw up a conceptual model to harmonise them' – with the occasional question, raised in the context of a general acceptance of structural change – 'Who determines what our needs for information are? does the tablet descend from on high? does enlightenment arise out of an ideological system? or do we arrive at it empirically?', which received the simple answer that 'deciding what should be circulated to the majority is essentially a political choice.'

Yet it also brought together many of the people who are shaping communications policies, in Unesco and at intergovernmental level. What looks and sounds like an exiles' club, characteristically dedicated to 'revolution-first' policies, is in fact not the isolated or irrelevant group that it appears. This is one reason that Somavia, and ILET as a whole, cannot be dismissed. The other is that ILET has voiced many of the complaints, genuine, irrational or calculatingly political, of the Third World's leaders and some of its intellectuals. Its support for information as a social good fits cleanly into the governmental thesis of communications as part and parcel of a development strategy in which identity is unity, and rights are essentially collective. Final recommendations by the meeting were for 'a right to reply for Third World countries', the definition of international news agencies' rights and responsibilities, the 'formation of an international court of communications' and for action to 'formulate and implement national and sovereign communications' on the lines agreed a year earlier by the Intergovernmental Conference of Latin American countries, convened by Unesco in Costa Rica to consider communications policies (and which will be discussed in the next chapter). The ILET group also called for more active Unesco involvement in developing the news agencies' pool of the non-aligned countries. All these proposals connect to some degree with plans and policies being hammered out at the political level.

Unesco was represented at Amsterdam by Makaminan Makagiansar, its Assistant Director General for Culture and Communications. Also present was Germán Carnero Roque. In a way, Carnero's career illustrates the links between organisations like ILET and the Dag Hammarskjöld Foundation, and the policy-making arenas. Carnero was a Peruvian government press attaché, at one point concerned with the UN organisations at Geneva. He became closely involved with the Dag Hammarskjöld's early probing of communications issues: with Somavia, he was one of a small group of Third World 'journalists' to participate in the Foundation's seminar, held parallel with the UN Seventh Special Session in 1975, to promote 'another development' and also to call for a 'new order for information'. By 1977, Carnero had been appointed Unesco's Regional Adviser for Latin America and the Caribbean. And as such, he was one of the three-man drafting team which rewrote the 1976 Unesco Draft Declaration on the Use of the Media, for resubmission to its 1978 General Conference (See Chapter

5). Several other participants at Amsterdam advise Latin American governments on the formulation and content of communications policies; some represented the Non-Aligned Movement. And Somavia himself is a member of the sixteen-strong International Commission at Unesco on communications problems – a commission which is intended to have the impact on communications policies which the earlier Faure Commission had on education and which will, according to Unesco officials, profoundly influence the organisation's future strategies.

The criticisms of the 'transnational' system advanced by all these groups are basically anti-capitalist. The clear implication is that a transnational system which was *not* commercial, but state-operated; not 'centre-directed', but expressive of 'Third World solidarity', would be perfectly acceptable. What disturbs them is not the fact that power, as they see it, is concentrated in a few hands, but that they are the wrong hands. Just as economic power, when wielded by the OPEC countries, is something which Somavia finds both acceptable and progressive, the 'democratisation' of communications basically means a transfer, not a broadening, of the power to wield a microphone.

Some have no qualms about providing an intellectual framework for increased government intervention in decisions over the content of information. Those who claim that this is not their objective – that they march under worthy banners against *all* monopolies – are likely to find that governments listen to the part that suits them. And it is governments, the majority of whom keep a very firm grip on communications at home, who are translating theory into action on the international plane. This is inevitable: the demands for a New Order for Information, as the non-aligned governments' spokesmen realise, must be articulated internationally if they are to be effective. The most promising forums, on this reasoning, are the supranational organisations.

For this reason, both private and governmental groups are looking with increasing impatience at the UN and its specialised agencies. The UN, until 1978, had shown marked reluctance to involve itself with communications. But in Unesco, the Third World has been using its majority to press not only for technical cooperation, and Unesco's assistance with the development of the non-aligned news pool, but for ideological debate. They have met with a sympathetic response. The Unesco secretariat had, in fact, started to alter its own policies on communications – and to focus on the desirability of government involvement in national communications strategy – well ahead of the formulation of a new approach by Third World governments. Unesco, an organisation which was founded to promote international understanding, became in the course of the 1970's the strongest supranational backer of the policy of using the media to strengthen 'cultural sovereignty'. Because Unesco inevitably works with and through governments, this activity encouraged not only a narrowly nationalistic view of communications, but the tendencies towards structured state control of the news. The importance of Unesco's policies rests on the fact that national governments are anxious to implement its proposals by restructuring communications at the national level and by supporting any moves by Unesco for international legislation.

CHAPTER 5

Unesco—Medium for the New Message

In 1976, three inter-governmental meetings finally began to focus public attention on the degree to which communications had become a major political issue – and on the key role played by Unesco in this process. In Costa Rica that July, a meeting of Latin American governments convened by Unesco endorsed the principle of state involvement in national communications policies, which would 'integrate mass communications media with national planning,' and called for a regional approach to communications which would respect national sovereignties, non-intervention and cultural plurality. In a parallel but separate development, the Colombo Non-Aligned Summit a month later called for a New Order for Information, stressing that 'the emancipation and development of national information media is an integral part of the overall struggle for political, economic and social independence.' And in Nairobi that November, Unesco's Nineteenth General Conference passed a resolution sponsored by Tunisia recommending that Unesco, as an agency 'capable of assisting in liberating the developing countries from the state of dependence . . . which still characterises their communication and information systems,' should support the non-aligned initiatives on communications and give priority to activities consistent with their objectives.

But the debate which alerted international opinion at Nairobi was over a Soviet-inspired 'Draft Declaration on Fundamental Principles Governing the Use of the Mass Media in Strengthening Peace and International Understanding and in Combating War Propaganda, Racism, and Apartheid'.

The Draft Declaration, under preparation for three years, not only placed upon the media a 'duty' to mobilise international opinion behind the new international economic order (Article VII), but sanctioned the use of the media by governments as a matter of principle. It contained two clauses which directly threatened the independence and freedom of information. Article XII declared, 'States are responsible for the activities in the international sphere of all mass media under their jurisdiction;' and Article X said that states which considered that 'the circulation of erroneous news reports' hindered their pursuit of the high ideals of the Declaration should have a right to 'rectify' them through the mass media.

Under the guise of promoting morally worthy objectives, the Declaration in effect – and particularly through Article XII – justified governmental control of all media, domestic and foreign; exposed foreign correspondents to the possibility of reprisals for material published or broadcast by their organisations whether or not written by them; and made governments responsible, conversely, for the worldwide activities of news media based in their countries. The effects on international reporting could be predicted; Unesco's constitutional duty to 'promote the free flow of ideas by word and image' was implicitly flouted; and above all, perhaps, the Declaration would gravely have weakened the already precarious position of Third World journalists attempting to keep government controls at bay. Certainly, it would have had none of the legal status of a covenant; but the use of Unesco to give an international moral respectability to state control of the media was rightly seen by Western and several Third World journalists as threatening. And the restrictions on international reporting which could have resulted, as governments cited their 'responsibility', were obvious: reporting would be vulnerable to any bureaucrat's interpretation of a journalist's record in supporting 'international peace and ... the development of friendly relations between States'.

For all of these reasons, the Draft Declaration was bitterly contested at Nairobi. Predictably, it might have been thought: but diplomatic observers have commented that the vehemence of the reaction of the Western media and other journalists genuinely surprised the Director-General of Unesco, Amadou

Mahtar M'Bow.

M'Bow had taken over the Director General's job on 14 November 1974, in the middle of the previous General Conference and also in the thick of a set of controversial resolutions on Israel's cultural policies in the occupied territories which were to lead both to the withdrawal of American financial support for the next two years, and to a massive boycott of Unesco by major literary figures and intellectuals – from Ionesco and Sartre to Iris Murdoch. The first African Director General, M'Bow comes from the small town of Luga in Senegal. His background is education, and his life is widely believed to be politics – practiced necessarily at the international level, once it became clear that his domestic career was unlikely to take him further than the job of Minister of Education and Culture which he held three times. He had been Unesco's Assistant Director General for Education (a division which absorbs well over half the organisation's budget) since 1970. He brought to communications problems a conviction that they were capable of systematic resolution, like education; and a resentment of the international press rooted in the sense of African cultural dependence, and confirmed by what he described, in his first official report as Director General, as the 'incipient and growing campaign conducted against Unesco by certain sections of the information media ... the often incomplete or slanted information put out' following the discriminatory measures taken against Israel at the 1974 Conference. He firmly laid the blame for the boycott by Western intellectuals on a deliberate campaign by the international media aimed, he asserted, at crippling Unesco.

M'Bow had, in any case, taken over an organisation more sharply polarised and more vulnerable than at any time since its creation in November 1945. This he recognized – although he blamed the tensions not on Arab attempts to put pressure on Israel through international forums, but on the world crises of energy, raw materials, monetary system and economic inequalities. He saw as paramount the pressures which had produced, among other things, the demand for a new economic order. Unesco, he firmly stated, could not and should not be aloof from these: it had a contribution to make to the new order. But it is also true that M'Bow, head of an organisation which had lost considerable support as a result of the Israeli question and which had survived the withdrawal of US funds only through interest-free loans from the Arab world, was not seeking further confrontation in Nairobi. There was in fact an additional reason for wishing the Nairobi conference to run smoothly: it was the first General Conference outside Paris, and it was a matter of African prestige that it should be a success.

Once the strength of the opposition to the Draft Declaration became clear, M'Bow worked behind the scenes to mobilise the African vote behind a compromise. The only way to avoid a major political crisis – potentially even more damaging than that which had marked the 1974 General Conference – was to use the forty-plus African votes to put the Arabs and the Soviet bloc in a minority and, in making this clear, avoid coming to a vote. The mechanism was a Drafting and Negotiating Group of twenty-five nations, to which the Draft Declaration was referred. This group was a face-saving innovation, intended to defuse issues on which M'Bow feared confrontation; it was the ideal vehicle for arriving at an agreement to postpone consideration of the Draft Declaration. Its decisions could however easily have been overturned in plenary session if work had not also gone on to create the political consensus behind what was then dubbed the 'spirit of Nairobi'.

The end result was that M'Bow was 'invited' to 'hold further broad consultations with experts' on the Declaration, 'with a view' to producing a draft 'which could meet with the largest possible measure of agreement' for submission to the 1978 General Conference. The final Resolution 4.143 – the only official consequence of the debate – also gave M'Bow leeway to propose any other action which he might think appropriate. The formula was worked out entirely through the Drafting and Negotiating Group, where western liberal views on the media prevailed with strong participation from Japan. Iraq and Algeria attacked the 'spirit of Nairobi', which they rightly interpreted, observers commented, as a tacit understanding not to create problems for the West. The Soviet Union on the other hand, partly because it was under attack from the Chinese over other issues at the conference, partly because it was not anxious to appear to create problems for Unesco, decided that the game wasn't worth the candle and even suggested that the Draft was merely intended to underline governments' responsibility for their own state-controlled media, and was not aimed at the freedom of the press in general.

The outcome of the conference was hailed by the international press as a victory for freedom. It was in fact a respite – certainly created to some extent by the spirited defence of Western values put up by Third World and Western journalists outside the doors of the conference; and assisted by diplomatic efforts to shift the centre of the argument from the ideological plane to questions of material assistance to the Third World's media. But it was only a respite, because the issue was due to come back to the next General Conference and, more importantly, because it was only the most dramatic of a large number of resolutions which tended cumulatively to reinforce the notion of information as a weapon in the service of development and subject to policies which integrate information in the whole structure of the national interest as perceived by governments. The international press had woken up very late to the implications of the Draft Declaration; and failed on the whole to perceive the undercurrents of *dirigisme* affecting the whole trend of Unesco's approach to communications. The American press, which had followed the Costa Rica conference, was an exception; but they too treated the 'spirit of Nairobi' more as the happy end to a troubled tale than as the temporary diplomatic pause in a confrontation between two views of the nature of information which was just beginning.

The Draft Declaration is in fact a separate issue which had taken root in this political jungle almost by accident. It is a product of national – in this case, Russian – obsession, rather than an integral part of Unesco's strategy on communications. Its origins go back to 1970, when Byelorussia introduced a curiously-worded recommendation to Unesco's members, in the General Conference of that year, affirming the 'inadmissibility of using information media for propaganda on behalf of war, racialism and hatred among nations' and inviting 'all States to take the necessary steps, including legislative measures, to encourage the use of information media against propaganda' of the kind, 'and to provide Unesco with information on the subject.' The initial wording had been 'to forbid the use' of the media for such purposes; Western objections effected a change into 'positive' language; but the resolution was, curiously, passed without strong objections to the reference to 'legislative measures'. The widely recognised motive for the Byelorussian resolution was Soviet concern to stop the activities of US broadcasting stations beamed into Russia and Eastern Europe. The references to racialism were perhaps merely an afterthought: a resolution which existed to serve essentially Soviet goals could include references to racialism which would swing African and Arab support behind it while enhancing Russia's reputation for solidarity with Third World causes. The only immediate outcome was a round robin from the then Director General, René Maheu, to member states. The answers he brought back to the 1972 General Conference from the fifty-four countries who had bothered to reply revealed that although some countries thought legislation unnecessary – Kuwait for the reason that 'the information media in our State serve, actualise and correspond to the general policy of the State' – twenty-four countries reported the existence of constitutional or legal provisions making such propaganda liable to prosecution, and another fifteen reported impending or existing legislation 'encouraging' their media to restraint. A further nineteen countries replied that they had no legislation *encouraging* the use of their media against racism, etcetera.

But only three – Norway, Sweden and the UK – actually took issue with the principle the Unesco letter raised. Sweden said that legislation to persuade the news media to a particular course of action would be contrary to the principle of press freedom; Norway considered that 'freedom of information is in itself considered as a defence of peace, democracy and human rights' and added that 'the guarantee against misuse is the control exercised by the free public opinion of a democratic society.' And the UK government replied first, that 'since in any society the ideas of government about what may be desirable will frequently not coincide with the wishes of the people, it is inappropriate to enact legislation designed to direct the information media in specific directions'; second, that such action would directly conflict with Article 19 of the Universal Declaration of Human Rights; and ended by pointing out with a certain irony that legislation to prohibit propaganda on behalf of war would 'restrict the ability of the information media to discuss the possible use of force in Southern Africa' and might even prevent them reporting certain UN resolutions 'regarding the provision of assistance to liberation movements which seek to attain their aims by the use of violence.'

The concept of state involvement in the media – as a matter of policy – was however already gaining ground in Unesco. For Maheu, nearing the end of his career as Director General, communications were the last in line for a comprehensive over-haul. From the start of the 1960's, there had been conferences and campaigns to persuade states to adopt education policies; science had followed and, despite some Western objections that culture was not a proper area for state involvement, Unesco had taken the stand that countries should develop a basic framework for cultural policies, within which to provide state help for the arts. This stand, Maheu believed, had been under-stood in the end even by those who argued that those who pay the piper are apt to give him directives (but who had simul-taneously to admit their support for state help for the arts in their own countries). The resulting declaration on cultural rights created a precedent for Unesco: communications after all are integral to cultural life. It also produced the kind of self-contradictory language which was to plague Unesco's pro-nouncements on communications. At the world conference of Ministers of Culture, in Venice in August 1970, a much-debated resolution finally read: 'Whilst respecting the freedom of artists, States will assure that the media of mass communi-cation are not employed to propagate material which is sub-versive of agreed values.'

Other factors were important. Until the mid-1960's, it had been accepted that the United Nations was the appropriate forum for political activities, including the drafting of any declarations or conventions to be agreed by member states. 'In Unesco', a key official recalls, 'we confined ourselves to activities we *thought* were apolitical. But the UN got nowhere – and we began to realize that we couldn't deal with the medium without dealing with the message.' Maheu himself was the more inclined to listen to such arguments because – as he had written in the 1940's, when still Director of the division dealing with the 'free flow of information' at Unesco – he believed that the right to communicate would be the great issue of the end of the twentieth century.

This belief had been reinforced by a particular event. Maheu was in Geneva in 1962, to address a meeting of the UN Economic and Social Council, when the news that Telstar – the first communications satellite – had been launched. 'He was electrified by it', says a Unesco official who was with him. 'He tore up his prepared speech, and went into the meeting with a passionate statement that this "monumental advance" must be properly used, and that Unesco was the body to do it.' This thinking was to influence Unesco's education programme – and also encouraged Maheu and others to see all communications – including news dissemination – as aspects of mass education. The existence of revolutionary tools implied, for Maheu, ambitious strategies to ensure their 'usefulness'.

In 1970, Maheu obtained a directive from member states to assist them in the formulation of mass communication policies; that General Conference had before it Unesco's first effort at longterm planning, an outline covering 1971–6. This document was sent back for reworking by the General Conference, because as a long-term plan it was found to be insufficiently competent. But some of the key ideas in it were vital to the future policy of Unesco, and they were not challenged. One of them dealt with the media. In the outline, Maheu had written 'the time has come to embark on a line of development which will give priority to the *content* of communication, rather than to the *techniques* for communicating it, upon which work until now has tended to be focussed. Freedom of information, the progress of communication techniques, and the development of communication media are all attended by a corresponding responsibility as regards the use made thereof, the importance of which in promoting respect for the individual, social progress, international understanding and peace itself is becoming daily more obvious.'

This statement both marks a watershed in Unesco's approach to communications; and clearly indicates that the initiative came from within the Secretariat, rather than through pressures from member states. By 1972, Maheu was describing a revitalised communications programme as a step which would complete 'the process which, beginning with educational planning twelve years ago' systematically directed national efforts in support of Unesco's policy of ' "comprehensive planning for total development".'

The Long-Term Plan had also urged that 'the denunciation of the errors and wrongs of racialism, which represents the most militant part of Unesco's programme on behalf of human rights, must therefore be continued unremittingly, and even intensified. . . .' The Byelorussian reaction to Maheu's 1971 circular letter on policies to 'encourage' the mass media was to say that the mere provision of information by member states was not enough. They requested the Director General to submit a Draft Declaration to the 1974 Conference on 'fundamental principles governing the use of the mass media' for a string of laudable aims. The recommendation fitted closely enough with Unesco's policies on racialism – and with its new activism in relation to the content of information. The fact that a forest of UN conventions and Unesco resolutions – including the International Covenant on Civil and Political Rights – already prohibited war propaganda and incitement to racial hatred did not prevent the Conference from mandating Unesco to start work on a Declaration which was to associated it directly with state control of the media. At the time, the vote went un-reported.

In the usual manner, the job went first to a consultant, the Swedish lawyer Professor Hilding Eek, whose initial draft was first submitted to two other consultants (one of whom, Bogdan Osolnik of Yugoslavia, later played a crucial political role) and then to a 'meeting of experts', in March 1974.

Unesco's meetings of experts are a convenient formula; they make possible informal discussions of complex subjects – and their recommendations can be (and have been) disowned by Unesco if politically expedient. The March meeting was a relative success: the Eek draft was considerably altered, to minimise the pretexts for states to intervene in the flow of information, and to acknowledge the need for the media to be independent of government control. After bitter argument, a move to establish a version of the future Article XII was defeated. The 'use' of the mass media became the 'role'. The Draft Declaration which went to the Eighteenth General Conference was a relatively cautious affair. (Significantly,

Unesco altered the experts' agreed text to include two specific references to the 'responsibility' of the news media.) But the discussions that March already indicated the lines of the political debate on the news media taking shape in Unesco. Third World participants 'particularly stressed the problem of promoting a more balanced flow of information and opinion, so that the cultural integrity of their countries would not be submerged or dominated by foreign sources.' The international agencies came under attack – as 'privately owned, often mono-polistic in nature, and like other multinational enterprises, beyond the jurisdiction of any one State.' Warnings that governments could use the pretext of protecting national integrity to suppress dissent were met by arguments that legislation to correct 'imbalances' would not threaten freedom of speech if, regardless of content, it focussed on 'the balance of information and opinion from foreign and domestic sources'. The Draft Declaration, from the beginning, touched on issues which went far further than its narrow terms of application, and explicitly set up 'freedom of the press' and 'responsibility' as opposing principles. And the debate inevitably turned, even at this stage, on the merits and propriety of the exercise by states of protectionist policies against the international flow of inform-ation: the question of 'content' was now on Unesco's agenda, in a highly political context. It was a development against which several key Unesco officials had fought determinedly – and successfully – until the end of the 1960's, on the ground that concern with 'content' would fatally politicise and hamper Unesco's work.

The 1974 text never reached the plenary of the Eighteenth General Conference: in the Communications Commission, the US and some other countries opposed certain phrases in the existing draft, while formal amendments intended greatly to toughen it were proposed by Bulgaria, Byelorussia, Cuba, East Germany, Hungary, Mongolia, the Ukraine and the Soviet Union – a well-orchestrated choir in which Mongolia had the part of introducing the fatally controversial wording of the future Article XII. Peru and India, tabling the only other amendments, formally introduced for the first time specifically Third World demands: India insisting that only major inter-national assistance to the developing countries' media, and better communications facilities, would create a two-way flow of information; Peru paddling its national canoe in arguing for 'the transfer of the ownership of the mass media to the social sectors' and – the shape of things to come – calling for 'international governmental control of the privately-owned major information agencies'.

Thus festooned, the Draft Declaration was referred by the General Conference to a more formal Unesco meeting of experts – representing, this time, governments – which was convened by the new Director General, M'Bow, in Paris from 15 to 22 December 1975. In the general furore over the resolutions on Israel, little attention was still paid to the issue.

The meeting, attended by eighty-five countries and the Palestine Liberation Organisation, was opened by Unesco's Deputy Director General, an American international civil servant called John Fobes, with a statement which made it perfectly clear that the point of the Declaration was not fundamentally to do with the principles to which it was formally pledged, but with pressures at the 1972 General Conference for international 'guidelines applicable to the media', as an extension, he suggested, of the concern to regulate direct satellite broadcasting which had produced an agreement that year. The rest was politics. Within two days, Yugoslavia produced an amendment to the preamble of the Declaration, referring to the United Nations Resolution 3379, passed in New York a month earlier, which equates Zionism with racism. The Yugoslav amendment was only one of several which had been informally circulated dealing with Resolution 3379, and the attempt to table it was predictable. The Italian ambassador to Unesco, Ludovico Carducci Artenisio, attempted first to secure a twenty-four hour postponement of action on the amendment and then the suspension of the session, but Algeria successfully forced a vote and the amendment was adopted 36 to 22, with seven abstentions. The Yugoslav who introduced 3379 was Bogdan Osolnik, the politician-cum-journalist who had been consulted on the Eek draft – and who in 1977 was to be selected by M'Bow as a member of the International Commission on Communications.

Whether or not this was the intended effect, the vote resulted in a walk-out by the US, the EEC countries, Canada, Australia and Norway. (The Japanese government instructed their delegation to remain, in the hope of remaining fully informed and if possible of influencing the content of the final text.)

The decision to leave the meeting, arrived at over late-night arguments on 17–18 December, created a public storm. It was taken in the knowledge that the Draft Declaration would then be altered without reference to the amendments tabled for the meeting by the missing delegations, and along Soviet lines. It also had the effect, once again, of deflecting attention from the substance of the Declaration. But aside from the view held by several diplomats that the reference to 3379 made a Western withdrawal inevitable, there was a strong feeling that the Soviet Union was using the entire debate to draw back from the agreement to permit the 'freer and wider dissemination of information of all kinds', to which it was committed under the Helsinki Final Act of August 1975. The best course was therefore to boycott a meeting which would undoubtedly produce a more restrictive document, saving the final battle for the Nineteenth General Conference. Here, it was hoped that the Declaration could be postponed.

The Europeans were also strongly influenced by their conviction that a united front was needed on another issue. Virtually parallel with the Byelorussian Declaration, another on Race and Racial Prejudice had been called for at the Eighteenth General Conference, and was to come up at another meeting late in January 1976. As a result of the uproar in December, M'Bow was persuaded by a group of Unesco diplomats that this January meeting should be cancelled, and the Declaration on Race simply referred to the next General Conference. It was a delaying tactic which backfired: when the Declaration on Race came up at Nairobi, it was indeed referred back for further consideration – but by that time it not only included provision to give states legal powers to 'prevent, prohibit and eradicate racialism' (at best, a clumsy attempt to eliminate prejudice by banning it), but specifically extended recommendations for legislation to cover the media. And at Nairobi, Resolution 3.173 which referred the text back for amendment agreed that the Secretariat should provide an explanatory gloss interpreting the Declaration. Published in August 1977, the new Declaration included a formal gloss which made the following specific points (in summary):

- the mass media were not only, if the Declaration was correctly interpreted, to be prevented by law from 'contributing to the spread of racialism but (made) into effective instruments for its eradication'.
- they must refrain from stereotyped images; from specifying racial origins unless strictly necessary for the understanding of an event; 'from presenting any particular social group as "a problem" '; and all reports dealing with race must provide 'detailed factual accounts of the social and historical background of specific ethnic groups'.

The April 1977 meeting which approved these provisions included Sean MacBride, future Chairman of the Unesco International Commission on Communications. The irony of a draft which was clearly intended to promote good race relations and to combat racial prejudice was that its restrictions on press reporting – if adopted, and endorsed within countries – could make debate on racial problems impossible: from articles on unemployment among black youths in Liverpool, to reporting of the racial tensions caused by Malaysia's Bhumiputra policy (a policy set up to prevent Malays being exploited by Chinese, which has caused great hardship to the Chinese community and accelerated, in the view of many observers, the growth of Malaysia's communist insurgent movement). And, like the Byelorussian Declaration, it introduced the principle of controls on the press as a major vehicle to achieve generally laudable goals. Unlike it, the Declaration on Race was approved at a final meeting in March 1978 by ninety-nine member states without a vote, and was expected to attract little opposition at the Twentieth General Conference that autumn. Both Declarations raise the question whether controls on the freedom of debate, once accepted as a means of governing, are likely to be limited to particular objectives. And both, by serving as the focus for political forces with much broader aims, acted as catalysts encouraging Unesco's participation in the politics of the New Order.

Circulated to governments in the summer of 1976, the Draft Declaration on the Use of the Media finally alerted the Western public to the threats posed to the independence of the press. But Declarations are, in a sense, the passive face of Unesco. Even though it influences their content by selecting the 'experts' who draw them up, and exercises its powers to alter drafts, the Secretariat is basically correct in asserting that it is simply giving life to the specific requests and ambitions of member states.

This is not true of the broad sweep of Unesco's policies on communications. Here again, Unesco officials are fond of repeating that the Secretariat merely reflects the wishes of its membership – but this is at best the necessary hypocrisy of an international organisation which must put its views into the mouths of others. There is convincing evidence that Unesco has shaped its communications policies, from its Paris headquarters, and brought its members into line as partners. The General Conference proposes, the Secretariat disposes; but the Secretariat drafts the proposals for the General Conference, above all when it outlines strategic shifts in policy. This is not to suggest that they may not coincide with, and sometimes reflect, governments' aspirations, but it is to say that Unesco can and does initiate. And it was essentially the Secretariat, with the experts which it coopted for the purpose, which set the pace in transforming Unesco's approach to communications from that of technical assistant to the media, to that of architect and chief engineer of a strategy in which communications are integrated into national planning, and find their place there as servants of the development process and of 'national identity'.

There are arguments both for greater activism in UN agencies, and for Unesco's communications policies. Broadly dismissed as well-meaning but insignificant where communications were concerned, the new policies have given Unesco a new vitality not unconnected with its deliberate decision to enter the arena as a firm partisan of a new international order. It can also be argued that a strategic approach to communications by Unesco was necessary – that its piecemeal (and practical) contribution to the improvement of the Third World's media was too small-scale to be effective without being strategically coordinated. It can be added that, as an organisation of the United Nations, Unesco has a duty to promote a new international economic order, within its sphere of competence. It can be held that development is obviously such an urgent priority in many countries that the undoubted influence of the media should be mobilised behind it. If politics enters in, this is an inevitable corollary of efforts to effect structural change and Unesco's 'sphere of competence' must therefore be understood to be broad enough to encompass that reality. It can, most forcefully of all, be argued that the developing countries are short on effective forums in which to organise the necessary steps to full independence; Unesco is therefore fulfilling the deeper requirements of its international mission in providing ideas and organisational ability to assist them to achieve their goals.

And when all of this is said, it has to be recognised that in involving itself, through the governments with which it must work, with communications in the strategic sense, Unesco has involved itself at national level in an area where national sovereignty may conflict with the promotion of international understanding (for which Unesco exists) and where individual liberties and national priorities, seen through governmental eyes, have a weighting in which the independence of inform-ation and freedom of choice tend to be light in the balance. All Unesco's research into access and participation does not alter the fact that it sits on the government side of the desk.

Latin America was selected by Unesco as the testing ground for the formulation of national communications policies, with the aim of convening an inter-governmental conference in 1975. To help Unesco in 'defining the agenda', a small group of communications 'experts' met in Bogotá, from 4 to 13 July 1974. 'Unesco thinking,' at this time, observes Professor John Lent, was that through national policies 'waste would be eliminated'. In short, all communication planning in any given nation would be systematised to act as an agent of planned education and social change.' At Bogotá, Unesco's advisers were reminded that in Maheu's view, progress would be 'slow and difficult' but that the innovation would have 'far-reaching consequences'.

They proceeded to make it more difficult – by removing any illusions the Secretariat could ever have nourished about steering clear of politics in the communications field, and by making clear their view of what those politics ought to be. So difficult, in fact, that Unesco subsequently not only disowned the whole meeting as a collection of personal opinions over which it had no control (even though it had selected the participants), but eventually struck all reference to the meeting off its annual chronology tables, and directed the keepers of its Paris archives to withdraw the report from their files. Bogotá became for public purposes a non-event. Yet the outcome was hardly the 'experts' ' fault: the themes which they were invited by Unesco to discuss included 'the ideological context of a communication policy. . . . Communication as an area of development policy. . . . The difficulty of applying a national communication policy without the participation of the government.'

This is what they said:

• 'a communication policy is always inseparable from an ideological framework'; communication is 'auxiliary to development'.

• policies should reflect 'the express wish of the nation and the State'.

• 'the formulation and execution of a national communications policy should be the exclusive concern of the State'.

• commercially owned media, by providing the people 'with amusement and means of escaping from reality which tend to deaden their critical faculties and stultify their potential for action to bring about social change' fail to promote development.

• if therefore, a State decided to permit the continued existence of private broadcasting media, it should 'impose certain services and programmes, thus controlling their operations as regards messages, content and the frequency of advertising, etc.'

The Bogotá meeting also referred rather in passing to the desirability of a 'deep respect' for the Declaration of Human Rights and, with greater enthusiasm, to the need for the participation of the masses and the nurturing of critical awareness. But the overriding impression to emerge from their recommendations is that resentment of the international agencies, and their co-conspirators the Latin American press and broadcasting stations, made state control their priority. Communications must be activated by government as a 'necessary public utility'; access and participation would in fact, integrated into communications policy, be 'the exclusive concern of the State'. And, in a system which was designed to serve development, there must be no more 'amusement and means of escaping from reality' – no more cakes and ale. Actually underlined in the report is the statement that 'The need for political, economic and cultural independence is forcing the Member States of the region to assume overall control over their national mass communication policy', ensuring by this means 'that freedom of expression is a right which belongs to the entire community.'

A year later, in June 1975, a second preparatory meeting was called by Unesco in Quito – this time on a more formal basis. It was to consider international news-flow and the role of news agencies. This meeting had before it a paper prepared by Professor John McNelly of the University of Wisconsin, which provided a sympathetic and practical statement of the problems which building up national and regional agencies would present – and included a description of the actual working of the international agencies which cut the ground from under the feet of the more xenophobic and anti-capitalist orators. But in opening the meeting, Unesco's Gunnar Naesselund went out of his way to emphasise that this was not offered by Unesco as a working document. Naesselund's speech, while insisting that Unesco was 'never the sponsor, supporter or initiator or one cause or the other' but merely 'the exponent of alternatives and options', went on to give a fairly clear statement of Unesco's expectations from the meeting.

One might, he said, ask why Unesco was involving itself in this 'highly political' area; the answer was first, that Unesco, having found 'that certain principles of research and planning as well as in formulating policies can be seen as modules which will fit into different socio-political systems' considered that this discovery 'justified the attempt . . . to define the rules that shape these modules.' Secondly, he said, there were 'international constraints' which affected national planning, such as 'transnational transactions in the communications field': here,

Unesco could take action on individual countries' behalf. And the Organisation felt confident that it was 'able to establish the contemporary as well as the foreseeable needs of information . . . to identify the strategies for information transfer, collection and dissemination, which is the immediate concern of this meeting.' To help the participants concentrate their minds, he added: 'we wish you to talk a great deal about news values. This indicates not only what you think is important to people in your country, but what content, what messages you would find relevant under the given circumstances to the people or groups of people whom you intend to serve. . . .' And, although he told them they were 'not here to judge the services rendered by foreign agencies, but to find out what it is you are *missing*' he added: 'You have also to dissociate yourselves from the models you know of today. The world agencies . . . are not relevant models . . . government's information needs and services . . . must be partners in the sort of services we have come here to consider.'

After the presentation of the 'options', the participants were invited to consider recommendations presented by Marcos Ordonez, Director General of the Latin American research institute CIESPAL which was hosting the meeting for Unesco, in a paper with the scholarly title, 'International communication and ideological contamination'. Their conclusions, contrary to some Western press reports, were surprisingly moderate in the circumstances.

Not, however, thanks to the influence of Unesco. One of the most remarkable passages in the final document comes in page 6 of the 'recommendations'. The Unesco Secretariat which drew up this report inserted the following paragraph: 'It is recommended that governments take the necessary steps to ensure that the national news agencies are exclusively empowered to disseminate news from outside the region referring to the internal affairs of each country, in order to avoid the distortion of news that is so frequent on the part of international agencies.' This, one of the most radical statements, was placed in the record by Unesco as a recommendation, in spite of the fact that – as a note in brackets following the paragraph records – 'a majority view was expressed against this recommendation on the grounds that it was inconsistent with the free flow of news.' The formal niceties of most meetings require majority approval for a resolution. The fact that it was so recorded suggests that it was put in the minute because the Secretariat wanted it there, rather than because the participants did. The effect is to suggest that Unesco not only formulates its own policies, but is prepared, on occasion, to record the fact that it is ready to run against the sense of a meeting in order to advance them. In this case, Unesco clearly intended to insert into the report, on its own initiative, an idea which straightforwardly restricts the free flow of information which Unesco is constitutionally obliged to foster and protect.

The participants at the Quito meeting, while they did not back such a concept, still agreed on a basic design which was bound to confirm the fears of those disturbed by the Bogotá meeting: national news agencies should be within the competence of the public sector, and conceived as 'reliable tools for development and for national and regional integration'; their objectives 'should be in line with the general intentions and aims governing the overall development strategy of the individual countries.' They should provide not merely political and economic information, but cover other aspects of national life – naturally enough. Not just because this too was news, however, but to disseminate 'all that makes for expression of the loftiest national objectives.' And they recommended Latin American governments to ask Unesco to prepare handbooks for news agencies 'laying down standards with regard to ethics and style, designed to increase the objectivity of the information put out ... and to improve relations between the countries of the region, by avoiding, in any case, the dissemination of items and commentaries likely to impair good relations between the said countries.' Clearly, the world agencies were not being taken as a model. The tone was moderate: but Quito also endorsed fully the 'pluralistic and democratic criteria' prescribed for national communication policies at Bogotá, within which the creation of national news agencies would exist to 'adapt information to the interests of the national majorities.' The Quito report, like that of Bogotá, has been withdrawn from Unesco's files, although the event is still acknowledged in its lists of meetings for 1975.

What significance should be attached to these meetings? First, for all Unesco's disclaimers, its official working document for the Inter-governmental Conference finally convened at Costa Rica in July 1976 states that 'the implementation of (Unesco's) programme for communications policies' was based on them – plus 'case studies' and research conducted by various specialists (including Herbert Schiller). Secondly, many of the 'experts' present at both are closely connected with ILET, and their work has directly or indirectly influenced both the non-aligned programme and Unesco's research and planning. Thirdly, these meetings and the Costa Rica Conference were explicitly intended to set the pattern for Unesco's longterm plans to promote national communications which, in the words of its Costa Rica working paper, would 'strengthen national sovereignty in all its aspects, particularly with regard to culture.' (What Unesco meant by this is spelt out a few pages later: 'When the mass communication media are used for the transmission of traditional values . . . they can be an invaluable instrument for the assertion of a country's national identity. When they are used consistently to convey information based on alien forms of behaviour and value systems, they deform the national character. . . .'

They are therefore the clearest indications we have of the general trend of Unesco's efforts to encourage systematic policies on communication in cooperation with governments. And the meetings of experts, in particular, illustrate one of the dangers: these were not gatherings of fanatics and would-be dictators, but of intellectuals disturbed by the 'irrelevance' of the media to what they perceived as the acute problems – poverty, inequality and 'dependence' – of their societies. Few knew anything, in practice, about the daily work of journalism; what united them was a generalised conviction that the entire structure could and must be overhauled to make it serve nationalistic goals, to mobilise the people; only a small minority, to judge from their conclusions, were troubled by the conflict between such purposeful social engineering and the individual's rights to choose. Concerned with national and collective rights, they understood their recommendation that communications policies 'should be the exclusive concern of the State' to be an expression of their support for 'pluralistic and democratic criteria'. The terms of reference given to both meetings by Unesco also demonstrates that the organisation was in no sense merely seeking advice on investment in the infrastructure – the hardware – of communications, but on their content, and the uses to which they could be put. Unesco's structural approach essentially encourages policies of the kind suggested at Bogotá and Quito; the meetings were not aberrations, nor was Unesco justified after them in proclaiming its neutrality.

Quito was also to have been the site for the Inter-Governmental Conference. But as the reports of the two preparatory meetings circulated, and when the provisional agenda for the Quito Conference was issued in March 1976, the Inter-American Press Association and other organisations launched a campaign against Unesco's policies and the conference itself. The Inter-American Broadcasters' Association and IAPA issued a joint statement on 27 April that the conference was contrary both to Unesco's constitution and that of many of the participating countries. Ecuador withdrew its invitation, and the conference was switched to San José.

Amadou Mahtar M'Bow opened the Costa Rica meeting on 12 July with a spirited attack on the protesting organisations (which were ensconced in campaign headquarters across the street) and the proud assertion that 'the fact that Unesco . . . should thus find itself involved in a reflection process which has caused so much disturbance in certain circles . . . shows how useful it can be to Member States when they decide to use it as a forum.' From this doubtful proposition, he continued by saying that Unesco was 'resolutely in favour of freedom of information' but that when this was supplied by media purveying 'systems of values foreign to the countries of a given region' they endangered national life. 'It is in this sense that one can say that uncontrolled development of the mass communication media makes it difficult for many countries to assert their own cultural identity.' The implication must be that M'Bow was prepared to put his authority, and Unesco's reputation, behind *controlled* development. As the Costa Rica working document put it, in a section on access and participation and the right to communicate, 'it seems to be desirable to . . . determine the rights to and limitations of the international use of certain media' and domestically to 'define as far as possible, the obligations of communication.'

M'Bow acknowledged the view that 'any rationalisation in

the field of communication carries with it a danger to freedom of expression;' his reply was that 'the development of modern societies requires the rectification of certain ill-defined or irrational situations.' The 'irrational situation' which he had in mind was the position of the international press. As the Unesco working paper for Costa Rica put it, 'the economic imbalance between highly industrialised countries and developing countries is reproduced in the cultural sector, establishing an invisible but more deeply-rooted dependence basically through control of the information media and the communication system.' 'Rationalisation' would therefore imply intervening against the international media, in the name of cultural sovereignty. The more 'invisible' the influence, the easier to invent reasons for eliminating it. And in fact, in some countries of Latin America, the fact (thought not the effects) of imported entertainment is easily established, and in overwhelming quantities. Unesco's formula of 'communications' enables entertainment to be lumped in with news: it is all 'cultural' material, after all.

The San José Declaration, a brief statement of principles, was diplomatically bland; it nonetheless predictably offered a perspective on the role of communications dear to all governments. They should 'contribute to knowledge, understanding, friendship, cooperation and integration of peoples . . . respecting national sovereignties and the international legal principle of non-intervention in the affairs of States . . . with a view to achieving world solidarity and peace.'

It was followed with thirty recommendations, which naturally agreed with the earlier meetings that 'the right to formulate national policies and plans in the field of communication pertains to States' – although 'the opinions of the various sectors concerned in communication processes at the local level' might be taken into account. Governments' general objectives should include 'definition of the social responsibilities of both the public and the private sectors,' coordination with 'the other sectors comprised in the overall process of planned development' and 'protection of the historical and cultural identity and sovereignty of States.' They also emphasised 'the responsibility and right of countries to strengthen and develop State-owned mass communication media in order to ensure the effectiveness of planning in this field'. Other resolutions took into account the desirability of plurality, the need to increase access to information and to make low-cost means of communication available. In thirty long recommend-ations, however, the best clue to the governments' interpretation of the meanings of 'access' and 'plurality' is contained in a single, self-contradictory phrase. It recognises 'the validity in a democracy of dialogue between governors and governed, constructive criticism and the contribution made by communi-cation media to peaceful coexistence and social solidarity, as bases for development'. The expression of what John Lent calls 'commitment journalism' in a nutshell – journalism which makes 'social solidarity' and not objective truth its guide. It was in this spirit that the governments agreed to create or strengthen national news agencies, and requested Unesco to call another meeting to establish a Latin American news agency. The conference did, however, attempt to reassure the Western opposition that, the 'protection of cultural identity' notwithstanding, this news agency would 'in no way impair the free operation of existing agencies or their future develop-ment.'

To assist Latin American governments in carrying out these plans, and to liaise with the Secretariat in Paris, Unesco proceeded to appoint a Regional Communication Adviser. It selected the Peruvian journalist, then attached to the Peruvian embassy in Paris, Germán Carnero Roque. The choice indicates Unesco's approach. A lengthy article by Carnero appeared in August 1976 in *Le Monde Diplomatique* titled 'Information in the Third World: means of subjection or instrument for liberation'. Carnero's views were already well-known to Unesco, which had followed his statements in a series of international meetings. But this article brought them together. In it, shortly before his appointment to the Unesco position, Carnero attacked the international agencies for controlling the flow of information in the Third World, and imposing on it, 'by manipulating the news, a biased interpretation of reality which suits imperialist interests. . . . Their criteria for selecting the news are such as to result in a systematic deformation – amounting to disinformation – of reality. . . . Their values . . . support the existing system of domination and nullify all critical and reflective abilities, *therefore all capacity for revolution.*' (my italics) He quotes Somavia's 'headlights' metaphor, to strengthen his attack on information as a 'merchandise', and on the whole range of media, from comics to TV, which 'exalt the false values of capitalism.' In the familiar chain of argument Carnero then turns to the complicity of elites and repressive governments within the Third World; 'rare', he says, 'are the countries which have had the wisdom to place the mass media at the service of the true interests of their peoples – a step which is a pre-condition for genuine liberation.'

The hopeful signs, for Carnero, are the non-aligned statements at New Delhi, the work of the Dag Hammarskjöld Foundation, and Unesco's 'remarkable task' of research into structures and systems in the Third World, 'where information must be made to accord very closely with the objectives and planning framework of development.' The non-aligned news pool, he adds, has the virtue of 'a precise idea of the kind of information required' even if in practice the product is too full of official speeches. He then comes to the heart of the matter, for him: 'What type of information does the Third World need, and for what purpose? It will only be effective if it becomes an instrument of liberation and historic change, in the service of oppressed peoples ... a free information system, conferring freedom, which rejects the fallacious criteria of "objectivity"' and which is created by journalists whose 'commitment to the will for liberation of the underdeveloped peoples must be total'. And the counterpart to efforts to create this new information order within the Third World must, he concludes, be international legislation to 'define the responsibilities and the limits to act of the major transnational press agencies.'

It is in the light of such views, held by people exercising key positions in the execution of Unesco's efforts to promote national communications policies, that the explanation of the Unesco strategy – given by Alan Hancock in 1972 for a collection of essays edited by John Lent should be read: 'Such a policy is not visualised as a piece of legislative censorship. ... It is intended to be a pragmatic design ... with no more attempt to impose an autocratic structure than the culture and tradition of the country endorses. The policy ... must be based upon a view of the communication process as a *total* process, looking at media in the widest possible economic, social and political setting. . . .'

Unesco's response to its critics has always been that governments who wish to control the press will always do so, and have the powers to do so without Unesco. Discussing the next intergovernmental conference, due to take place in Kuala Lumpur early in 1979, a Unesco official murmured soothingly in the Spring of 1978 that: 'Many people think communications policies will be government policies. But I don't think governments are that foolish; and we aren't telling them anything they do not know. We are saying, look at your communication networks; integrate them, to make them act as instruments of planned social change; make policies. Have you not thought that governments with policies might even be inhibited from blackmailing newspapers by withdrawing advertising or newsprint in an arbitrary way?' (There were signs, in fact, that those responsible for the Kuala Lumpur conference in Unesco were attempting to include ideas such as the importance of diversity and pluralism of a nation's media in the debate. But the first part of the Kuala Lumpur agenda – the part intended to establish an intellectual framework for communication policies – nonetheless stressed the 'role of media in an integrated approach towards development', and 'communication as a means of affirming and preserving cultural identity and as an instrument for national integration'.)

Pierre Navaux, an old hand in Unesco who now heads its department for the Development of Communication Systems affirms Unesco's neutrality: 'We *don't* advise on communications policies. We have simply promoted the idea that they are needed, as technology becomes more complex and media more influential. Our assistance is really limited to the methodology and the techniques – we talk about the infrastructure, the availability of frequencies, the sort of thing that involves economists and radio engineers, not theorists.' Yes – and no. Navaux's division has traditionally been responsible for the wide range of practical training work, technical advice and investigation of solutions to the physical obstacles to communication which predates Unesco's involvement with the 'total approach', and which continues to be a valuable support to developing countries.

The link between these two very different disclaimers is provided by Hamdy Kandil, head of the 'Free Flow' Division. He points out that Unesco only assists in the formulation of communications on the specific request of a government – 'but once we are invited, we *do* advise them on the content of those policies. The strategic decision, however, is political; it lies with governments, and no blame can attach to Unesco. We first establish what degree of control the government wants to assert – across the spectrum from liberal to highly regimented – and we advise within that framework.' Some officials argue – with some truth – that Unesco is criticised whatever it does – for having policies on the one hand, and for working within national guidelines on the other. Many insist that it would be 'unfair' to expect Unesco simply to concern itself with the technical side and, more to the point, that basic choices as to ownership patterns, the education/entertainment ratio, and decisions on programme imports, are integral to communications policies and are 'content' decisions.

Unesco, in other words, encourages countries to coordinate their implicit or explicit policies, in the name of efficiency and national development objectives, without however attempting to influence strategic attitudes to control of the media. At national level, at least: because in general policy terms, and speaking in its 'international voice', there is a widely-held view in the communications division of Unesco that poor countries cannot afford a free press.

'The conflict between you Westerners and us in the Third World,' says one key Unesco official, 'is the conflict of a time gap. If the choice in our countries were between total freedom of the press and government control, I would opt – whatever my personal views about freedom of expression – for the latter. We can't afford newsprint for a *News of the World*; we can't invest in networks and then let them carry just news and entertainment; and we can't afford divisiveness.' All of which raises some questions: first, whether Unesco has come to view itself purely and simply as an extension of the Third World; second, whether it is responsible, on the part of an organisation dedicated to an international outlook, to encourage the 'total approach' without any pressure on a government to think beyond a narrow nationalism, or to reconsider policies of press controls?

Is compromise with Unesco's constitution the inevitable price of activism in the communications field? The internal confusion in Unesco is illustrated by the official who said publicly that 'Unesco is pledged to uphold the freedom of the press. But [I am] willing to risk suppression of the true facts to see a flow of news operating between member states.'

The Western answer to Unesco's 'Third World spokesmen' is that the conflict does not have to do with a time gap at all: it has to do with control of the press and of freedom of expression, which restrict the civil liberties of the poor just as they would those of the rich. They argue that nobody is too poor to be free; like King Lear to his daughter, they say

> Oh, reason not the need! The basest beggar
> Is in the poorest thing superfluous.
> Allow not nature more than nature needs,
> Man's life is cheap as beast's.

Yet in arguing that countries poor in foreign exchange cannot afford a *News of the World*, the Unesco official was making a plausible point. The questions remain: who makes that decision? and secondly, has Unesco any business in putting forward such value judgements?

It may be true, as Unesco often asserts in its defence, that national communications policy-making is becoming the norm, in industrialised countries as well as the Third World. But this skips the central point, which is that Unesco is encouraging policies which focus attention, not on the 'physical infrastructure of communications, but on their content and social purposes. It is no defence to say that it is 'unfair' to suggest that Unesco should concentrate, as it did before, on the technical side – because it is concerning itself not merely with the use of media for education, but with an exercise in social engineering which takes the entire structure of society as its proper concern.

Unesco's 'neutrality' must therefore be interpreted in terms of its record, during this decade, of active promotion of purposive, 'developmental' theories and strategies covering the entire range of communications. The attitude of neutrality, deeply ingrained, is being replaced by a commitment to assisting countries, as M'Bow expressed it in Unesco's Medium-Term Plan for 1977–82, 'to pass from a contingent interdependence, which favours certain elements to the detriment of others, to an actively sought solidarity.' Unesco is very precisely in the business of 'giving governments ideas' – however 'neutral' its assistance to them in translating those ideas into actual systems on the ground. It is within the context of Unesco's commitment to the systematic use of communications to promote national development – and of M'Bow's publicly stated belief that the Western 'monopoly' of communications 'is opposed to the establishment of a New International Economic Order'– that we must understand the Secretariat's insistence that it does not seek to influence the overall character of the policies its spends so much energy to promote.

A good deal of that energy has been spent on an extensive research programme, launched on the recommendation of a meeting of experts convened by Unesco at Montreal in 1969 'to identify the ways in which the mass media can best serve the needs of present and future society.' This meeting, which of course was working to an agenda very carefully drawn up by a member of the Unesco Secretariat, was a watershed. The evolution of Unesco's research since that date has been, as John Lee expressed it in one of the most comprehensive and clear products of the programme (a paper published by Unesco called 'Towards Realistic Communications Policies'), from 'a theoretical approach into an international action programme'. To non-experts, much of the vast output of the past eight years reads like a cross between newspeak and academic jargon; most of it seems wholly irrelevant to the actual problems of communicating in the societies Unesco exists to help.

But to dismiss it for that reason would be to ignore the purpose of Unesco's new research programme: as Lee also suggests, it is geared to 'informing the policy-makers'. And from the start, it has deliberately included 'all aspects of the communication process – as an integral total'. It has also emphasised consistently that national policy on communications 'entails control to an extent which ensures that the [mass media's] operations are directed towards the public good.' To that extent, with the admirable general aim of helping developing countries achieve economic growth with popular participation, and develop their sense of national identity, Unesco has become involved in extending the state's responsibility to decide on the 'public good' to an area in which collective rights must clash with the right of the individual: if *everything* carries the message, where is his escape?

The Montreal meeting asked some questions, and stated its conviction that new forms of research were needed. The response – which has basically shaped Unesco's policy since – came from another 'panel of consultants' who met in April 1971. They included Luis Beltran (the architect, at Unesco's request, of the basic form of the Bogotá meeting's agenda), Kaarle Nordenstreng, Lakshmana Rao, the only 'journalist contaminated by a Ph.D. in Communications', as he describes himself (and the most realistic voice present), and eight other professional communications researchers.

The new strategy for research, they agreed, should be geared to the requirements of national development planning, embracing even 'inter-personal communication activities'. It should include questions of content and quality, because the aim of policy-directed research should be to discover 'opinion and information *trends* in the media which can then be compared with . . . the aims of national development'. The key questions asked, therefore, should be:

- Who are the owners of the mass media: nationals, or foreigners? What is the ownership pattern? What is the sponsorship pattern? Is sponsorship national or foreign?
- Who decides what is communicated and how (owners, managers, journalists)?
- What are the *values* – attitudes in relation to development – of owners, managers, journalists?

From these 'action-orientated' questions about structure, the group moved briskly to content. They distinguished ' "developmental" versus "non-developmental" ("significant" versus "trivial" materials)' and asked, 'what kind of norms and values do the media "teach" the people and to what extent are they functional or not tor development? . . . Do media actually contribute to social cohesiveness and national unity or not?'

The progression of research along these lines might already suggest that Big Brother was on the march; the next questions, the group thought, should consider whether the media were instilling 'alien' values, and whether, 'through advertisements, news and other materials' they were 'inducing people to engage in "irrational" consumption behaviours' (*sic*).

The point of all this would be to analyse the agenda-setting functions of the media: but the process should not stop there. To establish a really clear view of the pictures forming in the public's collective consciousness, all other forms of communication, and indeed culture, would require examination, and 'this approach would not preclude a study of the general population; in fact some general survey would no doubt be necessary to identify the various sub-cultural groupings for further intensive study.' There could be legitimate reasons for such research: the preamble to the report talks about the importance of reaching rural communities, and establishing an effective two-way flow of information. But the wording makes it hard to repress an irreverent suspicion that the direction and purpose of the whole report is to find jobs for the boys into the next century.

The group then turned to the international arena. Here, they correctly focussed on the technological revolution – from direct broadcasting via satellites, to the range of devices such as cassettes, facsimile, cable television, etc. The implication of all these, they suggested, would be vastly to increase the range of individual choice in ways which would 'operate almost independently of national production capacities.' Therefore, they must be brought into national communication policies. 'What should be national policy regarding "cultural privacy" to protect the fragile pattern of autochthonous cultures against the massive intrusion of foreign mass media contents? Where is the demarcation line between a "protective screening" and a harmful "isolationist" policy which would deprive the nation of the cultural achievements of the "universal" world?' The important, silent rider is that in the view of the group the question was not *whether* a line should be drawn, but *where*.

The disturbing thing about this outline for research is not that it fails to ask important questions. The report includes, although not very centrally, reference to the necessity for infrastructure planning which would enable choices between alternatives – national/regional organisation, *lingua franca*/ dialects, rural or urban development, new networks or the refurbishing of old ones. But the purposes of most of the questions which the outline stresses can only be the regulation of content and the shaping of national values by governmental *fiat*. Studies on the imbalance in the news-flow lean towards cutting out the dominant partner – the international agency or broadcaster – where the national interest requires it, rather than emphasising the creation of a greater plurality of sources. And there is no suggestion in the report that the news media are in any functional sense different from either entertainment, education, or government information services, no acknowledgement that, as Lee defines it, the principles of news selection 'are derived from the concern for the truthful reflection of objective reality, not from the concern only for the "balance" of all kinds of social interests – justified and unjustified.' This omission has tended to characterise Unesco's research, and its attitude to policy.

There are plenty of academic critics of Unesco's earlier promotion of the 'free flow of ideas by word and image'. They argue that the whole idea was American-inspired in the first place, that its effect has simply been to allow the strong and wealthy international media to 'invade' the developing world, and that Unesco's technical assistance in building up the Third World's own media simply created infrastructures which – for lack of local skills and materials – enabled more efficient 'penetration' of the Third World by Anglo-Saxon voices. Large and laboriously-researched books, like Jeremy Tunstall's *The Media are American*, 'prove' the thesis by recording the progress of the international media since World War II. Where entertainment is concerned, the case can be made to look very strong. But it hinges on two assumptions: first, that the under-educated populace of the Third World cannot distinguish soap-opera from life. There exist Latin American theses in which internationally-educated intellectuals claim to have observed just such gullibility in the *favelas* of Brazil or the *callampas* of Chile. Yet these same urban poor have shown amazing ingenuity in tapping water mains, creating jobs and houses with nothing and where nothing existed, and putting pressure cooperatively on governments to obtain legal recognition for their settlements. The thesis is not merely condescending; it is unrealistic.

In by far the sanest paper on this question published by Unesco (in *Getting the message across*, 1975) Lakshmana Rao comments that concern about the imbalance in the flow of communications, and with the corrupting influence of foreign media, tends to forget about the talents of the audience: 'The receiver is neither passive nor helpless. He is extremely active person, opening his eyes and ears to things that appeal to him and closing them to things which he considers uninteresting or irrelevant.' Changing the diet without taking these audiences into account – their preferences, as well as what is 'good for them' – requires a more sophisticated approach than that implied by the 'significant versus trivial' categorisations of Unesco.

The second assumption underpinning the 'cultural imperialism' case is that home-grown alternatives will flourish in a climate which protects the people from alien influences: hence emphasis on the content and quality of the media to be produced – and the insistence by governments that controls will be necessary to change the relationship between the state and the media if they are to be 'integrated into the development process'. And that these alternatives can be educative, 'contribute to social cohesiveness and national unity,' and produce rational patterns of ambition and consumption, all without boring the citizenry into a state of apathy. If Unesco's policies of the 1960's are to be criticised as unrealistic, its policies of the 1970's should be watched with sceptical misgiving. As Rao warned in that paper, 'what is the alternative? And where such an alternative is available, who should choose? . . . Those in power over the channels or those paying for such services and having the right to "escapist" entertainment?'

By the Nineteenth General Conference in Nairobi, Unesco's campaign to promote 'developmental' policies on the media had picked up tremendous momentum. If the flagging reader thinks he has been dragged through too many Unesco meetings, he has been spared all but a handful; from Manila to Hawaii, Baghdad to Finland or Florence, Unesco has been spreading the word and planning the means to make it flesh. He has been spared not so much out of charity, but because it is the cumulative effect that matters, the way in which Unesco language and the peculiar 'logic' of its chosen 'experts' have come to dictate the terms in which highly sensitive things like 'news values', 'balance' and above all 'cultural identity' are discussed by Third World governments and their advisers. But Nairobi forced a pause.

The Draft Declaration was sent back to the drawing board, with instructions intended to neutralise it politically. Without discounting the importance of the economic sanctions which the US (which contributes a quarter of the budget) would - at the least – have exercised had the Draft Declaration been accepted as it stood, 1976 was also the first year in which journalists had got their views across to Unesco's essentially political forum on the issue of institutionalised government controls of the press. The Editor of the *Chicago Tribune*, Clayton Kirkpatrick, emphasised that a Declaration which supported one of two opposed ideologies governing the state's relations with the media was 'contrary to the spirit of tolerance and pluralism by which Unesco should be guided,' commenting that developing countries, with particular and concrete problems, were being dragged into an argument essentially concerning East and West. The actual politics were, and are, more complex: the warning that Unesco had no business with them was still effective in the context.

But the General Conference also gave Unesco all the mandate it could have desired in pursuing its general strategy - enough to justify M'Bow's claim, as the conference ended, that, 'We can now speak of a new order in communications.' In the 'guidance notes' on the Medium-Term Plan, the delegates approved the concept of 'a free and balanced flow of information' on the international plane; the formulation of national communications policies; and directed that 'studies should be made on the content of media messages and on the role of the media in strengthening peace and international understanding.' And, in the long resolution which approved the main lines of Unesco's future strategy, the Conference said that efforts to help the Third World build up its media 'should be based upon deep deliberation, taking into consideration all the problems of communication in society, and taking account of those things which are needful for the establishment of a new international economic order.'

There were also some important reservations – above all over Unesco's investigations into the 'right to communicate', where delegates warned that 'the aim should be to broaden and strengthen the application of existing rights rather than to seek to substitute a new right for the acknowledged right to freedom of information.' And, reflecting either some scepticism about the increasingly universalist tone of Unesco's research programme, or the determination of governments to control the product, they recommended that Unesco confine its probing into the 'effects of communication in society' to strengthening 'the research capacity of Member States' and coordinating their efforts.

But, translated in the 'guidance notes', the reference to 'deep deliberation' became a request: 'A review should be undertaken of the totality of the problems of communication in modern society.' M'Bow interpreted this by setting up an International Commission for the Study of Communication Problems, headed by Sean MacBride and officially billed as the successor to the influential Faure Commission on Education which Unesco had created to provide new thinking on education policies and which reported in 1972.

The first meeting should have been in the spring of 1977; but it was December before M'Bow opened the first session. Since the Commission was due to submit an interim report to the Twentieth General Conference in the autumn of 1978, at the end of only three meetings, its scope for independent formulation of the problems was limited. A final report was due in 1979, for the 1980 General Conference and also to fit Unesco's plan for a World Conference on Communications in the mid-1980's. The sixteen-member Commission was supposed to represent the world's main geographical areas, and the major related 'disciplines'. It was to take in everything from folksongs to satellites – expressly placing the news media in the context of a 'total approach'.

Its composition is geographically well-distributed; the rest is less certain. From Latin America, no journalist is included: the two members are Juan Somavia, and the distinguished novelist Gabriel Garcia Marquez. The Africans are a Nigerian regional commissioner for 'Education, Social Development and Sports' (who happily proclaimed to the Commission that in his country, the State took care of the social status of journalists); and another, familiar figure from earlier meetings, Agence Zaire Presse's Director-General Elebe Ma-Ekonzo. The only international news agency represented is Tass, in the person of the formidable Leonid Mitrofanovich Zamiatin, Director-General of Tass when the Commission was appointed, but moved from the job in an unexpected reshuffle in March 1978. From Eastern Europe, Unesco turned to a long-established 'expert', Bogdan Osolnik. This said, the North American and European representation is strong: Elie Abel, formerly of NBC and Dean of Columbia University's School of Journalism, Betty Zimmerman of the Canadian Broadcasting Corporation, Hubert Beuve-Méry; and the former Dutch Minister for Development, Jan Pronk (who had so strongly supported ILET). The Asians – after China refused to be involved by failing to reply – form a distinguished trio: the Indian writer George Verghese, Mochtar Lubis – a Board Member of the International Press Institute and a journalist whose fight for the right to 'constructive criticism' led to the banning of his newspaper *Indonesia Raya* and a decade under house arrest or in prison, and Michio Nagai, a columnist with the *Asahi Shimbun* who is also a leading expert on educational problems and former Minister of Education.

The Commission, loosely referred to as the Wise Men, is supposed to be totally autonomous: it is, however, permitted 'to make recommendations to Member States' but required to submit its report not to the General Conference, but to M'Bow, for his consideration. Opening the first session, M'Bow tactfully laid down his priorities. Above all, he said, communications must be considered as a 'socio-cultural problem', to meet which mere material assistance, or even the mobilisation of human and financial resources, would be inadequate without exploration of the 'political, ideological and philosophical' aspects. And, with a bow to Article 19 of the Universal Declaration of Human Rights – which was important because of the Soviet insistence on deleting all reference to it in the Draft Declaration – he laid stress on the need for balance in the flow of information. From this unexceptionable beginning, he continued: 'the information which is presented to the world is often . . . out of touch with the deep-seated realities and the genuine needs of the countries to which it relates. Erroneous or distorted, incomplete or blown up out of all proportion, the picture of those countries which the media present is some-times not very pleasant and helps to spread unfavourable opinions and stereotypes in regard to them . . . these countries are generally dependent on a small number of major foreign centres. This being so, might they not rightfully consider that the messages which reach them from outside sources, conveying ideas and values which are alien to them, may well falsify their cultural identity and undermine their integrity and specificity as peoples. . . . ?' The Commission was invited to pay more attention to the responsibility of 'communicators', and the use of the media for objectives ranging from education to 'safe-guarding peace'.

What does this mean? Any of the Wise Men who wished to find out could refer to a pile of background papers prepared for them by Asher Deleon, the Yugoslav who was Secretary to the Faure Commission and who in the summer of 1977 was called back from India to serve on the MacBride Commission. Deleon's entire background, after leaving the Trades Union movement in Yugoslavia to join Unesco, has been in education – like M'Bow's.

An admirer of Ivan Illich's work on education – and Herbert Schiller's on the media – Deleon is fiercely committed to a didactic role for communications. He recognises the need to decrease the political tensions which surround the subject, but insofar as he has freedom to draft the Commission's report, will seek to extend it 'from coca-cola advertisements to wall newspapers and even door-to-door canvassing'. He sees no problems with legislation for the purpose of protecting cultures: the priority is to break, he says, the 'monopolies' over communi-cations – whether of the international agencies, or of privileged groups within countries. And in the context of national priorities, and of information 'viewed as a basic need', he thinks that 'there may have to be decisions about content. And to secure access to communication, I am fully prepared to admit that the consequence in some countries may be that the quality and freedom of information may suffer. I would rather see the maximum spread of information than worry too much about its content, or even government control; literacy programmes, too, can expose people to indoctrination. We should reach for policies which bring people into the process – even if the information they receive is limited and deformed – and as a second step, they will learn to use their access.'

Put into Unesco jargon for the Commission, the result of this line of thinking is to outline a programme which covers everything from the 'need to communicate: biological, ecological, sociological, psychological and linguistic', to the analysis of obstacles to communication ('notably by comparing normative texts with realities' – meaning, presumably, distorted press reports compared with official versions of what took place?), the responsibilities of journalists and means of making communications serve 'the legal equality of nations, reciprocal understanding and the intellectual and moral solidarity of mankind.'

The translation of all this into recommendations will depend very much on Sean MacBride, the Commission's Chairman. What was clear from the beginning was that MacBride, an old soldier of international affairs who has been the UN Commissioner for Namibia, a Chairman of Amnesty International, and who holds both the Lenin and the Nobel peace prizes, intended to put his personal stamp on the report.

MacBride starts from the belief that 'eighty per cent of the Third World complaints are justified,' as he told a press conference when he attended the International Press Institute's 1978 General Assembly in Canberra. In the first place, because the international agencies were not able to adapt to Third World requirements; secondly, because 'powerful financial, economic and political forces seek to dominate communications,' blanketing small countries with an alien cultural civilisation. 'Many people,' he says, 'in many countries assert that their independence, identity and integrity are endangered. These are concerns which no one should ignore or underestimate' and 'minor inaccuracies' do not weaken the case. A firm believer in the importance of the independence of the press, MacBride would still prefer to see the media owned by governments than by international interests. In his view, 'a tremendous change has been taking place ... which has altered the centre of power from secret diplomacy and governments, to public opinion. .... The media can therefore both inform, and exert pressures on governments. They therefore have great powers, and great responsibilities.' MacBride thus approves of the notion of treating communications 'globally'; and believes that Unesco's discussions – particularly of 'balancing' the flow of communications - have been useful because they have drawn attention to the inadequacy of the existing system. MacBride's own scepticism about the international press was revealed by his suggestion, in Australia, that the press was soft-pedalling on the disarmament issue because the news industry had a vested interest in the continuing arms race.

Whether or not the Commission establishes a language and approach distinct from that of Unesco, in the very limited time available to it, the brief may shrink at least to what Gunnar Naesselund calls 'manageable communications'. (Before leaving Unesco in the summer of 1977, Naesselund drew up a working outline which excluded personal communication: there are still people in Unesco who recognise that there are limits to the practice if not the desireability of control.)

The second meeting of the Commission, held in Stockholm in April 1978, was combined with a four-day meeting – a sort of evidence-giving session for the Commission's benefit – of some ninety representatives of news agencies, newspapers, broadcasting organizations and professional bodies. A new batch of documentation was provided by Deleon's team, including monographs from the agencies and a carefully drawn up 'overview' of the 'world of the agencies'.

The meeting was supposed to discuss infrastructures; it did so to a limited extent, but the real focus was on the content of information, the rights and responsibilities of journalists, and the desireability of international codes and regulatory bodies. Perhaps this was inevitable: as the 'overview' put it, 'the controversial issues relating to balance and imbalance in news flow are closely linked to the basic question of news values.' In any case, MacBride set the tone. Arguing that the feeling of 'the "information poor" countries ... that their independence and identity are threatened' could not be ignored or under-estimated, he went on to pose three questions: 'Does the concept of a free flow of information necessitate any limitation? Whether or not it involves any limitation, is it not desireable that the free flow should be a balanced flow of information? Are there areas of information in regard to which the news agencies and the mass media have a special responsibility towards the public?'

The most encouraging thing to emerge from Stockholm was that the posing of these questions did not – as it would probably have done a year earlier – launch a sterile argument about 'balance' versus 'freedom'; there was, instead, at least some discussion of the genuine difficulties which different national and cultural perspectives create for international news reporting. There was even some agreement that access to the political opposition in a country was important for a rounded picture – until Zamiatin firmly blocked any reference to such a heresy in the final report. (It was impossible, he said, to include any reference to the 'opposition' because 'in the constitution of some countries, there is no opposition. In the Soviet Union, the opposition ended in 1922.') But one of the outcomes of a four-day session – aside from demonstrating to non-journalists in the Commission the complexity of the issues, and the ideological passions behind them – was that the 'Wise Men' were asked to look into the question of codes of ethics, and the possibility of setting up an international body to monitor the behaviour of both journalists and governments.

The agenda for the private session of the 'Wise Men' which followed the public meeting was chiefly remarkable for leaving nothing out – making the range of subjects impossibly wide for what was supposed to be a meeting to establish the broad structure of the Commission's interim report. The real work, however, was done in Paris: a small team of outsiders, led by Professor James Halloran of Leicester and Fernando Reyes Matta of ILET, was invited to draw up a 'systematic framework' for the interim report. They listed such 'perceived areas of concern' as the omnipotence and remoteness of the communications structure, cultural contamination and cultural imperialism, the vulnerability of special groups and of the ill-educated, the relationships between communications and the State, and between the media and development. The report, they suggested, should deal with 'positive communications objectives' – the beneficial and social use of the media and the 'role of communications in the socialization process'. It was,

Halloran reported to a meeting in London shortly afterwards, a bid to ensure that the Commission widened its brief to encompass 'the economic and political dimensions' of communications. It seemed likely that the Commission was to be presented with this 'framework' on the eve of approving the interim report which it would in theory have drawn up itself. There would be little scope – because of shortage of time – for strategic changes.

The Commission's report may thus – as some in Unesco hope – provide 'independent' endorsement of the general course which Unesco is setting. The future direction of Unesco's strategies is indicated by the tone of its research programme. The communications budget, still a relatively minute $5.6 million a year, was given a 5–6% increase at Nairobi – significantly excluding the research division. The Division of the Free Flow and Communications Policy at Unesco – which deals with research – reports in relation to the budget that all the pressures from member states are for technical assistance, for consultants, equipment, or help with their own research programmes. Nevertheless, the ambitious flow of research continues. The work plan for 1978/9, drawn up early in 1978, aligns itself with the pressures coming from the governments of the Third World in one important sense: it is explicitly geared to 'promoting the establishment of a New International Information Order.' Although officials claim that Unesco is *not* planning to involve itself with the demands for international legislation on the subject, according to the work plan 'the role and impact of transnational corporations and industries will be studied' (language which betrays an acceptance of the Schiller/Somavia thesis); and research will lead 'to the development of principles for international media distribution and news exchanges, including legal and economic aspects, and thereby to the reduction of the present dependencies. . . .' Internal discussions were continuing, in the spring of 1978, on the possibility of Unesco's 'establishing an intergovernmental committee on the free flow of information.' Internal sources explained that (like the International Commission) such a committee could divert some of the fire from Unesco itself; its existence would however unequivocally suggest that Unesco viewed freedom of information as a matter for the judgement of governments. Preparations on codes of ethics for journalists would continue.

The division of Unesco which has traditionally concentrated on practical, infrastructural work has also adopted, for the 1978/9 programme, a more committed tone: its purpose is 'to ensure a fuller contribution of the media to the development effort ... the establishment of communications systems that are relevant to the needs and aspirations of the people they are designed to serve ... favour endogenous development and self-reliance' and contribute to the 'new international information order'.

There can be no doubt that, after Nairobi, Unesco officials are anxious to avoid further confrontation with Western countries; at their backs, too, the Soviet Union is unenthusiastic about the extent to which Unesco's policies increasingly reflect and coordinate the newly forming demands of the Third World. At Stockholm, an open rift developed: the Soviet Union, while happy to use Third World grievances as a political weapon, is far from pleased by the more 'supranational' aspects of their demands. Already in December 1977, in closed session, Zamiatin had insisted that the 'New World Order for Information' was something the Soviet Union had never heard of and considered meaningless and irrelevant. At Stockholm, he astonished members of ILET and Tunisia's Mustapha Masmoudi by dismissing it openly: 'What is this New Order? I have never heard of it. We had our New Order – under Hitler'. The Russian position was later clarified (not before Zamiatin had also included the New International Economic Order in his condemnation) as support for the development of national news structures – but only insofar as 'they assist the independence and growth of developing countries against colonialist and neo-colonialist domination.' There was conspicuous silence on the other aspects of Third World aspirations – to re-examine the 'social functions' of the media, and to gain direct access to the media of the industrialised countries, for example. The 'New Order for Information' has come up against Soviet distaste for too much debate, under any circumstances, on the role of the media. Unesco's officials, therefore, will have to be cautious in their endorsement of the 'New Order' – without offending Third World governments. But this does not mean that they are prepared to renounce two essential aspects of Unesco's strategy.

First, the integration of the media into the development process. This cannot but have the implication that the 'balanced content' of information should reflect national goals. And Unesco's whole programme is shot through with ambiguities about the distinction between government information (and the educational uses of the media), and objective news. In the former category, the process is purposive, and the citizen is intended to respond in a particular way. The fact that so many Unesco people know far more about education than they do about journalism inclines them naturally to a 'purposive' view of all communications. And there is, built into the 'developmental approach', the risk that the state becomes the arbiter of what 'uses' of the media best serve development.

Second, the principle that communications between states – through the media – should be based on the respect for national sovereignty and cultural diversity. This is where the difficulties with the 'total approach' most obviously enter. It is easy to say that folksongs should be cherished, even that Western entertainment programmes swamp indigenous cultures; and from there a short step, but a qualitatively vital one, to say that the alien values of Western-style news reporting should be replaced by something indigenous and appropriate, reflecting 'national culture'. The research programme is to include an analysis of 'national and international news values in different cultures and societies' – with the aim, according to a Unesco staff member, of demonstrating that news values adjust to cultural circumstances. Truth becomes the 'truth' of a society.

Much of the citizen's map of the world is determined, by local codes of national law and custom; but he is still left a certain proportion in which to find his own way. Unesco's programmes, and the public statements of its staff, raise doubts as to whether it sees the proper role of information as maintaining, or even enlarging, those areas. Since governments everywhere prefer to impose national perspectives on local ones, there is more than one kind of cultural imperialism. And in the conflict which arises between national sovereignty and the promotion of international understanding, Unesco seems to be veering from its constitutional duty to 'further the free exchange of ideas and knowledge' towards support for a supervised flow of the news, in the cause of fostering cultural identity. Such attitudes can create a narrow parochialism, even where they are not used by governments to censor the international news-flow.

Unesco's commitments, essentially political, to shaping a new order, may put it on a collision course with Western governments. Can this be avoided? Having decided at the end of the 1960's to involve itself strategically with the content and structure of communications, Unesco has inevitably become the conduit for the resentments channelled into the call for the New Order for Information. As a forum, it institutionalises these feelings and transforms them. But – unless the Director-General succeeded in sidestepping the whole issue – it was probable, in the summer of 1978, that the immediate confrontation would not centre on these long-term changes in the function of the organisation, but on the particular question which started the public controversy: the Draft Declaration.

The politics surrounding the preparation of the revised draft, work on which began in the summer of 1977, were carefully kept out of public view. The principal drafters were Kaarle Nordenstreng, Germán Carnero Roque, and Clement Jones, a British journalist and president of the Commonwealth Press Union's Press Freedom Committee. A draft prepared by these three in July was shown during the autumn to about 150 people – journalists, governmental advisers on communications, and professional organisations – by a number of emissaries sent out by Unesco. Their reactions were then compared at a fresh drafting session lasting from 17 to 22 December 1977. Throughout this process, to immunise Unesco from controversy as far as possible, the whole exercise was carried out at a strictly 'technical' level, without in any way involving M'Bow.

The objections to the summer draft resolved into two main patterns. In the West, and Japan, there was pressure to abolish the Declaration altogether. Much of this pressure came from a number of institutes – the International Press Institute, Freedom House, the World Press Freedom Committee which links a number of organisations and newspaper groups under the chairmanship of George Beebe of the *Miami Herald*, and the Inter-American Broadcasting Association – and from such influential quarters as Gerald Long at Reuters, and William

Harley, the active and respected member of the US Commission for Unesco. At the other end of the spectrum, there were strong Russo–Arab pressures, supported by a handful of Asian countries, to retain the specific reference to the Zionism resolution; the Russians reluctantly agreed not to reintroduce the reference themselves, but warned that they would support any Arab initiative.

At the end of December, the draft which was finally submitted to M'Bow on 17 February 1978 omitted all reference to the 'use' of the mass media (substituting the word 'contribution' in the title and elsewhere), or to the Zionism resolution (except under a general formula referring to 'UN resolutions' on racism), or to the controversial Article XII which made state responsibility for the mass media explicit, or to 'legislative measures'. As a counterweight, it brought in Unesco's formula of 'free and balanced' information, emphasised public access and participation (which could, under the terms of a resolution which had slipped peacefully through the Nairobi Conference, imply 'taking measures against the harmful effect of "commercial mass culture" '), and, reflecting in particular the demands of the Vietnamese, several references to 'colonialism and neo-colonialism'.

There were still passages which are dangerously ambiguous – such as the call on the media 'to expose propaganda for these evils thus contributing to their elimination.' (An example: if the Libyan press, condemning President Sadat's visit to Israel, calls for unremitting struggle against the Zionist enemy, should the Egyptian press: expose the warmongering propaganda coming out of Libya – thus falling foul of another requirement of the Declaration, that the 'philosophies' of states should be respected, and indeed exacerbating tensions rather than promoting peace between them – or should it exercise its responsibility to respect States, and stay silent?) But the draft sent to M'Bow, while totally irrelevant to the practice of journalism, at least seemed unlikely greatly to hinder it.

There remained a strong possibility, in the charged atmosphere of the Middle East after the opening of negotiations between Israel and Egypt in December, that one or the other of the 'confrontation states' – such as Iraq – would insist on introducing the Zionism clause at the General Conference.

This would have sealed the fate of the Draft Declaration – but could also be guaranteed to reopen the sores of the 1974 confrontation at Unesco. Aware that the US, having left the International Labour Organization, could remove itself from Unesco, several officials were saying that the easiest course for M'Bow would either be to use his discretion not to present the Draft Declaration, legally within his power despite the mandate of Nairobi; or, if a Western government suggested it without attacking the content of the new draft, shelve it, pending the report of the Wise Men. M'Bow's initial reaction to these possibilities was to sit on the draft, reporting to Unesco's Executive Board in April 1978 only that there were still differences of opinion which made it impossible to say that a consensus had been reached.

No such hesitancy was evident in the US diplomatic mission to Unesco, when it first obtained the draft. It may be that the US does not assign to Unesco diplomats who might be prepared to go beyond the reiteration of dimly-conceived points of principle; but a diplomat with a watching brief on the Draft Declaration was saying in the spring of 1978 that the US would fight it to the last ditch – because it mentioned the 'responsibility' of the media. What if the context were neutral? 'That makes no difference to us; we are just basically opposed to *any* connection between the media and responsibility, however expressed.' This crude and cliché-ridden confrontationism fails to touch on the genuine issues; and could, if carried to the General Conference, isolate the US as markedly as, at the 1976 World Employment Conference, it was isolated in its opposition to the principle of a 'basic needs' development strategy on the grounds that it was inconsistent with a *laisser-faire* economic system. The irony is that if the US does not like the general trend of Unesco's policies, it has largely itself to blame. Between 1968 and the Nairobi General Conference of 1976, there was, to put it kindly, a benign neglect of Unesco by the State Department, except when the Zionism issue was raised. Whatever the reasons, this created a vacuum – which was exploited, many diplomats and former Unesco officials emphasize, by the Soviet Union. Among these former officials, several believe that the launching of the 'communications policies' was an error – because it almost inevitably would encourage censorship. But, they say, there was a large measure of inadvertence – which some alertness in the West would have prevented. 'The West missed its chance to move in on communications policy, at the beginning', says one of them; 'if it had done so, it could have posed the vital question: "Do these policies really mean the extension of freedom of expression to more people?" '

The fate of the Draft Declaration, if the Zionism issue did not recur and clinch the matter, depended on whether Western governments wished to use the issue to warn Unesco that it should back out of the political front line on the communications issue. Much depended on the Declaration's final content. During the summer of 1978, it began to appear that M'Bow might be ready, after all, to risk a showdown on the Draft Declaration. Under private pressure from the Soviet Union to present a draft to the Twentieth General Conference, M'Bow also agreed to a supplementary redrafting of the December version which would toughen the document and make it an inevitably controversial one. This redrafting, carried out by Kaarle Nordenstreng and an adviser on communications to the Polish government, was reliably reported to include a reformulation of Article XII – the article giving states responsibility for the mass media 'under their jurisdiction' which had created the furore at Nairobi in 1976.

There was also the question of how much weight Western governments attached to the *étatiste* trends in Unesco's communications programme as a whole. The lack of realism of much of that programme, and the theoretical language in which it is set out, have diverted attention from the consequences it could have for freedom of expression. These consequences are already clear in some countries of the Third World: Mexico has established, according to John Lent, a Central Communications Office whose aim is to 'nationalise public opinion'; and in Peru, Costa Rica and Venezuela legislation has either been planned or effected since the San José Conference which reflects the goals of Unesco's communications programme.

Unesco's involvement in national and international communications policies conditions, at the same time that it reflects, an important shift in Third World politics. It echoes not only the changes in governmental attitudes to the media – from random censorship to systematic control, in the case of many countries

– but towards human rights generally. There are certain ideological positions which are irreconcilable, because they concern the relationship of government to society, and the individual to government. The significance of the Draft Declaration is that it marked the point at which Unesco became the forum for a purely ideological issue.

The only avenue for Unesco, if it wishes to withdraw from the ideological front line, would be to concentrate on research into some of the issues which need clarifying (the effectiveness of the use of the media for educational purposes, for example, or for rural development) and, on the active side, to revert to its role of technical assistant. This would imply ditching its commitment to national communication policies, except at the infrastructural and technical level. This is deeply unlikely to happen; not just because it would require rethinking an entire strategy already well advanced, but because the strategy is gaining Unesco credit with the majority of its member governments. There, for the Secretariat at least, the heart lies.

Those who believe, like Richard Hoggart, that Unesco should always have been concerned with 'the uses made of the media systems they have helped to establish', and the 'social and ethical implications and options' of plans drawn up by Unesco for member states, put the other side of the issue. This is that if Unesco adopts a more active stance, it must accept the responsibility that goes with it: a member of the Secretariat would have to 'see that, though he may easily join in the chorus of criticism of mass media dominance by the West he can, unless he stakes out a new third position, soon find himself sanctioning state control and conniving at the yet greater reduction of free speech or free circulation.' The case against Unesco is that its present activities in communications are already having precisely that effect.

The demand for recognition of a New Order for Information came firmly onto the agenda of the United Nations General Assembly in 1978, in a resolution which commended Unesco's pioneering role, and called for consideration of 'Cooperation and assistance in the application and improvement of mass communications for social progress and development.' The action confirmed the importance and effectiveness of Unesco's efforts to create, out of disparate national dissatisfactions, an international politics of communications – a politics which did not exist before this decade, and which by 1978 was firmly entrenched.

CHAPTER 6

The Village, the Nation and the 'Global Village'

The summer before the victory of the Pathet Lao put an end to the independent press in Laos, John Lent sketched its portrait in an article for *Gazette*.

> The press in Laos today is capital city oriented, elitist, politically motivated and plagued with problems (mostly economic in nature). . . . The average Lao editor is working in cramped, dingy, ramshackle quarters without the benefit of teleprinters, adequate type fonts or presses. The four printing presses in use are old flat-bed types, some predating the World War II years. The calibre of personnel Lao editors are working with is pitifully low, the average staff member having barely a primary school education. These same editors . . . hope to make enough money monthly to pay staff wages; rising prices of newsprint . . . even make this difficult.

Journalists' monthly pay, when they received it at all, was equivalent to one sack of rice at the 'expensive' rainy season period.

The oldest and largest circulation paper, *Xat Lao*, had a print-run which had dropped from a peak of 6,000 to less than half that as a result of newsprint shortages and costs. Advertising covered only eighty per cent of costs, but cover-prices could not be raised because of the already acute problems of local purchasing power. Not even all government officials could afford to buy a newspaper. Few copies moved outside Vientiane, the capital. One paper managed to move about ten per cent of its print-run to outlying provinces - by relying on what its editor called 'the Lao way of circulation', which meant bribing an airline clerk with a couple of free copies to slip them on board without charging. Moonlighting as compositors, across the river in Thailand, kept many of the papers' staffs solvent.

The Lao press was a copy-book example of the financial, political and structural problems of a Third World press. Yet oddly, it was also an example of the ambitions, and the developing nationalism, of developing countries' approaches to the relationship between public opinion and government. In Laos, it came out in three ways. There existed a monthly magazine, *Lane Xang*, 'devoted to "teaching Laotians the new face of development - political, socio-cultural and economic" ', which actually sold half its 2,500 print-run (the rest was given to village headmen), and which otherwise kept going because it was staffed by middle class professionals on a voluntary basis. And, in late 1973, the Laotian government was being criticised for having signed an agreement with the French for a Laos TV service: 'some officials explained that because the French are funding the new service, a great deal of the programming will be in the French language, dealing with French, not Laotian, custom.' And thirdly, there was talk of setting up a university in Vientiane with a journalism course, and journalists were keen to learn about training schemes elsewhere in Asia.

Laos – a small, landlocked country at the tail end of a long and debilitating civil war, its radio transmitters drowned out over much of the country by Hanoi and Peking – still serves as an example, strangely caught in amber. It shows the unreality of much of the expert theorising, and also demonstrates the degree to which the which the basic elements of the struggle for a 'new order', or at least a distinctive kind of journalism, have penetrated the developing world. A country, utterly without the resources to set up its own TV network, concerned over the effect which French programming might have on its cultural identity; without the economic or distributive foundation for a healthy press, hoping for formal journalistic training at a yet-to-be-founded university. A country which in miniature, and *in extremis*, presents three aspects of Third World reality: physical difficulties, psychological and structural ones (including self-censorship), and the ambition across both of these to develop a distinctive model, free as far as possible from government control, professional instead of amateur.

The physical problems differ in degree, but they are roughly similar in most developing countries: they are illiteracy – the world total is now over 800 million, and rising – and language problems (dozens of markedly different languages, not just dialects, may be spoken in African countries; several in Asia ones), they are poor distribution systems and low purchasing power, together producing a situation in which in many Third World countries, one newspaper is produced for every hundred people on the national average, with the proportion vastly lower in rural areas. Language difficulties affect not only the written press, but result in whole areas of some countries being cut off from any kind of news service, or from basic programmes covering health and nutrition, birth control, weather warnings or agricultural advice.

It is horribly easy to talk in North–South clichés, backing them up with solemn and authoritative-looking international statistics. The developing countries, according to these, with more than 70 % of the world's inhabitants, were provided in 1974 with 2.2 television sets, 7.6 radios, 2.6 newspapers and 0.8 cinema places per hundred people. The lack of facilities affects the transmission of news at both national and international levels. According to a 1978 Unesco study, for example, there are 1391 direct telephone circuits linking the USA with Britain, only two between India and Malaysia, 'while most new and developing countries have none at all'. Where such links exist, they are expensive: it has been calculated that if you weighted telephone charges in Africa – domestic as well as international – by per capita GNP, they cost 267 times as much per unit as they do within the EEC. What this means is less certain, in terms of the degree to which people in developing countries have access to information. India had at the time of the State of Emergency around 12,000 publications of one kind or another; yet on all the statistical indicators, huge numbers of Indians were totally deprived of any channel of information. The curious fact remains that – whether at first, second or third hand, Indian villagers had by the 1970's become accustomed to the sense that they knew what was going on; and at the elections in 1977, the freedom of the press was proved to be a genuinely popular issue, popular with peasants commonly supposed to be 'outside' the national communications systems. It should also be said that, while there are plenty of flat-bed presses around, the leading Jamaican paper went computer-offset while Fleet Street still hesitated; between heavy government investment this decade, and technological developments which have assisted even the private sector to reach wider audiences, the Third World is not always as bereft of physical means to communicate as some research suggests. But broadly speaking, the cost of newsprint – above all in terms of scarce foreign exchange – are inhibiting and in some cases deadly to the growth of a written press. And the economic base – adequate advertising revenue and sufficient purchasing power to assure viable circulations – is often missing. Many countries are not in a position to exercise the principle of plurality of information, even if their governments permitted it, for the lack of entrepreneurs willing and wealthy enough to invest in what must look like a losing commercial proposition – and, often, a politically risky one.

Against this background, it is understandable that governments insist that the structure and content of the media must reflect national political, social and economic goals. To the international dimensions of their demand for a New Order for Information, are added concepts of relevance, balance and responsibility on the domestic front. What this means in practice differs widely; 'balance' is a two-edged sword, one turned towards the international press and the other – much the sharper – edge turned inward. Julius Nyerere of Tanzania says that 'while other nations try to reach the moon, we are trying to reach the village.' His response has been twofold: since 1967, Tanzania has been pursuing a social and economic policy based on the *ujamaa*, or village commune, which is intended both to organise rural production along socialist lines and to create a pattern of life which will encourage ideological awareness. Since 1973, the movement to villages from scattered communities has been compulsory, although the setting up of a *ujamaa* communal system within the villages is not. The programme has much to be said for it, in the sense that more compact communites make the provision of health, education and other services much easier, whatever problems the coercive element has created, and although effects on food production have not always been positive. But Nyerere's ambition is to build a new society, not merely a fed and housed one – 'with few socialists . . . to build socialism; with few people conscious of the basic requirements of democracy . . . to achieve change by democratic means; with few technicians . . . to effect a fundamental transformation of our economy. And with an educated elite whose whole teaching encouraged motives of individualistic advancement . . . to build an egalitarian society.'

The second arm of policy, therefore, is the organisation of a communications structure to encourage 'peasant ideological development . . . and support for party and government agents and institutions to safeguard and build on results to date'. In November 1976, the Tanzania News Agency was created. As described by Ludovick Ngatara in the IoJ monthly, *The Democratic Journalist*, it was to be 'capable of taking countermeasures against imperialist news dissemination,' and aware of 'the need to promote national policies and the aspirations of the people of Tanzania and to uphold, support and justify confidence' in the government.

The agency's powers to do so are impressive. It is the sole receiver and distributor of foreign news within Tanzania; and it 'controls and regulates' news gathering and dissemination domestically. 'No person other than itself, its agents or the holders of written authorisations issued by the Agency' can circulate news domestically, whether it originates in the country or outside it; or 'distribute or cause to be distributed' Tanzanian news abroad. Agency and all other foreign correspondents may be granted 'some access' to news sources, and some material is allowed in, but all 'have to obtain authorisation . . . under special conditions.' The success of this venture, Ngatara concludes, will largely depend 'on the support it will enjoy from other agencies in Africa and throughout the progressive world, especially those countries pursuing a socialist ideology.' Meantime, the International Press Institute reported at the end of 1977 that six Tanzanian journalists remained in jail; two of them, Victor Namunera and Otini Kambona, had been detained without trial for ten years. But, ironically, what Ngatara did not report was that the Tanzania agency was created according to a blueprint prepared by Reuters, which had also crash-trained reporters for it.

Tanzania at least takes communications seriously enough to have created an organisation which is rapidly building up regional and sub-regional offices, and to run two-year training schools for journalists. There, 'emphasis is laid on active rather than passive journalism . . . the facts must be actively sought out – whether they relate to planning for a big self-help scheme or the reasons for the abrupt resignation of a public official' (the report, in the second case, would presumably have to be written in such a way as to 'justify confidence' in the Republic). 'Accuracy, objectivity and balance' are stressed, and in addition to courses on economics, politics and sociology, students are given a grounding in 'press responsibility, newspaper law and press ethics' and the role Africa's media 'can play in promoting national development' and literacy. The underlying assumption is that development is by way of ideology, that socialism and development are coterminous – a concept common to the leaders of several developing countries which have stressed communications policies, and possibly valid; but it means that information has a special meaning. 'Democracy' is promoted while 'individualism' is held in check. The deck is stacked.

'Reaching the village', to some governments, means controlling it. In a West African country a few years ago, the President decided to visit – for the first time – a province on the edge of the national territory. The presidential plane touched down rather bumpily on the crops growing outside the principal village, the only cleared area. The dancers began. The President stood at the door of the plane: '*Merde, quel pays.*' Persuaded to mingle with the welcoming villagers, of whose language he understood not a word, he returned half an hour later to the aircraft unmoved: '*Merde*, how can we talk of *this* as a country.' An old man appeared in the doorway. He wanted to know who this stranger was, who had come to his village and omitted to greet him, the chief.

The chief had simply been told by the regional administrator that 'another chief' was coming to visit him. Useless to explain further – unreached by radio, the villagers were not aware of the existence of the 'country'; the institution of the President meant nothing. On return to the capital, the young head of the national radio drew up plans for regional stations, cheap to install and capable of translating news programmes into languages – and terms - which would reach villages such as this. He put his plans to the cabinet, all military men. They asked one question: 'How do you propose to control the content, in these languages not spoken in the capital?' The project died.

A combination of such wariness and the existence of other, compelling priorities put investment in communications structures near the bottom of national investment plans for the first decade of independence in most countries. Non-governmental organizations, such as the International Press Institute, conducted training schemes in Africa and Asia; the written press remained largely an area of private initiative, with governments controlling, generally, only important factors such as newsprint or official advertising, or intervening to prevent embarrassing political stories from reaching the public. Such actions could be harsh, could lead to closures of newspapers or the imprisonment of editors; but they tended to be rather *ad hoc*. Where official steps to assist the development of the media were taken, they were geared to international prestige or to the demands of a growing urban elite; the huge potential audiences in rural areas tended to be ignored, and the severest language problem in the Third World is still the one which divides town and country. During the 1960's, in Asia, a group of journalists began to promote the concept of 'development journalism' – in a bid to reach rural areas with information which was relevant, clear and competent; and to steer journalism towards informed discussion of the economic and social problems central to developing countries's situations.

In the Philippines, then enjoying a riotously free, politically *engagé* and irreverent press, the Philippine Press Institute headed by Juan Mercado combined with the Philippine News Service to run seminars on development topics and train reporters to analyse development plans or academic research into social or economic problems in lively and plain language; Indian and Japanese press institutes were working on the same lines, and the Press Foundation of Asia (PFA) was launched in 1967 with the express aim of creating a corps of 'development journalists'. It was an attempt, remarkably successful for some years, to create a new kind of journalism for the developing world, focussing on the economic and social issues arising out of the struggle for 'exponential growth'. At the same time, its originators hoped to give journalists, often demoralised by government censorship or repression of political reporting, an outlet for serious reporting in areas which were less 'sensitive' than politics and at the same time arguably more important for the growth of democratic debate.

The success of this campaign was limited; ten years later, the former director of the Press Foundation of Asia, Amithaba Chowdhury, lamented that the one-way flow of news was still a reality in the Philippines: 'Only a trickle, and an inconsequential one at that, flows from the village to the urban centre. . . .' And, he added, 'the Kuala Lumpur or Bangkok based newspapers cover the rest of the country – their own world – with the same attitude, style and haste as they allege the wire agencies apply to the global flow of news.' But the PFA's contribution to a development news structure continues in the form of *DEPTHnews*, a regional features service in several editions which circulates valuable background material for use by the Asia media, and well-written features on development themes; and the effort proved that Third World professionals can with funding assistance (in the PFA's case from the Ford Foundation) do an impressive job of raising standards and redirecting efforts within the profession.

In an important sense, though, the concept of development journalism backfired: its successes alerted governments to the importance of economic and social reporting – and its potential usefulness, if systematically applied, to mobilising mass support behind government policies. Intended to enlarge the area of free debate, the concept has been taken over by governments, extended to cover all communications and integrated into an official variant of 'new' journalism.

A great deal of liberal ink has been spilled over the question of ownership of the media, on the grounds that government-owned press and broadcasting spell death to the freedom of discussion. It is unfortunate that the argument has been advanced in this way: because for many developing countries it is a fact that for the next decade at least, investment backing for privately-owned media will simply not be forthcoming except from foreign sources; because it plays into the hands of those who argue that the issue of ownership is linked to Western 'free market imperialism'; and because there are many serious journalists trying to find room for manoeuvre within a 'public' information system that they have no hope of seeing in private hands. In any case, the real issue is slightly different. It is that with a few exceptions, the basis in law or custom for the independence of the press is being eroded. This is a question not entirely of ownership, but of control – and the largely unavoidable involvement of government money in the media thus carries with it a forced collusion between the press and the ruling ideology.

Many governments have made this quite explicit and have also taken steps to transfer existing and commercially viable media to 'public' ownership: in 1975 Guyana's Prime Minister, Forbes Burnham, rationalised moves of this kind by saying that freedom of the press was a myth and that the media must be 'an agency for pushing the development of the nation in the context of Government policy.' With no historical justification whatever, governments are tending increasingly to equate control of the press with political stability; and to take the argument a crucial step further by equating support for government policies with a 'healthy' press. By 1974, Juan Gatbonton, a Filipino columnist and one of the proponents of development journalism, was writing that 'it is becoming more and more difficult to earn a living as a professional journalist in our part of the world, and I for one am afraid that things will get worse . . . Asian governments of the future are going to be even more 'authoritarian' than those we now have to live with – and even more intolerant of the free critic's role that has been until now our tribal reason for being.'

The crux lies not in the fact that, for example, only a small handful of Arab and black African states permit private ownership of the media. In some of these countries, lack of funding – and the notable vulnerability of media owners to government displeasure – would in any case mean no private takers. It lies, as Gatbonton says, in official attitudes to the 'free critic's role'. What has changed is that the intolerance of criticism which characterised most authoritarian governments has evolved into a positive philosophy: the press is required not merely to be discreet, to avoid 'divisive' themes, but actually to participate in the indoctrination of the people. The journalist as educator is an extension of the political will to create a new society. This evangelical role is buttressed by governmental arguments about the vulnerability of society, rationalised by redefinitions of democracy (*à la* Nyerere) and accompanied by references to the need to build a cultural identity. The new thinking is enthusiastically supported by inter-governmental and international organisations.

These arguments exert some power even over experienced journalists in the Third World who have long championed the free debate of national issues. Some, inevitably perhaps, have changed their views about the proper degree of government involvement when those they support have come to power. At the International Press Institute assembly in Australia in March 1978, a journalist and proprietor from Sri Lanka who had bitterly fought Mrs Bandaranaike's efforts to control the press began an apologia for national communications policies with the telling slip, 'We became the government.' A different situation, with similar results, obtains in Liberia, where government-owned papers are dominant and where, as one Liberian explained at a 1977 IPI seminar in Nairobi, 'we cannot criticise the government because we are part of the government.' Others continue to fight the concept of government involvement, while seeing a case for reform both of the free market structure of the press and of 'media values'. Amithaba Chowdhury attributes the present dilemma of the press to earlier failures 'to know, to formulate and finally to develop and market the new domestic product of information . . . to find a concept of journalism that will be valid and consequential in the context of [developing countries'] social realities.'

He argues that it was not without reason that 'the newspaper editor and the entrepreneur have both been held responsible . . . for contributing to the cumulative frustrations that arose out of sluggish economic growth, political disarray resulting from fractious and divisive debate and the atmosphere of an enfeebled culture.' But government meddling, he adds, has been proved totally counterproductive as a means of effecting reform: the media, he says, remain as city based as ever, simply satisfying the government with 'dull announcements of new economic projects and the ritualistic daily chanting of growth achievements', and reassuring the business elites by refraining from disclosing news 'that might stoke up labour or consumer discontent.'

Chowdhury's professional experience gives considerable weight to his view that 'no intelligent man in the government or in business fails to perceive ... the fact that information today must constitute a national resource' – and his own feeling that the media must be seen 'as a resource, and not merely a service industry ... a constituent part of the gross domestic product.' But news of the 'new quality and character' – reporting, for the grass roots as well as the urban intellectual, on health, education, agriculture etc, employing information as an 'input for economic and social growth,' should not be confused – as he warns that it is being – with the idea that remoulding the citizen is the legitimate business of government and that it is therefore entitled to use the media for the purpose. Because of this trend, he says, 'development journalism' has become a phrase which he and his colleagues regret having coined. Yet still, he says, 'the kind of news that has resource potential can be produced ... even under varying conditions of authoritarian rule and the demoralising restrictions they impose.' And it can perform a service needed by Third World peoples without implying that the media simply transform themselves into obedient servants of the ruling ideology.

To the long-running debate between (generally Western trained) journalists and the governments of developing countries, a new dimension has been added: a gradually more evident division between those Third World journalists who now believe that news should serve the interests of the state, and those who believe the state is better served by media free from state control. It parallels the international dialogue, and is closely related to the almost universal desire to counter the dominance of the international media with a form of journalism which meets different needs in different ways. And, with the question of state involvement in such a 'reform' looming ever larger, the discussion, even at the professional level, has become highly politicised.

Writing in *Asiaweek* in 1976 about the trends in the ASEAN

(Association of South East Asian Nations) press, the Indonesian journalist Rosihan Anwar discussed an ASEAN press seminar, due to be held in Bali and attended by the Permanent Committee on Mass Media of the ASEAN governments, plus 'selected chief editors' from the five nations which make up the group. Aside from questions of training and logistics, he said, they would doubtless 'stress cooperation to promote "a healthy, free and responsible press".' For most ASEAN journalists, he added gloomily, the issue was really settled if they wanted to stay in business: 'They are told by the powers-that-be that the freedom of expression endemic to the West is not applicable to their societies ... the younger journalists should grow naturally enough into their new role.'

Anwar added a gentle reminder, 'as one belonging to an out-going generation of journalists in the region': he recalled a UN meeting on Human and Social Development, held in Tokyo some months earlier. Emphasising that 'development must ... begin by identifying human needs ... provide all human beings with the opportunity to develop their potential,' the meeting had stressed that these included non-material needs, including 'the desire for self-determination and political freedom'. He hoped, without much conviction, that discussions on a 'healthy press' would take this into consideration. At the time this article was published, the Singaporean media had taken warning from another round of arrests of journalists – followed by 'confessions' by some of them on TV; Malaysia's media were well harnessed into campaigns to promote the national ideology along with the government's development plans; the Filipino press, operating under the martial law in force since 1972, was routinely promoting President Marcos's New Society and his personal leadership; and the Thai press was going through one of its frequent periods under tight control. In the spring of 1978, to make sure that no unhealthy attitudes to the intended re-election of President Suharto surfaced, the Indonesian press was closed down almost in its entirety for a period, and permitted to start up again under conditions which some – like Mochtar Lubis – found totally unacceptable. Lubis refused to publish: for an increasing number it is the only alternative to being forced to deceive their readers.

The transition from professional discussions aimed at finding ways to bridge the language gap between urban elites and their audiences, to a more explicitly ideological argument, was marked in 1975 by a curious gathering of Third World 'journalists' (including Juan Somavia and Germán Carnero Roque), assembled by the Dag Hammarksjöld Foundation in New York while the Seventh Special Session of the UN was in progress. It was this meeting, the ten participants later claimed, which first enunciated the concept of a 'New Order for Information'. The 'consensus statement' which, in true diplomatic style, they produced does not substantiate this claim: but some demands which were to become familiar in subsequent ILET meetings and among the non-aligned were certainly made. They were: to 'break the hold' of the international agencies, to liberate communications 'from the market-oriented sensationalism approach to news' (*sic*) both in the developed and the developing world, and to 'protect' Third World nations from the distortions of their way of life implied by their 'communications dependence'.

It was hardly a gathering of the best and the brightest, any more than it was geographically or culturally balanced; but it was the first meeting billed as purely professional to invite the wolf through the door: 'governments should take action within their own countries to create, foster and strengthen national structures, based on self-reliance, for information and communication that will enable them to change existing systems in this field.' Words which fell on fertile ground: the meeting is cited, in the non-aligned booklet on a *New World Order for Information*, as evidence of widespread professional backing for development-support journalism. It is still far from proved that the majority of journalists in developing countries, given any choice in the matter, support the notion of a guided press. Most of them have suffered too much from uncoordinated efforts to ensure professional subservience to governments to welcome the evolution of a better-organised straightjacket. Most do not attend international conferences: they are not invited, and in many cases they could not be spared from organisations functioning on shoestring budgets, with small staffs, battling against the daily realities of inadequate equipment, communications and – increasingly – difficulties in getting at the information they need to function at all.

Nor has a satisfactory case been made out for the usefulness of government involvement in the content of news media. On the whole, the more independent of government the better. One of the more remarkable examples of 'development journalism' has its origins in a sex education seminar in Francophone Africa, which requested the Canadian International Development Research Centre to support an educational magazine. *Famille et Développement*, launched in 1975 and edited by a Senegalese social scientist called Marie-Angélique Savane, started as a magazine for 'grass roots' workers, teachers and district health officers, in countries which have huge illiterate populations and in many cases no newspapers or irregular broadsheets; but it rapidly addressed itself direct to the public. After two years, it had an official circulation of 25,000 in a dozen French-speaking African countries, and an audience many times that size through the broadcasting of articles on national radios, use in schools, and up to fifteen readers for each copy sold to individuals. It is a model of 'self-help' journalism far removed from the ideologising in New York or Colombo. It concentrates on practical talk about nutrition, health, and solutions to problems of rural life. Certainly, it steers clear of formal politics and has thus gained the blessing of the region's governments; but, Stewart Dill McBride reported in the *Christian Science Monitor*, the magazine plays a highly political role in emphasising the role of women in development, and writes with authority and frankness on 'taboo' subjects like 'polygamy, teenage abortions, pornography, drugs, and the negative impact of Western tourism.' Its enormous popularity may be partly due to the fact that, relying on no government (and refusing advertising), it defers neither to official views of development nor to pressures from urban elites; and it is under no obligation to fill the front page with a particular minister's speech. The Achilles heel is that, to continue, it relies on foundation money.

Devilling the argument between pro- and anti-governmental media in the Third World are two things: the first is a confusion, which arises at least in part out of the search for 'relevant' news, between government information services and news – a confusion which Unesco does much to promote. The second is the desire to find a middle road between Soviet and Western styles of journalism – as Hilary Ng'weno put it in a brilliant article in Kenya's *The Weekly Review*, 'to get the good aspects of government control of the press and marry them with the good aspects of an independent press.'

Ng'weno's article appeared during the 1976 General Conference of Unesco in Nairobi, after one by Kenya's Information and Broadcasting Minister, Darius Mbela, arguing for 'totally committed African mass media based on African socio-economic-cum-political policies and not a replica of either East or West.' The sensitivities of the Third World over the performance of the Western press, Ng'weno argued, were natural enough. 'Many young countries have fragile political structures that cannot withstand endless scrutiny by the news media of the shortcomings of those in power or the failures of economic and social development programmes.' The Western media, he added, concentrated on the 'negative and unseemly side' of life in the developing countries, and did so often in crudely cold war terms.

But whatever the force behind such resentments, Ng'weno continued, the crucial issue for Third World countries was the flow of information within their own boundaries: and there, the proposals in the Draft Declaration before Unesco would 'replace one kind of distorting factor – that of Western bias – with another, that of governmental or bureaucratic bias.' Politically, he wrote, there might well be a distinctive Third World route between the two systems of the industrialised countries, 'but on the issue of the press there simply happens to be no middle ground ... Third World nations will have to stop trying to sit on the fence hoping for an opportunity to present itself which would help them establish a halfway house between government control ... and independent media.' Governments were in the business of influencing people, and 'for them information is not information until its probable impact on select audiences has been ascertained ... the truth or untruth of the information is of secondary importance.' And, when governments claimed that they did not need a rebellious press, it had to be remembered that it was the 'spirit of enquiry which most Third World nations today consider to be rebellion.' It was always possible to argue that a government-controlled press could operate freely, he said, putting the public interest above those of the group in power; in practice, it had never happened – and the argument that the government knew what was best for the people, 'often used in defence of systems where the press is controlled, only goes to show that one cannot have both control and freedom.'

Where governments could and should help, Ng'weno urged, was in upgrading the journalistic profession in the Third World, where they were 'not only poorly paid, [but] poorly regarded by authority ... treated as glorified messenger boys for those in power [or] shunned as dangerous purveyors of untruth, half-truth or truths which are unpalatable to the powers that be.'

The lack of understanding of the journalist's role in a developing society to which Ng'weno (putting it kindly) referred is a central problem, and one which the promotion of 'nation-building' communications policies is likely to exacerbate. While many newspapers and broadcasting stations are short-staffed, it is not for lack of talent in many developing countries, but because the talent finds other, safer, more profitable outlets. Journalism courses have sprouted in many countries, efficient regional centres provide training, and others exist both in the West and in Eastern Europe and Russia specifically for journalists from developing countries. (Those in the communist world are geared to producing anti-imperialist journalists in the approved mould; but Third World editors report that the trainees often return passionate advocates of total press freedom, and that their chief difficulty is in calming them down to keep them out of jail.) The talent does not stay in journalism for two reasons. One is that 'yes-man' journalism is not very interesting, and independent journalism is risky. Another is that advertising agencies, press attaches' jobs and government information services offer better financial rewards in many developing countries, and much less exposure to possible pressures or arrest. And, as Ng'weno also pointed out, countries which were willing to invest in expensive infrastructures for their broadcast media generally failed to allocate appropriate budgets for the development of programmes; simply acting as a funnel for imported programmes is not a career which attracts the most lively talent.

For all these reasons, C. J. Irani of *The Statesman* of India argues, not too much can be expected from training. 'We need the *right* training,' he argues, 'and we cannot afford to do without it. But training for what? Approach and attitudes are all-important, and these are best learned in the marketplace. But propaganda training is much more teachable than scepticism.' The arguments for 'appropriate' training, Unesco officials report, reach them from governments concerned with the 'authenticity' (to borrow a phrase from Mobutu) of their national media. The conflict between cultural identity and universal values is again implicit. Those who, like Irani or Ng'weno, assert that the best support and assurance for national dignity and identity is a freely informed public risk being branded – even when, like Irani, they have fought for their rights in their countries' courts, and won – as elitists who have sold their souls to the imperialist store. Irani pinpoints the centre of the conflict when he says that the case against an independent press 'rests on an incomplete analysis, which argues that in order to further economic development, it is part of the role of the state to participate in the building of a new order for information which would ensure that governments are able to communicate their ideas adequately to their people.'

The result, he argues, would be –

> to put development above human rights; the links between social values and news are talked about, but what is really at issue is the control of information. To seek to build national identity on such shifting sands is illusory. Besides which, the demand to assume the powers to do so is hypocritical: the objective is political power, held without check. What is wrong is not that governments put out propaganda, but that they call it news. Information bureaus are not news bureaus. Spokesmen are not journalists. And the role of a journalist is not to build nations, but to report the truth, with courage.

Is this fair? At an Asian journalists' meeting in Manila, in July 1977, convened by Unesco partly to publicise its important restoration work at the great temple of Borobodur, in Indonesia, and partly to mobilise professional support for 'mass communication for social progress and development in Asia', the

Philippines' Secretary of Public Information, Francisco Tatad – the same man who had warned foreign correspondents that martial law was none of their business – gave the 'keynote' address. Efforts to redirect the mass media, he said, had been 'much criticised in the West for its perceived implications to press freedom, and the evident erosion of adversary relationship between media and government. But it is very clear that this loss, if real indeed, has meant the alignment of mass communication to national endeavours and achievements, resulting in more palpable service to enormously greater publics.' The media should retain their ability to probe and analyse, he continued, but there should be 'a reorientation towards the issues that truly matter to our societies.'

Some 'reorientation' in the Philippines there has certainly been. When martial law was declared in 1972, all media were closed down (and 150 journalists arrested). In 1978, Bernard Wideman wrote in a special issue on the Philippines in the *International Herald Tribune*. . .

> Of Manila's four daily newspaper chains, one is controlled by the president's ex-military aide, one by Mrs Marcos's brother, one by a fraternity brother of the president, and one by Mrs Marcos's official biographer. Of the country's five television networks, four are controlled by the fraternity brother.
>
> Most news and commentary simply repeat and reflect government press releases. A survey commissioned by one martial-law daily showed that readers are simply bored by the papers. Newspaper readership . . . has dropped to about half. . . . Meanwhile, reading of comic books has greatly increased.

It is not the best advertisement for Filipino awareness of 'the issues that truly matter'; but, it could be argued, only a small proportion of the 43 million Filipinos read newspapers anyway; and it is only the opposition, deprived of any coverage prior the carefully controlled elections permitted in 1978, who really protest. The vital thing is spreading news about health, nutrition and so forth to the rural areas.

But the system allows no criticism, in the new, nation-building media, of the facts that 37 % of all Filipino doctors and 46 % of all nurses work in Manila, or of the expenditure by

Mrs Marcos, Governor of Metro Manila, of $50 million on a heart sanatorium in a country which has the highest rate of tuberculosis in the world, (a situation directly linked to under-nourishment, which on government statistics affects 60–70 % of all Filipino children). Government advice on nutrition may have been stepped up; but how helpful is this when the average family is spending even more of tiny budgets on less food now than before martial law, and when the minimum wage (for those lucky enough to earn it) is one-third of the amount the government reckons a family of five needs to spend on food? The press was not in a position to report the attack by one of Marcos's few outspoken opponents, former foreign secretary Salvador Lopez, on the restrictions of human rights (such as the right to organise labour movements) which went with the new 'orientation': 'Juan has been deprived of his rights, Pedro is still without his full bowl of rice. . . . The chances are that if a man opts for food without freedom, he will end up without food as well. . . .' At the Manila meeting, once Tatad had left, a number of journalists from South East Asia talked about their shame at the way their newspapers had accepted state control, and their own forced acquiescence. Meantime, a leading Filipino columnist in the 'reoriented' press, Teodoro Valencia, headlined an article with the advice, 'Asian nations must ignore Western press.'

The Unesco meeting grouped journalists who agreed on the need to balance the worldwide flow of information, and who were not in principle opposed to a Third World news pool or other cooperative arrangements. But as they discussed the repressive condtions under which most of them worked, they were sceptical about the value of swapping government-controlled news, arguing that the priority was greater freedom of public debate inside developing countries. Meanwhile, down the road, the more conformist Association of ASEAN Journalists, at a gathering addressed by Marcos himself, issued a call for the establishment of an ASEAN news exchange network. The local press gave them prominent coverage.

As two Yugoslavs from the national agency Tanjug put it to their colleagues from the Arab news agencies, over breakfast in a Baghdad cafe on a warm April day in 1973, the idea of a Third

World News Pool was a simple device to enable developing countries to 'splash the news' on a world scale. For Pero Ivačić, Tanjug's General Director, and Mirko Aksentijević, it was the first public airing of a project they had been nursing for a decade, and which the enormous growth in the number of national agencies in the Third World now made practicable. Their proposal, at this stage, was that national agencies should select a few items a day, and file them to Belgrade where they would be assembled as a Third World news file and redistributed internationally by Tanjug. There would be no editing: Tanjug would simply act as coordinator and distribution network. The aim was twofold. The Pool would enable news of the Third World to reach the industrialised countries 'carrying the authentic, honest voice of the Third World' and balancing by this means the 'distorted' images disseminated by the international agencies. And through it developing countries could, as Ivačić put it, exchange an 'alternative' kind of news with each other, 'news for countries preoccupied by starvation and acute poverty and the problems of underdevelopment'.

From the first, some reservations were expressed: wouldn't such a pool imply a sacrifice of sovereignty? Wouldn't it mean that small countries, those with the least developed national agencies, would simply become dependent on another agency, exchanging one form of reliance on external sources for another? This system would be different, reasoned Ivačić: with the international agencies, they were in a consumer-producer relationship; with the Pool, they would be equal partners. But doubts of this kind were to influence the future structure of the Pool – and the scope of its operations. It was after that April meeting that the Tanjug proposals were scaled down to a non-aligned framework; a world service would have to wait.

The official origin of the Non-Aligned News Agencies Pool dates from the Fourth Non-Aligned Summit, which took place in Algiers in September 1973; but although the conference warmly endorsed the principle of cooperative action to form a pool, the actual initiative came again from Tanjug. By January 1975, it had begun relaying items from a dozen countries within its normal transmission, coding them 'Pool'. By the time the next Non-Aligned Summit met in Colombo, eighteen months later, and formally established the Pool, Tanjug reported that around forty countries were already exchanging news through Belgrade.

Western reactions to the formal institution of the Pool were in many cases violently hostile, and obscured much of the subsequent, necessary, debate about the New Order for Information. The timing didn't help: the Costa Rica conference was just over, and Westerners were newly aware of the threats to freedom of information contained in the Soviet-inspired Draft Declaration due to come up in Nairobi. Nor did the heavy-handed endorsement of the Pool by India, then in the thick of a campaign to control its domestic press, or the Indian Government's abrupt cancellation, that August, of the contracts of the Indian news agency Samachar with UPI and the Deutsche Presse Agentur. (What went unreported was that there were serious arguments, almost amounting to a rupture, the month before at New Delhi, when the Indians had demanded that they should be the central organisation for the Pool against the stubborn opposition of Yugoslavia and of Tunisia, which had by now become a secondary distribution centre.)

Nor did the rhetoric which surrounded the Pool's christening. The eighty-five nations of the non-aligned movement, while they had in fact done no more than to agree to exchange news, features and photographs with each other, and 'also to provide objective and authentic information relating to Non-Aligned countries to the rest of the world,' stated this intention in the context of a declaration that the imbalance in the existing flow 'has created a situation of dependence and domination in which the majority of countries are reduced to being passive recipients of biased, inadequate and distorted information.' At New Delhi and Colombo, there were denunciations by politicians of the principle of the free flow of information; and the governmental emphasis of the new arrangement was underlined by the report which Tanjug submitted to the New Delhi ministerial meeting. Tanjug commented that in some non-aligned countries, 'the daily press is still controlled by private capital and therefore persists on the traditional track of making exclusive use of news reports and information carried by the big services. This underlines the importance of creating a new mentality concerning reporting and editorial policy.'

The combination of hostility to the international news

agencies, and what could well have been taken as hints that they would be squeezed out in favour of official government news, led to cries of alarm in the Western press that in retrospect range from exaggerated to hysterical. After the New Delhi meeting, *The Sunday Times* of London editorialised, 'Next month in Colombo, the heads of state of Third World countries will be asked to approve a new and comprehensive system of information control ... replacing the news service of the international press agencies ... with their own government controlled "news" service.' The article went on to say that there was a case to be made against the Western press coverage of 'development' issues – but that the evident concern of governments was not 'the publication of truth', but control; their action originated in 'a genuine disbelief in everything which educated men understand by freedom.' And *Newsweek*, in a 6 September article, reported that 'many Third World countries have begun talking about banding together to replace Western coverage of their affairs with a collective, government-managed conduit of information to the outside world ... the trend is a profoundly ominous one – a portent of Orwellian mind control on a continental scale ... a joint Third World agency ... would supplant the Western wire services operating in their countries.'

The problem arose for two reasons. One was that the language used at New Delhi and Colombo was indeed the language of potential censors – and it obscured the force of the Third World's case for more, and qualitatively different, news. The second was that there was some confusion in the international reports: they failed to distinguish between what some developing countries' governments – although not all – would *like* to see happen, and the actual scope of what was agreed. Looking ahead, it is possible to project that as capabilities build up, a Third World News Agency might become the unique source for media in the developing countries, publishing what *Newsweek* called the 'sanitised version of events'. But such a projection would exclude the recognition of the enormous disparities between the outlook of the eighty-five countries of the non-aligned group. (Would Kenya accept Uganda's version of its 'national reality' without verification? Or India, Pakistan's?) and other unsolved problems of 'official news'. As

Keith Fuller of the AP comments: 'News is what every head of government wants; propaganda is what he would prefer others to read.' It makes propaganda difficult to export.

Secondly, the Pool was not and is not an agency: its constitution prevents it from being anything of the kind. It is, at one level, simply an expression of developing countries' resentment at having their international portrait drawn by foreigners – even knowledgeable foreigners – and their conviction that the selection of news by international agencies and foreign correspondents is not always relevant or adequate. As formalised, the Pool works to the following rules: participants, who must be members or have observer status with the non-aligned movement (a category which has been stretched since 1976, for Pool purposes), can all transmit or redistribute items within the Pool's framework; no partner is to be dominant; and all will cooperate 'on the basis of full respect for equality and democratic principles.' Limited amounts of information – theoretically not more than 500 words a day – will be selected for the Pool 'on the basis of mutual respect and common interest'; and each agency will carry the costs of its participation, whether of the preparation of the original news item, or translating and relaying costs which arise in redistribution of others' copy. This last point on financing means, for the moment, that Tanjug – which still does most of the distributing work – carries most of the costs of the Pool, adding about two hours a day to its transmissions in three languages on high frequency radio. While other regional centres are now operating, the most important is the Cuban agency Prensa Latina, which compensates for Tanjug's inability, according to a study of the Pool by Edward Pinch of the US Information Agency with which Tanjug has found no factual quarrel, to reach west of the Andes.

The questions raised by the Pool's constitution, Pinch notes, are the restrictions implied by the 'basis of mutual respect' for news selection. 'Pool participants,' he writes, 'may be faced with the awkward choice of either censoring themselves (and others) and breaking agreements to transmit copy without alterations, or of violating the spirit if not the letter of their own and possibly others' laws.' The problem would not arise if the emphasis were not on government-owned and controlled news agencies; while there are differences in the degree of control exercised in each country, the fact is that each article is interpreted abroad as the government's view, and is therefore sensitive material in diplomatic terms. Within non-aligned countries, therefore, never mind elsewhere, the Pool has what Westerners would call a 'credibility problem'. In addition, to the extent that Pool material reproduces government speeches and official accounts of policy, it will bore readers abroad as much as the same items bore readers at home; and there is an inherent weakness in the proclaimed philosophy behind the Pool: the mutual dissemination of 'achievements'. If political and economic difficulties are not frankly discussed in the Pool, the Third World countries will be less well informed about each other than they are now. Many governments within the Pool, united perhaps only on this one issue, see the balancing of the news-flow in terms of improving their public relations image, and of finding a way of getting across to the industrialised countries their common demands for a new economic order: their aim is in this sense increasing the views-flow; it has little to do with news.

If the Pool is intended to be a central feature of the new order for information which is described by some non-aligned leaders as the essential precondition for the achievement of a New International Economic Order, it is hard to see just how successful it can be. Its basic structure reflects an approach to the media which could even be counterproductive in terms of that goal. If the Pool is to be effective, its output will have to interest readers, rather than satisfy governments; yet its constitution, the emphasis on governmental sources, and the fact that nothing can be edited, all make for stories in which the likelihood of attracting readers is the last criterion for selection, not the first.

Essentially, the Pool has less to do with being better informed of brother-countries' mutual achievements, than with news exports: it is the expression of a longterm ambition, legitimate and not to be ignored whatever the present or future means employed, to 'splash the news'. The trouble is that it will not, on present form, be the 'news' that is splashed; and nor, probably to the increasing bitterness of developing countries, will the product make much of a splash unless it looks to the world's professional wholesalers like news.

It has been widely criticised by developing countries' journalists on professional grounds: because it is not concerned to meet the needs of the consumers; because it ignores for political reasons the poor performance of many of the agencies within the network (in fact, Tanjug journalists have privately admitted that they reject about threequarters of copy sent to Belgrade as wholly unsuitable); because it circulates copy late – meetings of ministers are often only reported by agencies after their own minister has returned to the country – and because the only 'new' aspect of Pool news is the absence of critical life.

In the spring of 1978, however, the Pool had become a qualified success: membership had grown (although a mere seven countries still provided sixty per cent of the news file) and, although no study had yet been published of the level of 'take-up' in the non-aligned countries' media, Yugoslavia at least reported that it was making extensive use of the material. The Pinch study provides an analysis of content and quality, based on a careful sampling from the first three months of 1977. Nearly a fifth of the total copy concerned the Middle East, 'explained by the fact the eleven of the twenty-six active Pool participants are Arab news agencies' who supplied ninety per cent of Middle East copy. Just under half covered development issues, from economic policy and investment to education and the arts (which compares favourably with the Reuters and AFP African services, which according to another sampling allocate 23–33 % and 35–41 % respectively to African development). On quality – which Pinch recognises to be a subjective and elusive criterion, and by which he means acceptability by Western media – the sampling produced 22 % of 'high interest' material, and 26 % of 'medium interest', with Qatar, Jordan and Cuban agencies all scoring higher than more democratic media in Cyprus or Sri Lanka, on grounds of 'solid news content' and professionalism. Over half the file contained news of interest to all or part of the developing world, but not beyond: to that extent, the Pool was providing the 'alternative' news Ivačić claimed it would (along with some items of purely local interest), but not speaking to a global public.

By this time, the international agencies in particular were saying publicly that they welcomed the Pool, as they would welcome any increase in the flow of information. One reason was that it was now clear to most that the Pool was performing a different kind of role, and one which did not threaten the services they provided. Privately, however, they were still concerned about their most vital interest: access to developing countries for their reporters, freedom to export news from them. The spectre they raised was the possibility that Third World governments, finding that the Pool's output was not being carried in the press of the industrialised world, might block other sources in an endeavour to see that their version of events was the only one in circulation. There was some justification for this view: the explicit goal behind the New Order for Information, of which the Pool is a partial consequence, is to develop a distinctively Third World voice – and one which is listened to.

The best protection against such a development – which would above all affect the ability of Third World publics to be informed – may be active encouragement of professional standards in Third World news agencies. Because of the sensitivities about 'dependence', this will be difficult; and it will certainly be expensive. 'Professionalism,' one director of a news agency connected with the Pool says, 'is something we are trying desperately to encourage. We know, some of us, that the success of the Pool depends on depoliticising it, and gaining for it an international credibility. At the moment, the myth of professional standards is maintained, but it's a matter of bluff and faith.' He adds a warning: 'The early reaction of the Western press, and above all the agencies, has made the job immeasurably more difficult for those of us who see the Pool as a genuine instrument to improve the news-flow – because we are already a minority, and every outburst shrinks support within the Pool countries for the realism we are trying to promote.'

The Pool started functioning in 1975; three years later over twenty new national news agencies had been created in the non-aligned countries alone. Pressures for 'each country and its news agency', as Ivačić phrases it, 'to realise the right to report the real facts of interest beyond its frontiers about the most important events of its daily life, and sovereign development' continued to grow – and in some countries were being equated with export controls. At a New York conference,

Biola Olasope of the Nigerian Broadcasting Corporation put this openly: 'Nigerian news organisations accept reports of British events by Reuters [which he had earlier accused of being supported by the British government] without doubting the integrity of British journalists. The British must be willing to do likewise to the News Agency of Nigeria. To do otherwise would be to expose the British to charges of arrogance based on prejudice. After all, it is always better to hear it straight from the horses' mouth.' At the time, the international press had in fact little alternative: the only correspondent of the 'Big Four' still in Lagos, after the Reuters man was floated out of the country (literally – in a canoe without a paddle) was AFP's – and as he was under instructions to stay there, he was filing little.

Efforts to improve the exchanges of news within the Third World are not a new phenomenon: from the early 1960's, regional meetings have produced pious resolutions on inter-agency cooperation, ranging from the dream of a Pan-African Agency to the creation of a regional pool in Asia (which stayed alive – barely – through subsequent years only because the Japanese agency Kyodo sustained it). Sukarno had ambitions for an agency to serve the 'New Emerging Forces'. But only in the Arab world, with the Arab Radio Union and Permanent Committee on Information of Arab States, was cooperation a reality – and even then the major news agencies such as the Egyptian Middle East News Agency established news exchanges not through a pool but on the basis of bilateral (and commercial) contracts.

What changed in the 1970's, above all after 1973, was that desultory efforts became determined. Parallel with measures to strengthen the non-aligned pool were meetings at governmental level to improve the Afro–Arab news exchanges and, in Kampala in November 1977, to put lifeblood into the Pan-African Agency. The Kampala participants declared their commitment to information as 'an irreplaceable instrument for the education, the mobilisation and the conscientising of the African masses' and their support for non-aligned efforts to build a New Order for Information. A less charged declaration from a group of Asian journalists (convened at a Unesco conference in Colombo a month later as part of the preparations for Unesco's Inter-governmental Conference on communications in Kuala Lumpur in early 1979) backed the principle of activating an Asian news agency. The problems of technological development are formidable, especially in Africa, where the communications system linking some countries is still nonexistent, and where (an important qualification in the Third World view) national agencies have not yet been set up in all countries.

But by 1978, there was little doubt that regional agencies, pools and – eventually – a Third World agency were on the way to creation. Because the impetus remained political, the tone of some meetings suggested that the principal concern of the Third World was the building of 'international solidarity' rather than specific measures to improve information. And the rhetoric of 'international solidarity' was no more reassuring in 1978 than it had been in 1976. At a meeting of the Inter-Governmental Council for the Coordination of Information from Non-Aligned Countries, held in Havana in April 1978 largely because Cuba was due to take over the presidency of the Movement later that year, some useful suggestions to cut tariff rates for telecommunications and to establish more training courses were overshadowed by discussions about establishing a code of ethics, of which 'the aim would be to give non-aligned countries sovereignty over news flowing in and out of their borders'. The aim appeared to be constant; there was simply greater realism about the means, forced on the participating governments by the fact that technical meetings which followed grand statements of intent were often inventories of the need for more information on actual communications structures and facilities before progress could be made.

Some Third World journalists continue to fear that the domination of the news-flow by the international agencies, which they are largely united in wishing to see reversed, could be replaced by the domination of national bureaucracies, which they already spend much of their professional lives struggling to escape. At the first meeting of broadcasters from the non-aligned countries which took place in Sarajevo in October 1977, and which laid the basis for a newsfilm pool patterned after the news pool, a carefully conciliatory speech made by Tunisia's Mustapha Masmoudi still emphasised support for governmental information; the press indeed guaranteed the individual's right to freedom of speech, 'but the press must be there to defend the interest of society as a whole and the right of whole nations to make known their preoccupations, difficulties and their aspirations to a better life . . . it is the task of the press to promote the advancement of society.' This Sarajevo meeting also agreed that there should be a joint approach by the non-aligned countries at the 1979 World Administrative Radio Conference (WARC). Called by the International Tele-communications Union, WARC will review access to the entire electronic spectrum. Third World countries will press for a reallocation which 'accords with present realities'. In other words, they will demand that some frequencies currently used by major international broadcasting organisations be turned over to national broadcasting corporations for their present (or future) use. Such action – which will have the backing of socialist countries – will affect the ability of, say, the Voice of America or the BBC to reach Third World audiences.

Governmental or not, the ambitions symbolised by the developing countries' emphasis on national agencies and inter-governmental cooperation lie close to the heart of Third World awareness of the need to muster a collective identity against the rich, an identity forged much along the lines of 'class struggle'. To adapt Chairman Mao's advice about walking on two feet, the New Order for Information and the New International Economic Order are being developed, in tandem, as the twin pillars of bargaining strength. As one editor-bureaucrat of a national agency puts it, 'we need not only to be accepted in our demand to be heard, but to be seen as an equal partner.' A Latin American journalist comments that this is the one point on which even Castro and Pinochet might agree.

Against the force of such essentially political demands, the voices in the Third World which fear that the means employed will result in the shrinking of their people's horizons sound like a whistle on the wind.

This does not excuse governments, whether individually or through Unesco, which dismiss them as unimportant. Eugenio Lopez, the publisher of the *Manila Chronicle* imprisoned by President Marcos for five years – until his escape in 1977 – condemns what he sees as a certain collusion between Westerners prepared to say, like the US diplomat George Kennan, that democracy 'is not the natural state of most of mankind,' and dictators for whom this form of condescension 'fits their plans for self-perpetuation in power.' It confuses, he says, the Western forms democratic institutions have often taken, with the universal substance: 'freedom in Asia is not a borrowed value but an indigenous flame.' Marcos, he says, has used the argument that only the elite cares about such matters; the Indian farmers refuted it in 1977. And, whether they should be dismissed as an 'elite' or not, the Pakistani editors who were imprisoned and flogged in May 1978 – simply for going on hunger strike to protest against censorship – chanted as they were being flogged, 'long live the freedom of the press'. Governments, too, are 'elites'. Marcos, as Lopez reminds us, uses the alternative argument that the Philippine press 'abused democracy' and thus brought reform on itself. 'Why were we licentious? Because we told the truth, the good and the bad? Because in doing so we might have projected the image of an imperfect democracy? . . . George Gallup [has been] reported as complaining that the US press was succeeding in portraying to the world a very negative image of America.'

The people who are first harmed by the 'new' approach to information are those in Third World countries. The editor is increasingly engaged in a form of self-censorship, in the name of national development goals; the typical progression, as Mochtar Lubis sketched it at the IPI meeting in Australia, runs from printing official handouts, to printing handouts he knows are not truthful, to positive recommendations for policies which he believes to be wrong. Only to find he has not done enough: he loses his paper, but he has already lost his credibility with his reader. 'The editor has serious obligations to society: the question is when our governments will begin to understand that he can only discharge them if he is able to operate in a climate of freedom.'

CHAPTER 7

The Real Cultural Imperialism

In 1973, an audience in the Hong Kong Foreign Press Club was treated to a speech by one of the top executives of *Newsweek*; he drew the portrait of 'Newsweek man'. Nationality unimportant, a global stereotype, Newsweek man was easily recognisable. He was a 'decision-maker', a rising figure in business or government, a man who required a global perspective, who needed to make up his own mind on the basis of the facts – but who, being very busy, needed the facts packaged for him in a form which enabled him to digest and use them in the shortest reasonable time. To reach him across the world, *Newsweek* had launched its international editions, giving him the regional 'in-depth' coverage he required but catering always to the known needs of the composite world phenomenon, the cosmopolitan elite.

It was a classic, energetic and convinced *exposé*, and the largely Asian audience had few questions. In practice, it would be unfair to suggest that *Newsweek* knows no frontiers: the price of copies is, for example, kept deliberately high in countries where consumption – and advertising yields – do not justify the costs of circulation, on practical yardsticks which embrace Britain as well as India. It is also true that *Newsweek*, like *Time*, provides reasonably reliable brief stories on issues in countries where they would not otherwise get an airing. But the assumptions behind *Newsweek*'s confident expansion are close to those which are with increasing frequency being branded as 'cultural imperialism'; the portrait is one which governments insist that national policy must reject: the transnational soul is contained in it, and the spread of *Newsweek* man within their societies threatens their cultural identity.

Arguments about 'cultural identity', like those about 'balancing the news', run in two mutually incompatible directions. Where getting the message out is concerned, there is much talk of the interdependent world, of access and the importance of cultural exchange. But inward flows tend to be discussed in terms of national sovereignty, the protection of national culture, and the need to oppose freedoms to cross frontiers which benefit only the 'strong'.

In practice, where news at least is concerned, the idea that developing countries are helpless, 'passive recipients' is something of a myth. The Pinch study found that in 73 % of the non-aligned countries, the services of the Anglo-Saxon news agencies either were not sold at all, or were sold to governmental agencies; Reuters in Africa sold directly to only five newspapers, but to twenty-seven national agencies or government ministries. Agence France Presse, according to the report it supplied to the MacBride Commission, sells to sixty-nine national news agencies. Chowdhury judges that public complaints by governments create an impression that they are seriously worried, whereas in reality 'in the field of news imports, extremely high and almost impregnable walls have already been raised. The national news agencies in many Third World countries play the role of centralised importer and distributor, and offer most governments the service of liveried gatekeepers.' This leaves, he says, a few regional and international magazines, 'the remaining source of relatively unfettered information, the only link between the outside world and the developing country.'

The claims about cultural vulnerability therefore invite some scepticism: are governments concerned to protect their infant communications industries, to practice a policy of import substitution as they build up a distinctive image; or are they simply concerned to exclude foreign messengers which bear with them the bad news, the criticisms and the independence which are suppressed at home in the interests of national unity? Are the news magazines a favourite object of attack because of their alien cultural values – there is a case for this view which could be argued – and because they represent the interests of transnational business; or because of their information content? *Newsweek* was bitterly attacked by the Indonesian government in 1977 for an article which not only described the corruption which is openly admitted within the country to have reached the scale of a national crisis, but – fatal step – linked the President's wife with this special form of income redistribution. The repercussions of this particular row could seriously affect regional magazines in Asia; towards the end of 1977, a secret agreement was reportedly reached between the information ministers of the five ASEAN countries, which together form the major regional market: in future, action taken against a foreign publication would be coordinated, and a ban in one country would mean a ban in all five.

But although the concepts of 'relevant' content and 'balanced' flow, so strongly supported by Unesco, serve in a crude sense to give international respectability to controlled or at least 'guided' information, some of the essentially protectionist aspects of the bid to establish a New Order for Information have a more genuine social base. News magazines and imported television programmes, it is said, spread patterns of consumerism, which in countries with low *per capita* incomes accentuate social divisions; accelerate the flight from the countryside to cities (which, without an industrial base to support the immigration, are doubling in size every six to eight years); and at another level, encourage the departure of trained elites to richer countries. Industrial models which emphasise the cost-effective, capital-intensive and profit-orientated approach of the West become, through these alien cultural influences, more respected than models which would provide more jobs and require less crippling investment inputs. International influences inhibit a necessary search for indigenous approaches to education which emphasise basic literacy and appropriate skills. The encroachment of 'alien' models impoverishes not only 'national value systems', but the country itself: copying the West sinks governments ever deeper in debt burdens. These cannot in some cases be financed out of the national product – if at all – without the sacrifice of urgent programmes to meet the basic material needs of the mass of the people.

Economic self-reliance thus becomes entwined with cultural

policy. The response on both fronts, however, is rarely to take 'self-reliance' seriously on the domestic front – to encourage the capacity for self-help in creating purchasing power at the bottom, or inventiveness in cultural 'import substitution'. Most Third World 'solutions' to dependence imply more, not less, governmental control – and less room for manoeuvre outside officialdom.

Third World leaders complain, with justification, that their diverse and complex societies are stereotyped by the Western use of the term 'developing'. But when they unite to insist that they are at the mercy of a technological-cultural invasion, from which their 'fragile' societies must be protected, they encourage the stereotype. The idea that controls foster diversity, and the promotion of national 'values' – however seriously one takes the threat of homogenisation implied by the international spread of the consumer society – is a contradiction in terms.

An African politician argues the classic case:

> We are caught between the fact that fifty per cent of adults cannot read or write, and that our elite demands the maximum of liberty. And there are tribal hatreds just under the surface which erupt for for no clear reason, even though we have almost completed settling our nomads. We have to fight against certain brutalities, certain hatreds.
>
> If a regional governor nationalises a piece of land, to use the water beneath it for the community, that land was almost certainly owned by the ancestors of a local tribe. If somebody in the press or the opposition tells them they have the right to retain that land, they would not stop at words, they would take to arms.

Common ground there may be: many colonial frontiers were drawn which arbitrarily grouped disparate traditions, ethnic groups, or religions, and building a nation of them in a generation is a formidable task even without the handicaps of poverty and high population growth. But when governments argue that they are therefore compelled to use their powers to create a safe common ground of 'national consensus', they subscribe to the notion that the best way of averting social unrest and cultural conflicts is 'homogenisation' at the domestic level –

through policies which are markedly similar throughout the developing world. Such policies deny the benefits of creative debate to societies where the illiterate peasant certainly exists – alongside groups with considerable intellectual skills and technological expertise. A tiny elite conspires to limit the liberties of a larger one, in the name of the masses whom they thus hope more effectively to control. For governments to say that their countries cannot afford free debate – whether because the nomads will take to arms or because the siren of consumerism will lure their elites to alien shores – is to say that they cannot afford genuine cultural development. It may be couched in terms of a search for distinctive social systems and 'endogenous development', to use a favoured phrase of those who make a career out of emphasising the problems of multi-ethnic societies; the proper term is authoritarianism.

These fallacies drive out the validity of the facts – the fact that the enormous flow of imports (not of news, but of entertainment) from a tiny number of exporting countries puts pressures on rapidly changing societies both in the industrialised and the developing countries; and that it does so because so much of the material dumped in this fashion is cheap stuff in *any* culture. And it is not an adequate defence to say that the West feeds on the same soap operas or even, which is true, that the world buys American television programmes not just because they cost little but because they actually amuse people. The Third World objects to pre-cooked cultural diets: and the same material could bear some more critical scrutiny in the West.

The explosion in communications, above all since World War II, is not limited to information, or to the printed word – to the 1,500 books published every twenty-four hours, to the flow of 'fast' news which makes it the pride of UPI that they can push 9,600 words a minute across the Atlantic. The volume of international broadcasting doubled between 1950 and 1960, and doubled again in the next decade; by 1972, there were 1,365 shortwave broadcasting transmitters. The BBC transmits in thirty-nine foreign languages and broadcasts round the clock in English with its World Service; but it now ranks only sixth in the external broadcasting league. Voice of America, which broadcasts in thirty-five languages through 123 stations, reckons that it reaches around 25 million people daily, and up to 80 million during international crises. The Soviet Union and Eastern Europe together transmit nearly 10 million words a week to Western Europe and North America.

Part of the reason for this huge expansion in broadcasting is that it is extremely difficult, and expensive, to block. Jamming costs fortunes, even by the standards of wealthy governments. The Soviet involvement in a Draft Declaration aimed at providing grounds for protest against the various US broadcasting stations directed towards the East was in a sense an admission of defeat. As a Yugoslav study published by Unesco in 1977 pointedly commented, crude propaganda has a boomerang effect: and 'the more a society is open to the free flow of information the more ... broadcasting propaganda becomes obsolete and doomed to inefficiency.'

Hardly a single country, however poor, has failed to invest in external services. They carry not only propaganda – and in a few cases, none at all – but entertainment programmes, music, news and information on the cultural life of the sending country. International and regional broadcasting arguably provides the major opportunity for a wide audience to gain access to an open exchange of views. It also, in the view of some governments, represents a serious threat to national cultural policies. The man in the street, who, as Joe Rodrigues of Kenya's *The Nation* points out, has no choice in authoritarian regimes between government-controlled media or nothing, 'keeps in touch with the rest of the world by tuning in to free, uncensored radio stations – the BBC, Voice of America and, amazingly in many independent African nations, Radio South Africa.' Along with news, come attitudes and cultural styles.

But the fiercest allegations about cultural 'dumping' are reserved for television. Governmental anxieties on this score are directly proportionate to the enthusiasm with which they have invested in the infrastructure for the small screen – and to their expectations for the future. In the late 1970's, these fears must be seen in proportion: there are more television sets in Hong Kong than in the whole of Black Africa, where it serves 0.001 % of the population; China, which operates several TV stations, does so for a nationwide total of about 100,000 sets. Indian television is still at an experimental stage. But the potential of the medium is lost on nobody, and perhaps greatly exaggerated by some. Essentially, governmental concern centres on the fact that direct broadcasting by satellite – from space to the home, without the intermediary of ground stations – is already technically feasible and rapidly becoming commercially viable.

Given the restricted spread of television in many Third World countries, and its non-existence in some, and given the fact that electronic invasions of national sovereignty (via radio) have been an international game for half a century, the debate over direct satellite broadcasting principally demonstrates the degree to which communications have become a focus of nationalism. The problems fall into two main categories: the first concerns the ownership and operation of communications satellites; the second, direct broadcasting. Current technology requires the establishment of ground stations to receive the signal from communications satellites. The charm of this for governments is that, although there is likely to be some over-spill between neighbouring countries, the messages can thus be controlled – edited or totally rejected – before they reach the consumer. But community antennae are already a reality, and the 1980's will bring onto the market 'cheap' (£80 or so) receiving dishes small enough to stick on top of the TV set at home. Still too expensive, by far, for most societies; but the pocket calculator is an example of what can be done to bring these toys within the financial reach at least of middle-class families in the Third World.

The potential of direct broadcasting via satellite is clearly enormous; in the rosy perspective of Dr Delbert Smith, Editor of *Satellite Communications*:

> Lifestyles will be changed. . . . The office of the future will be primarily electronic. . . . Work locations will be changed to perhaps neighbourhood work centres, many business and financial transactions will take place in the home. Education will truly become a lifelong activity with courses, perhaps interactive in nature, being offered via satellite. Many medical diagnostic procedures will take place in the home. . . . Location will case to be a limiting factor. . . .

And there, for others, is the rub. No amount of talk about the possibilities for community programmes, education for remote areas, personally-tailored programming and two-way exchanges between producer and consumer obscure the fact that direct satellite broadcasting offers opportunities for 'commercial and cultural aggression' – for bypassing national control systems – of an unparalleled effectiveness.

This is where the first part of the issue interacts with the second. In 1978, the US and the Soviet Union still exercised a duopoly in launching capacity for large satellites, and therefore an effective veto on the number and kind of satellites allowed into circulation. Europe, China and Japan seemed the only challengers established in the field. Ownership and control has principally been used by both the US and the Soviet Union for national and military purposes to date. As a paper by Professor O. W. Riegel in *Mass Media Policies and Changing Culture* observes, 'the four satellites of the global public communications network in world service are like four lonely sunfish in a sea of eels.' This network, Intelsat, was originally dominated by the United States. Under an Act of 1962, the American private commercial company COMSAT was created, and other nations were entitled to investment ownership in the company roughly in proportion to the amount of traffic they generated. The spread of Intelsat under COMSAT was remarkable: by 1975, the consortium had ninety-one members and Intelsat was serving eighty-one ground stations in sixty-five countries. But the management pattern created bitter discontent, and the agreement which established a permanent Intelsat organisation, in 1973, limited US influence by greatly expanding the international membership of the Board of Governors and including representation for groups of small or developing countries; COMSAT assumed a management role limited by contract, and subject to review in 1978. The US investment share was reduced to forty per cent.

Intelsat is theoretically open to any nation who can afford the tariffs; Intersputnik, the Soviet system, is more tightly controlled. Neither comes near to establishing the global satellite system to which all have equal access, called for by the United Nations – a system which would probably not alter the balance of power between rich and poor countries so long as launching and research remain in the hands of a tiny number of states. The delightful language of footprints and transponders can be converted into national capacity only at prohibitive cost (met, in the US, by the development of the NASA programme and the military research on satellites for other purposes).

The touchiness of the issue is illustrated by one small anecdote. Réunion has a ground station, which receives French programmes by satellite and laces them locally with bits of domestic news to make up its television service. Two hundred kilometres away, Mauritius runs a television service which combines domestic production with foreign serials as filler. Most of Mauritius' equipment is French-supplied. It would be possible, some experts say, to link Mauritius into Réunion's ground station system via microwave for the minute cost of about $60,000 per channel, assuring it both of French TV services and a much more efficient telecommunications hookup. Surveys suggest Mauritians want access to French programmes; well-informed sources say that, precisely for this reason, the Mauritian government has refused to consider the deal.

Satellite broadcasting was one of the issues which led to the close involvement of Unesco in national communications policy. The question arose from the moment, in 1960, when NASA launched its first communications satellite and was being actively debated by the mid-Sixties. It came onto the agenda of both the UN and Unesco in 1972. At the UN, the Russians presented a draft convention governing the use of satellites for direct television broadcasting which required that nothing be broadcast without the express consent of the receiving country and without giving notice to the Secretary General of the UN and Unesco; and secondly, the exclusion of 'material publicising ideas of war, militarism, naziism (*sic*), national and racial hatred . . . immoral or instigating in nature or . . . otherwise aimed at intefering in the domestic affairs or foreign policy of other states.' The Soviet draft was rejected on a close vote, but at the same time the Committee on the Peaceful Uses of Outer Space was asked – against the opposition of the US but nobody else – to come up with guidelines.

Meantime at Unesco, a 'Declaration of Guiding Principles

for the use of satellite broadcasting for the free flow of information, the extension of education and the spread of greater
cultural exchanges' was agreed by the General Conference,
opposed only by the US, the UK, Canada and West Germany
although twenty-two states abstained. Despite the title of the
Declaration, and the reference in the preamble to Article 19 of
the Declaration of Human Rights, the key passage required:
'States, taking into account the principle of freedom of information, [to] reach or promote prior agreements concerning direct
satellite broadcasting to the population of countries other than
the country of origin of the transmission.' The principle of the
'sovereignty and equality' of states was built into a declaration
which both announced that 'the objective of satellite broadcasting for the free flow of information is to argue the widest
possible dissemination . . . of news of all countries', and warned
that 'cultural programmes' should 'respect . . . the right of all
countries and people to preserve their cultures.' It is the
paradox of controlled freedom which has since become familiar.

How justified are the fears of developing countries? Even
against direct satellite broadcasting, there are means – from
jamming to vetting the types of television sets on the market –
to protect the public from outer space. Where 'commercial
aggression' is concerned, transnational advertising of which
governments disapprove can always, at least in theory, be
countered with import quotas or restrictions on the national
operations of the corporations involved. It is expensive – and
will be for some time – to mount foreign television broadcasts
by satellite; nobody is likely to embark unless there is a good
political or commercial market, the means for reception exist,
and the government concerned is not hostile. This is not to say
that there are not serious problems of access and control
involved; but the issues have so far been treated, at Unesco and
the UN and even in the ITU, on a more narrowly political
basis. As Reigel says, most of those involved 'look at their own
nations and other nations not as peoples but as collectives of
power. Their main concern is not what would be best in
communications . . . but what will advance the economy and
enhance the security of the state . . . or, conversely, what will
prevent the importation of ideas and images and forms of
competition that, in their estimation, might threaten the *status*

quo. Agreements and cooperation remain predominantly forced marriages of convenience between rival nationalisms.'

But the problem stretches beyond the traditional insistence by governments – whatever their motives – on their right *not* to receive broadcast communications, to the fact of the current dependence of TV networks in many developing countries on imported programmes.

There is a relatively simple explanation for this dependence. Having invested heavily in the infrastructure of a television network, both governments and private corporations naturally wish to use it. But aside from the very high costs of television film production ($100,000 an hour is a rough estimate in the US, although costs in Western Europe are considerably lower), local talent and experience take time to build up. The gaps in programming are filled from abroad. Like most simple explanations, this fails to take account of the fact that developing countries are by no means leaders in the import league; Australia imports more than half its programmes, New Zealand seventy per cent. The only inventory which is even reasonably up-to-date – the Unesco study by Tapio Varis and Kaarle Nordenstreng, *Television traffic – a one-way street?* – shows that Western Europe imports a third of its programmes, and that Canada has had to introduce a policy requiring that fifty-five per cent of programmes must be locally produced. But the extent of imports is considerable in the Third World, even if it is not nearly as high on average as Western supporters of the 'cultural imperialism' thesis have argued. The Varis and Nordenstreng study showed that Africa, the Middle East and Latin America import about half of their programmes, and Asia slightly more if the highly self-sufficient countries, Japan and China, are excluded. The proportion of imports ranges from around twenty-five per cent in Brazil and Argentina, to seventy per cent in Singapore and Malaysia and a high of eighty-four per cent in Guatemala.

The vast bulk of this material comes from the United States, which in 1970 (the year of the Varis/Nordenstreng survey) exported some 150,000 programme hours; Britain and France came next, with 20,000 hours each. Overwhelmingly, what is imported is entertainment: if the US and Britain exert a strong cultural influence, they do so through exporting TV series and feature films – categories which accounted for about ninety per cent of the US export total. Series account for around half total programme time in Latin America and Asia, and about a quarter in Africa.

The lack of development of television in most developing countries makes it difficult, however, to argue that the society as a whole is being saturated with B-grade films, the cult of the pop star and television serials whose chief virtue is the bargain prices – anything from $50 to $500 per instalment of a series, for a small to medium-sized country – at which films initially expensive to produce are offered. And it is impossible to argue that the serials get there without being invited. If, however, this is cultural imperialism on a limited scale and by popular request, it is also big business with a lot of commercial energy behind it. And governments, who argue that they import these serials only *faute de mieux*, view the whole operation in terms of a much-resented technological dependence.

They complain, particularly in relation to the US, of the diet on offer. *Peyton Place* ('the town in New England . . . but it could be located anywhere in the world' says the blurb) for example, distributed by Twentieth Century Fox, is a leading example of the 'transnational culture' and not a very cultured one. And, since it runs to 514 episodes, a weekly dose for addicts would last nearly ten years. Latin American 'experts' in particular complain that *I Love Lucy* inculcates the lifestyle and values of the American suburb in the *barrios* of their cities, where such 'escapist' entertainment is taken as undiluted truth – an assertion without much research to back it. The same charge about alien values has been directed at the widely-praised British serial, *The Forsyte Saga*, which by 1970 had been seen by about 160 million viewers in forty-five countries; (something about the propaganda effect of exposing Soviet viewers to the British nineteenth century upper classes must however have occurred to the Russians; it was the first Western television series to be purchased by Moscow). The fact that NBC's *Bonanza* has a weekly audience of 350 million makes it a candidate for greater international fame than almost any world leader – and possibly, critics argue, a leading influence on lifestyles.

The Nordenstreng/Varis findings were presented to a seminar in Finland in 1973. It was opened by President Kekonnen with a stirring speech on the imbalance in the flow of communications, emphasising that 'two-thirds of the communication disseminated throughout the world originate in one way or another in the United States,' and the view that no communications are value-free. He quoted the warning of a 1946 US commission on the freedom of the press – a favourite quotation of critics of US media exports, largely because of the supposed shock value of its origin – which had warned: 'There is evidence that a mere quantitative increase in the flow of words and images across national borders may replace ignorance with prejudice and distortion rather than with understanding.' When communications were controlled 'by a small privileged group with control of both power and the channels of influence,' he concluded, 'a so-called free market economy which claims to offer free choice is in no position to point an accusing finger at societies it considers totalitarian.'

Others went further. A Canadian sociologist, Professor Dallas Smythe, charged that 'TV programme content has been developed as an important tool of cultural strategies in the capitalist nations for the expansion and defence of their respective systems as against each other and as against the socialist systems.' Importing TV in the Third World, he said, 'effectively creates outposts within their borders for the exercise of influence in the interest of the countries from which the programmes are obtained.'

Besides giving 'Lucy' a role she never dreamed of, the fallacy of this version of the 'cultural imperialism' thesis is that it relies on a conspiracy theory in which for example:

• RCA, which controls NBC, also holds defence contracts in telecommunications – and is thus uncritical of the US government (and therefore there must be something sinister in NBC's exports of *Dr Kildare*).

• The expansion of US television is part of an effort to subjugate the world to the military/industrial complex, via culture and the commercialisation of the global ethos.

• The proof of intended domination is to be found in the collusion between American industry, American advertis-

ing abroad (the top ten agencies spent $2,800 million in
1975) and American programme exports.
  • These three, together, intentionally subordinate
national interests to the demands of the international
capitalist system – a process which will be completed by
direct satellite television broadcasting.

Such a conspiracy theory not only looks at effects and deduces
intention, but assumes that with such grandiose designs, the
imperialists would field the Second Eleven – the slush diet of
which, precisely, developing countries complain. Most versions
of it produce the extreme examples of dependence on foreign
programmes – Guatemala, for instance – and leave it to be
assumed that the pattern is constant throughout the Third
World. And it fails to explain why so much emphasis should be
put on television as the ideal medium for cultural imperialism,
when it is so little developed in much of the Third World; or
why the populace which absorbs the imports, who are necessarily still largely the elites, should be considered so extremely
gullible.
  But the thesis is attractive to some Third World politicians
and broadcasters; it is more satisfactory as an explanation than
recognising that any alternative policy is going to pose serious
problems, and difficult investment decisions. National policies
for television, which balance culture, entertainment, education
and news, are inevitable. They raise two questions: first
whether home-produced films can be made to look genuinely
different from the highly-professional imported material, and
still attract their audiences; second, whether the effort will go
into rationing imports of foreign products and setting government criteria for the 'appropriateness' of particular kinds of
programme, or whether it will concentrate on building up
competitive national alternatives while adopting a liberal
attitude to imports. A strong current of xenophobia has come
to accompany complaints about 'quality'. A senior Unesco
official told a meeting of journalists in Venice that, as an Arab,
he would prefer to ban even good educational programmes like
Sesame Street than to see the children of his country subverted
by alien cultural values. (A longrunning attempt to 'Arabise'
Sesame Street has in fact run into a snarl of difficulties, not all

of them technical.) The findings of the Varis/Nordenstreng inventory (and these are not at all the authors' conclusions) suggest however that this may be something of a chicken-and-egg approach: the countries which import fewest programmes are generally those which already have the strongest cultural traditions, if those which exercise rigid state control are excluded.

Professor Elihu Katz of the Hebrew University suggests three approaches for policy-makers: imports, he says, are largely a result of the need to fill in time. Therefore countries could decide: a) to broadcast for fewer hours, with better programmes, b) to devote more of the domestic budget to documentaries, which can be done cheaply and outside the studio, and less to expensive studio-based entertainment c) to 'take purchasing seriously' by increasing the staff and status of the purchasing departments 'so that scouting and screening can be done throughout the world, with the smaller distributors as well as the large ones.'

Katz suggests that the third suggestion might appeal to policy-makers; to the extent that they are, in fact, the principal consumers of the international diet, he might be right. But the fears of cultural domination expressed by these policy-makers, and exploited by Marxist writers of West and East to encourage control of the international flow of all media, are rooted often in their own sense of isolation from the 'masses' which their travels and education have produced. The most likely deterrent is the expense of creating a competitive alternative – and the conflict between encouraging trained talent and controlling output. The Indian film industry demonstrates what can be done to provide 'authentic – and wildly escapist – entertainment, while some of its film producers have high international reputations for serious creative work. Hong Kong's *kung fu* films have carved for themselves a special category and a wide following in Paris and other Western cities as well as in Asia. In both countries, except for the period of the State of Emergency in India, the media – entertainment and information alike – are free.

The confusions about the role of television as a medium probably have quite as much effect on the performance of television in the developing countries as any deliberate effort at dominance by outside forces. It is one thing to see communications as the long arm of the transnationals, stretched over the earth to influence patterns of economic development and perpetuate dependence. It is another to decide what autonomy might mean. In the present state of the industry, a policy of import controls would be like shutting the stable door before you have a horse to put in it.

Third World politicans and journalists sometimes warn that the real confrontation will come in the next decade, when the men at the top are no longer those who were largely educated within the colonial system, or in the West itself. They, it is said, will be determined, and able, to break the umbilical cord of history and culture and free their countries from the dependence inherent in the transmission of the ideas, and the values, of their former imperial masters. Insulating peoples from culture, technology and information from outside, sets back the development process and damages the well-being of their countries in the short-term. But some will be persuaded to try the experiment nonetheless, in the convictions that imitation is a recipe for eternal slavery.

Insofar as there is some truth in this estimate, it is closely linked with the widespread doubts in the developing world about the appropriateness of the technological revolution – in industry and also in communications – to their societies. These doubts sometimes vanish in the face of specific projects; and they are uneasily coupled, particularly since the US did a *volte-face* under President Carter and supported the 'basic needs' approach to development, with suspicions that appropriate technology is a Western plot to keep thier economies in a permanent state of technical obsolescence. But the pressure for an 'alternative' and 'authentic' form of development is very strong in the cultural field.

On the infrastructural level, such policies make a lot of sense. A curious unreality creeps into many discussions which promote technological advance as the means of 'solving' the communications gap – even if messages do become much cheaper to send if bounced off a satellite than if pushed through the creaking networks of another era. Satellites will help to free developing countries from the need to channel their news via the old colonial centres. But the realities for newspaper editors and reporters, trying to get copy from rural areas – or to them – are often closer to moving from bush telegraph or rural bus to shortwave radio links. And better communications do not necessarily depend, within countries where they matter vitally, on the sophisticated techniques which smooth the job of foreign correspondents. Nor will the markets justify the high investment required. The sense of exploitation is not based entirely on myth, either; 'it has been estimated,' writes a British researcher, B. R. Webster, 'that twenty per cent of the price which a nation pays for the privilege of having a new technology covers the cost of the research and development' which has gone into it. Fair enough, in market terms, although more generous arrangements ought to cover transfers; but only if the new technology is really needed is it worth the price. The same report continues, '. . . there is a radio in every village in the world – yet grandiose experiments using television via satellites and elaborate video distribution systems are being planned where in some cases duplicated picture books linked to radio programmes would probably be as effective.'

Not that appropriate technology necessarily means the simplest technology: one of the misunderstandings which has commonly arisen is that Western use of the term implies condescension, and a 'second-best' approach. An invention which will revolutionise ideographic languages was reported at the end of 1977. Called Ideo-matic 66, it has been developed by two British lexicographers with the help of one of their son's Meccano set. Seeking a quicker method of completing the Chinese–English dictionary they were preparing, they discovered how to teach a computer to read and write Chinese.

Reporting the discovery in *The Times*, Philip Howard outlined the pre-computer situation: the Chinese alphabet consists of 50,000 characters (a conservative estimate, in fact), and a basic minimum vocabulary would include 4,000 – and still involve adding a high number of variables. 'Chinese compositors still have to select their type manually from massive racks . . . a really proficient typist can achieve only ten characters a minute. . . . It is said that it takes twenty years of assiduous application to become expert in the Chinese telegraphic code.' Although experiments in Taiwan have taken printing slightly further than Howard suggests, results have been only partially effective. What Robert Sloss, Director of the Chinese Language Project at Cambridge, and Peter Nancarrow, a physicist turned patent agent and amateur lexicographer, have done is to work out a grid system for a basic Chinese vocabulary – at this stage, 4,356 characters – and transferred it onto a revolving drum; the effect is to create grid references which a computer can understand and use.

The results: not only will Sloss and Nancarrow's modern Chinese–English dictionary, which they expected to take their lifetimes to produce, be published in 1979 but Cable and Wireless have developed the invention as an Ideographic Encoder and the process is expected to revolutionise everything from printing to the Chinese telegraph system. The computer can also translate, well enough to make them intelligible, articles written in Chinese. And it is of course also applicable to any ideographic language, simply by changing the grid.

But what of cultural 'authenticity', the promotion of which is a major political justification for the adoption of what will most often be intermediate technology rather than the shiniest machinery? Cultural authenticity is, paradoxically, a post-invasion fiction: essentially it implies a comparatist's view of society which itself is a Western concept. Claude Lévi-Strauss has described his journey to a remote tribe, untouched by the finger of 'civilisation'. He met them coming down river. They had decided to give up their unsullied existence and head for a new form of life. He persuaded them to return, and he studied them; but with a melancholy recognition that they had, after all left their settlement once. What was left was to conduct a carefully 'authentic' reconstruction.

There is more than a hint of isolationism running through such talk, too; if 'authenticity' involves giving new impetus to the social, economic and cultural development of a people, how far can governments afford to control the selection of what is absorbed from outside the country? And secondly, does it imply a determined effort to use traditional forms of communication to bridge the gap between rural areas and the cities? Or to get policies across – as puppets are being used, for example, to bring home the family planning message in Indonesia? Alternatively, is 'authenticity' a mask behind which governments can hide, suppressing a plurality of voices in favour of a centrally-based drive to rally support behind a narrow concept of the 'right choice'? This last approach could be self-defeating. Even in advanced societies, audiences are fickle things: just before the 1978 French elections, only four per cent of viewers watched a televised debate on the costs of the *programme commun*; the rest were watching *The Ipcress File* on another channel.

Kofi Awoonor, the Ghanaian novelist, poet and historian, sees 'authenticity' not in terms of 'cultural atavism', but of using the past 'to select the direction in which our culture is going to change,' taking from the past the 'good and beautiful – the way families and social institutions were organised' and avoiding 'what I call the deadly aspects of Western culture – the overwhelming respect for technology. . . . The base culture itself, which is a gift of all human societies, endures. Then the secondary culture, the things you pick up as you go along through history, provide you with the elements which you can use to expand this culture.' But the condition, as Awoonor sees it, is the evolution of a 'humanitarian political system' in which dialogue on these issues is possible. (This interview, one of the clearest expositions of the case for 'authenticity' put in the Western press, was published by one of the arch-priests of 'cultural imperialism', *Newsweek*).

A key question is what can be imposed through the exercise of political will. There are limits to the powers of the media. At the Amsterdam meeting of ILET, Herbert Schiller argued that 'communications either assist and support the totality of political and economic structures; or they change them.' It is a simplistic formulation, and principally because it leaves out the response of the public, who may or may not be won to the cause of changing the system. Another question is connected with the problem of the post-invasion fiction. As soon as you begin to think about 'authenticity', your culture, by that act, is modified; the notion of a return to the ancestral roots – however that notion is qualified by saying that progress will be achieved through the elimination from the national conscious-ness of the alien intervention – is Rousseauesque in spirit, even if Rousseau held no great brief for any collective identity.

Which is not to say that Rousseau's ideas do not hold their

attraction, as a cure for the post-imperial hangover. But their application implies a shrinking of the imaginative fabric, before it can assume a new form. René Grousset describes, in his history of China, how the Ming dynasty foreshadowed the collapse of China's cultures and political vigour. After the Mongol invasions, he argues, China's rulers became obsessed by the determination to restore and then protect the purity of Chinese institutions, as they had existed under the Sung dynasty. They fossilised into a form only broken, centuries later, by fifty years of civil war and revolution. When imperial domination fails, and the Mongol hordes of the AP, UPI and the rest of the international media have been beaten back, how will the restoration of ethnic/national purities fare?

Perhaps in another mode. 'Some of these countries,' observes John Lent, 'look to China as a model, with its heavy dependence upon interpersonal communication (*sic*), use of nearly 20 million cadres, emphasis on local community management of mass media (with its serious dedication to development), unity of communication . . . and the educational system.' But even so, if such a radical model has been 'perfected' in China – and since Lent wrote those lines, the model has been the subject of serious questioning within the country – China cannot serve as a model for the recovery of 'authenticity'. Not merely because of its size and the historical tenacity of its sense of itself; but because that was eventually modified by outside influences. China's modern 'authenticity' is the product of a society revolutionised in the spirit of a nineteenth-century German, Karl Marx, whose thinking was entirely developed in terms of the intellectual traditions and industrial structure of the Europe of his day.

A 'guided' culture is not the same as an 'authentic' one; when the two are forcibly merged through an effort of political will, the result is likely to be a deformation quite as marked, although of a different kind, as anything the conspiracy theorists carry in their philosophical baggage.

CHAPTER 8

Worlds Apart

The Indonesian Assistant Director General of Unesco for Culture and Communications, Makaminan Makagiansar, likes his office. It has, as he says, a view over Paris stretching from the Eiffel Tour to the Sacré Coeur up on Montmartre. And it is a long way from the small island, south of Mindanao, off the Celebes, where he was born. 'You have to think what brought me here,' he says. 'At Harvard, my friends told me I was too nationalistic. I was very nationalistic certainly, and with good reason: the world's recognition of the struggle for independence has brought me this distance.'

So, possibly has a habit of limiting himself to the higher generalities. (One Dutch journalist, hearing Makagiansar at the ILET conference, whispered that he was the perfect product of cultural imperialism – a few centuries of Dutch rule, and he talked just like a Dutch pastor.) But in some senses Makagiansar is the quintessence of the new style of international bureaucrat, and when he talks about 'the new stage we have reached, of using cultural indicators as we once used economic indicators,' he is talking the practical language of the new politics. 'I notice', he says, 'that you use the word danger, when we talk about the use of communications for national ends. It is a Western perspective: you are used to taking argument and confrontation as the root of progress. I might agree, intellectually; but I use the word less. We must, you see, use communications in the context of our historical necessity.'

Western opposition to the principle of 'guided communications' certainly has its blindnesses – nowhere more evident than in the American diplomat's insistence that 'responsibility' is an inadmissable word in connection with the media. It would exaggerate reality, and distort the proper meaning of freedom within society, not to concede that the mass media in the industrialised world have absorbed the private world to some degree into a political whole reflecting certain conformities, some generalised acquiescence. The fact of absorption confers responsibilities; and those who argue for the public's right to know imply that the media convey knowledge – perform, at least in this sense, an educative function. But there are degrees in this process, and they are connected with intent; the history of Western society has also been that of the distancing of the individual from the 'intent' of his rulers, and the press has been a medium therefore for the continuing dialectic between asocial instinct and the ordering processes of government.

The West therefore argues that the existence of a lively and independent press is vital to the shaping of a national middle ground of shared assumptions and openness to change. So, of course, do many governments in the developing world, who use precisely such arguments to insist that the importance of the 'mediating' role of the press requires that it be free – of private influence – and free, also, of the distorting 'sensationalism' of Western-style journalism. Both democracy and freedom have undergone certain redefinitions. The mildest version of this governmental approach was offered by L. K. Advani, India's Minister of Information and Broadcasting in the government formed *after* elections ended the State of Emergency. The adversary role of the press, he said, might be desirable in advanced societies; but in India, the press must be 'watchdogs, educator and social reformer all rolled into one.' At their extreme, these redefinitions equate criticism of political or administrative failures with an attack on national identity. If Westerners are in fact not alone in using the word 'danger', it is because journalists in developing countries – however proudly nationalistic – are aware that in societies where there are one party systems, the press is the only public adversary, the only outlet for debate on national issues.

What serves development? An Iranian journalist, who happens to be a firm supporter of the Shah, describes what he sees as the consequence of the failure to establish there a working public dialogue between governing and governed. Girls, who some years ago were crowding the universities, he says, have not only returned to Islamic dress, but no longer seek higher education in the same numbers. A tiny symptom, he feels, of a failure to develop a modern national language. In his rapidly changing society, archaic institutions – rural, tribal, religious – fail to evolve as rapidly as economic conditions require; and there is inadequate public debate to flesh out the skeleton of the changing order. Without a modern idiom, created out of shared experience, the citizen's choice lies between refuge in the familiar and still-revered traditions, or a break with the past which must adopt an alien language, 'Western' or Marxist. The confining of discussion of policy to 'court circles', he fears, increases the possibility that debate will eventually be forced by violent means. (A year after this prediction, Iran was shaken by unrest in many of its towns and cities; and significantly, the impetus came from conservative religious leaders who stressed the dangers of Westernisation and the value of adherence to Islamic tradition. The authorities castigated the movement as obscurantist and medieval; but responded not with decisions to broaden the possibilities for political debate, but with stern repression by the military.)

Ambiguities exist also at professional level; the same terms are used in mutually incompatible senses. An Asian journalist reports that in his country, 'the press is visualised as part of the social system . . . [it] no longer stands isolated from the other institutions in the community. The press devotes its potential to social progress and the achievement of national goals and aspirations. . . . Any assumption that the press can work independently of the social system of a given country is a fallacy.'

Many Third World journalists would disagree with this formulation, recognising the play on definitions it involves. It is too easy to oscillate from a broad sense of social system, in which the 'adversary role' can find its place, to the restrictive sense of 'system' as a form of government. It may be true that the press cannot work independently of the social system; but on one definition, it can still be independent of government; on the other, it cannot.

When government, in addition, moves from the casual

repression of dissent – the closing of newspapers and silencing of individual journalists – to an active approach to planned communications, the result is almost certainly that the areas of social control are enlarged in the name of the general will. The responsibility to the public, as it is understood in the context of an independent press, becomes 'a responsibility to canalise the will of the people'. And in this way, the 'potential' of the press – as Hedi Nouira, the Prime Minister of Tunisia, has so ably expressed it – becomes 'a weapon to which the developing countries are as entitled to resort as any other countries, in order to strengthen their regimes, defend their independence, increase their influence and ensure the success of their efforts for renovation and development.' The confusion between the uses of the word 'system' is part of the semantics of North–South confrontation; and, at the professional level, it is one of the sources of the growing ideological suspicion of 'Western' assumptions.

What bridges can be constructed between the news industries of the North and the often publicly owned media of the South, in order to counter a political trend which threatens to create a kind of international *apartheid* – a 'separate development' with opposing social rules in which the exchange of information appears likely to be increasingly difficult, increasingly partial? Much can be done in a piecemeal way. In the knowledge that no professional 'solution' will be adequate, but that many of the barriers to the flow of information are still technical and professional. There is at least some common ground in a commitment to the always inexact criteria of professional and intellectual honesty.

In the first place, though, the Western media must wake up to the fact that minor adjustments are inadequate, and that if they want access to developing countries, they must provide clearer evidence that they are seriously interested in what is going on there. This does not mean 'good news' reporting; but less 'spot' coverage, and editorial policies geared to more rounded coverage – and more space. *Le Monde* is one of the very few European daily newspapers with global reputations, together perhaps with the *Financial Times*, to give the space and resources to the consistent analysis of development issues, and to the social as well as the political life of Third World countries.

It does not do so because its editors happen to be inspired by an exceptional missionary zeal, or without recognising the particular problems of reaching the reader which development reporting must raise in an industrialised country. Jacques Sauvageot, the Administrative Director of *Le Monde*, warned at a conference at the Cini Foundation in Venice, in November 1977 that 'the first problem is the limited interest of *any* country's citizen in news which goes beyond the merely parochial; there is for this reason no common, worldwide language.' Nor, he added, can news be seen as an educative process; 'the teacher talks to small groups for a short time; the press to the masses, and constantly.' But the circulation of *Le Monde* has survived pages of detailed discussion of the situation in developing countries; and recent polls have demonstrated that the French public is far more alive to the issues of the North–South dialogue – even if no more prepared than any other Western community to make sacrifices for the sake of a new economic order – than is generally supposed. And a worldwide language urgently needs to be constructed, at least to the extent of enabling the publics in the developing and industrialised countries to understand each other's perspective. *Time* Magazine's coverage of the problem of drought, coinciding with the World Desertification Conference, is an example of what can be done – provided an organisation is prepared to release staff to sift through the mountains of documentation which subjects of this kind produce, and link the problems to concrete situations.

The international agencies are already providing more stories which attempt in-depth coverage of regional problems, and covering international conferences less in terms of Western viewpoints. In a discussion of 'Asian news values', the Indian journalist Pran Chopra argued at a 1977 Unesco meeting that 'most Western agencies which work in Asia give a great deal more of Asian news to their clients than the latter care to use.' (He added that some of the agencies' Western clients made more extensive use of the material than the Asian press.) But there is a limit to the agencies' potential for 'regionalisation', however they restructure their news flows and terminals, because fundamentally they operate for Western audiences and must use the language Western news editors think they can 'market'. What they can add to further efforts to improve their own coverage is greater determination to assist regional and national media to build up their professional competence.

All insist that they are willing to share their technology, that they conduct training assistance schemes, that their offices are never empty of Third World colleagues observing their operations and discussing the development of new agencies or the expansion of their activities. But the big agencies, in particular, reveal few details about the terms on which they transfer technology and offer advice; and in private, most admit that the commercial competition between them – whether they are non-profit-making cooperatives or not – would make the coordination of their activities with each other difficult. They also, like all the Western press, work under the difficulty that the dividing line between cooperation and domination, in the minds of Third World governments and 'partners' from national agencies, is extremely narrow.

Within these limitations, the agencies are often doing more than they are given credit for. They do their image – and the debate – no good by being so secretive about these activities. Reuters, which 'piggy-backs' Agence Zaire Presse's news to 35 % of its embassies, has also trained its journalists in Zaire, put senior staff through courses in London and Paris and provided technical advice. A Reuters man was seconded for two years as director of the school of journalism at Nairobi University, another to train journalists at the (fiercely anti-Western, in public) Libyan news agency. Some twenty-four projects of cooperation along these lines were listed in an internal Reuters document, in Africa and the Arab states alone. Other agencies, including the West German DPA and Italy's ANSA, have similar programmes.

At the back of many Third World complaints about the performance of the Western media, running across a wide range of structures and sociological approaches, is the feeling that the industrialised countries are indifferent to their problems. There is a lot of truth in this allegation. To the question whether the West would be more cooperative on the economic front if their publics were better informed, the answer could at least be given that clearer information would arouse greater concern, creating a market for more news – and that the interactions between the two might lead to a greater development effort. The hypothesis might be worth testing. A senior World Bank official, who was formerly a distinguished journalist, argues that 'the decisions on coverage, even if taken by journalists in an independent system, are essentially political. They should see reporting of the developing countries in terms of of the fact that the breach has been increasing between the organised Third World and the organised industrial societies – and that the North–South conflict is becoming stronger, even, on the political front than the conflicts created by the economic gap between North and South.'

There is a growing recognition of the need for major changes. *The Washington Post* has started a development bureau, including agricultural and economic specialists, and says that it is rubbish to suppose that Third World news can't compete with more local material, that there are a lot of good stories. *The Los Angeles Times* is setting up a bureau for European economic coverage, with emphasis on North–South questions. In the UK, several papers appointed development editors in 1978; *The Guardian* started a Third World news supplement. And there is also more willingness than Third World leaders believe to run news produced by the developing countries themselves. But for this willingness to translate into fact, Western editors insist, the quality of the coverage provided by developing countries has to change. From Italy to the North Cape, they report that the Non-Aligned News Pool has been almost totally unuseable – because it is too full of government speeches and the long, unedited, outpourings of propaganda. They do not demand 'adversary journalism'; but they believe that beyond the government handout lies an area of reporting which is 'public-spirited', but critical and analytic. And they add that news exchanges on a bilateral basis, with agencies such as MENA in Cairo, have been working smoothly.

For these reasons, and because the improvement of professional standards may be hampered by the ideological approach of governments to the role of the press, much coverage of the Third World will still for some time depend on how much access its governments are prepared to give foreign correspondents. It is the deteriorating picture in terms of visas, access to information, harrassment and expulsion which makes for much of the alarm with which the Western press first greeted the creation of the Non-Aligned News Pool. Their alarm is compounded by evidence of the shrinking room for manoeuvre allowed Third World journalists in many countries.

Agence France Presse, for example, reported to the MacBride Commission the difficulties which its correspondents – both foreign and national – encountered in many countries: '. . . the Agency's correspondents all too frequently fail to obtain information, even official information, for lack of sources and contacts.' Too much of what was obtainable, AFP added, was 'purely political . . . and quite inadequate as far as economic and cultural affairs – precisely those which international agencies are taxed with neglecting – are concerned.'

Another basic factor on which international coverage depends is the quality, and focus, of the media in the developing countries – because it is not always recognised what a vital source the national press is for all foreign correspondents. A sampling of Reuters' Africa file, in September 1977, showed that the service was certainly Africa-orientated; but that too much of the news dealt with what the French call 'protocol news' – visits of ministers and the like. Part of the blame may rest with Reuters, part with governments who, as AFP pointed out, make it difficult for journalists to get at economic and social stories – an attitude which is often reflected in the national media of their own countries.

There is enormous distrust on both sides. The political debate at Unesco and in other international forums has been orchestrated by a relatively small number of countries; but this should not be taken to mean that only a few governments are hostile to the methods of working ascribed to the 'Western' press. An example of the new thinking comes from Ethiopia. In February 1978, the ruling Dergue reversed its ban on visas for foreign journalists, to allow eighty-eight of them in to report the war in the Ogaden and the progress of the revolution. It was, reported David Lamb of *The Los Angeles Times*, a conscious effort to put Ethiopia's views across to the outside world. A country at war generally places some restrictions on the activities of foreign correspondents; the Ethiopians, however, went to spectacular lengths. Journalists were forbidden to leave their hotel without an escort, or to take taxis, or to eat in public restaurants. They were told that they must miss no event on their programme, at the risk of being viewed as counter-revolutionary. And in addition to these restrictions - the natural consequence, Lamb thought, of the regime's reservations about the outside world - 'the tone of press week was set by Tamrat Ferede, one of the ruling Dergue's most influential members. In his welcoming remarks ... he asked the journalists to report objectively on Ethiopia – despite their attitudinal inclinations, their prejudices, biases and tendencies to seek out the negative and sensational. But he did not sound very hopeful that they could.' The mass tour produced a huge volume of copy – on the war, on the government's land reform policies *and*, inevitably, on the 'red revolution' which was then openly taking the form of a government-directed reign of 'red terror' against 'dissidents'. Ethiopia undoubtedly had the material, in all this, for a *dossier noir* of clippings 'proving' the truth of Ferede's gloomy view of the international press. The problem is that the whole truth is never the revolutionary truth.

On the other side, journalists – unless retrained in terms of the national ideology – 'distrust the arrogance of power wherever we find it,' as a West German editor remarks. 'And governments have so much of it, that it is natural to us to watch what they do with it.' This is not the same as a conscious hostility to developing countries, but it is often interpreted in this way, and it makes fair reporting progressively more difficult. The editor continues:

In any country we also know that we have to work with the national authorities. What maddens us is that, increasingly, we are not able to work with them, often because of the refusal of petty officials to give us access to the most basic statistics; and then we are blamed for inaccuracy. In this climate, if we give governments a chance to formulate, through Unesco, guidelines for the international press, we shall have had it; and so will any reliable foreign reporting of their countries. There is an urgent need for meetings between journalists, government officials and government information services, to

illuminate the misunderstandings so common in developing countries about the nature of our work.

The same prescription may be required for the internal
relations between government and the press in the Third
World – to persuade governments that better relations with the
press would be in their interest.

Government officials complained, a Western journalist
reported on return from an International Press Institute
training session in Africa, that their national journalists were
incapable of reporting a budget speech; on investigation, he
found that the problem was at least two-sided: the way the
information is presented, the access provided to background
material, affect the quality of coverage.

Two last aspects of the piecemeal approach concern training
and professional debate between North and South. The first
has a long history, some of it highly successful; many of the
training schools in the developing world were started with
private Western assistance (and some are therefore under fire
from 'experts' for acting as Trojan horses for the Western
ethic). Deleon, speaking for Unesco, says that Western organisations should stop thinking in terms of assisting the Third
World; that 'horizontal cooperation' is more appropriate; and
that the job is in any case too large to be carried out by private
organisations. Certainly, not all programmes have worked on
the principle of *encouraging* self-sufficiency, or on the basis of a
clear understanding of the conditions in which journalists in
some countries have to work. A British journalist, Harford
Thomas, reports that when he had finished lecturing a group
of African journalists on the need to get out of their metro-
politan offices and down to the villages, one of the group
turned to him: '*How?*' he asked.

Communications problems of other kinds exist; many
journalists operate without telephones, very few newspapers
have libraries; a large number need machinery and printing
equipment. And, without subscribing to the concept of 'development journalism', their task is distinct from the Western
journalist's – if only because they need to explain to their
readers things which would be assumed, in the West, to be
part of the common background which needed no spelling out.

Professional misunderstandings about, say, the daily operation of the international news agencies on one side, and the pressures faced by Third World journalists on the other could be helped by discussion, not at the level of editors but of 'gatekeepers' – news editors from North and South, who are often the least aware people in the profession about the news values operating outside their own countries or regions. Cooperation on development coverage is possible, but only on the basis of a better mutual understanding: of the criteria for the selection of news, of the problems of reporting processes as well as 'facts'. And with a willingness on both sides to provide the kind of material which fits the other's needs.

Such steps, and many others on the technology and equipment front, together with increased cooperation with Third World journalists to discover and meet their interests and requirements as equal partners, can be useful. But perhaps limitedly so, in terms of improving the quality and quantity of information moving from South to North or within the South itself. The issue has become too politicised for it to be soluble at the professional level; and in terms of the world picture, the forces making for confrontation are stronger than professional goodwill. It is important to define the areas where changes are necessary, to discuss the relevance of the technological revolution to known obstacles to the flow of the news. But the limitations to this approach emerge from the fact that journalists, shut in a room together – and whatever their ideological differences – tend to agree on most points of conflict, make speeches about the freedom of the press, and return to their offices to find that their discoveries make no impact on government or sub-editor, whichever it is they must deal with. Agreement on 'professional' grounds is important because it can help to defuse the tensions which surround the creation of a New Order for Information. But the battleground is essentially political – and it is far wider than the area in which journalists traditionally operate.

Launching his proposal for a Charter of Economic Rights and Duties of States in 1972, President Luis Echeverria of Mexico called for the creation of mandatory agreements, binding on all parties, to protect weak states from exploitation by the

industrial powers. His aim was to 'remove economic cooperation from the realm of goodwill and root it in the field of law.'
The profound distrust of the language and assumptions of
Western liberalism which permeates most political speeches by
Third World leaders in this decade is a key element in the
demand for a new political order. The revolution in the politics
of communications must be assessed in terms of this overall
situation.

The roots of confrontation lie in the bitterness felt by many
governments at the close of the United Nations First Development Decade in 1970. Economic growth in that decade had
added about $200 a year to *per capita* income in the indus-
trialised countries – and nothing, or less than $1 a head, to the
purchasing power of the poor in the developing countries.
Not only had the poverty gap widened, but in their efforts to
attain growth targets, Third World economic and technological
dependence had increased. After ten years of often successful
pursuit of growth measured in GNP terms, the poorest two-
fifths of the world's population was receiving around fifteen
per cent of the total income, and the developing countries'
share of world trade was a mere seventeen per cent.

The central political effects were to create widespread dis-
illusion with 'Western' economic models, mistrust of the
concept of interdependence, and a conviction that the Third
World must pool its ideas and its voting power to obtain a more
equitable share of the cake. Political independence, governments agreed, was a hollow achievement when illiteracy,
malnutrition and unemployment continued to grow in defiance
of national policies. The redistribution of wealth could only
base itself on a real increase in purchasing power; and cooperation from the rich countries must be extracted on terms
which did not tie national development to foreign business
interests.

This newfound unity produced in 1974 the formal demand
for the creation of a New International Economic Order –
which was essentially a demand for better and more equitable
terms, rather than a revolution in economic thinking, although
parallel with it there has been a search for 'alternative' development models. Perhaps because of its economic conservatism,
this essentially political demand united governments with the

most varied (and sometimes mutually hostile) political philosophies, diverse economic needs and different levels of development. The oil price rise of 1973 provided some leverage power against the countries of the industrialised North, and effected far-reaching changes in the international bargaining structure. But the effort of political will predates what the West insists on calling the oil crisis.

Western hostility to the New International Economic Order convinced Third World governments, as serious negotiations revealed how effectively the rich countries could drag their feet over meeting what seemed to them self-evidently just demands for change, of the need to exploit communications to get their viewpoint across to a larger public. Press coverage of the Seventh Special Session of the UN, in 1975, had put the outline and scope of their strategy on the international map. But the forum of the United Nations, as a rule, can produce resolutions and even covenants for the numerical majority more easily than it can assure public awareness of what most developing countries believe to be the critical political evolution of the late twentieth century. The international purpose of the efforts to establish a New Order for Information is therefore based on the need to gain access to the microphone in order to increase the pressures on the industrialised countries. The harder it proves to extract agreement on the economic front, therefore, the more solidly unified the support for a new structure in communications is likely to be.

Political instability in the developing countries is closely related, in the view of many observers, to the persistence of the economic gap. Growth has not only not matched popular expectations, but has conspicuously failed to satisfy basic human needs for food, shelter, and – above all – the jobs on which personal self-sufficiency depends. In the mid-seventies, nearly 300 million in the developing countries were under-employed or totally unemployed, eighty per cent of them in rural areas. The situation of permanent crisis created in many countries by internal economic inequalities, and the growing 'marginality' of up to half their populations, has encouraged more authoritarian political structures and thus contributed to the control of the domestic press. But another factor emerging in the second half of the decade was the growing support for a view which placed economic and collective rights above individual freedoms.

'Developmental journalism' is one element in this approach, which fits naturally with the rejection by most developing countries of parliamentary democracy. On 16 December 1977, at the end of President Carter's first year of 'human rights diplomacy', an overwhelming majority at the United Nations passed resolution 32/130 on 'Alternative approaches ... for improving the effective enjoyment of human rights', calling for a full report from the Commission on Human Rights and deciding to include a debate on the subject on the agenda of the 1978 General Assembly. The resolution redefined human rights to give priority to the following concepts:

- Equal attention and urgent consideration should be given to ... civil and political, and economic, social and cultural rights.
- The full realisation of civil and political rights without the enjoyment of economic, social and cultural rights is impossible ... progress ... is dependent upon sound and effective national and international policies of economic and social development.
- The international community should accord ... priority to ... the massive and flagrant violations of human rights of peoples and persons ... resulting from apartheid, from all forms of racial discrimination, from foreign domination and occupation, from aggression and threats against national sovereignty, national unity and territorial integrity ... [and] the refusal to recognise the fundamental rights of peoples to self-determination and of every nation to the exercise of full sovereignty over its wealth and natural resources.

The predictable conclusion was that: 'The realisation of the new international economic order is an essential element for the effective promotion of human rights and fundamental freedoms and should also be accorded priority.'

It is the classic 'bread before freedom' approach, expressly linked to the North–South dialogue. And, in placing collective rights – including national sovereignty over natural resources – ahead of the civil and political rights (this was the Third

Committee of the UN, which is in principle devoted to the protection of individual rights), the Third World directly confronted Western assumptions about pluralism, choice, and freedom of expression. *Le Monde* reported that 'the Soviet Union manoeuvred skilfully to exploit the distrust of the Third World as to the self-serving motives of the West in supporting human rights. Economic and social rights, which are debated in the General Assembly and in half a dozen other commissions, gained nothing in this exercise.' The main purpose was not, clearly, to upgrade debate on the new economic order – although the opportunity to include references to it was naturally taken – but to make clear the extent to which Western values are minority considerations in the new international political system. It is also an example of the determination of the Third World to advance their cause on all fronts, demanding that all issues be treated as inalienable and inseparable; and it is this which is tightening the links between information and the new economic order. And the passing of this resolution again demonstrated the continued importance of Soviet involvement, as a catalyst for Third World ambitions which match its own political interests.

These interests, it became clear at Stockholm in April 1978, are not coterminous with the more revolutionary aspects of the Third World's bid for an independent voice. The Soviet Union is indeed concerned to combat Western dominance in media technology, and the market appeal of Western news media. But it holds no brief for grand designs to secure genuine independence, economic or cultural, for developing countries. Third World leaders should not have been surprised to have a demonstration, at Stockholm, that the USSR is a thoroughly conservative Great Power or that it can pick up, and drop, Third World causes at will.

The linkage of human rights to the new economic order parallels the wording of another resolution, which put the issue of national communications policies and a New Order for Information onto the UN agenda in 1978. Under it, communications are tied not only to national development but to the active promotion of the International Development Strategy and the new economic order. The same committee which altered the perspective on human rights also, in 1976, called for the consideration 'with appropriate priority' of the issue of Freedom of Information'. UN sources suggested that enormous pressures were likely to be applied to postpone both items until 1979, to avert what many diplomats believed would become a crisis in American – and possibly even Western – relations with the whole UN structure. What was increasingly clear in New York, however, was that communications and the future of the North–South dialogue would dominate the international forum, as interlocking aspects of a process of confrontation between the under-developed majority and the culturally and economically affluent world.

How effective are these pressures likely to be? There is a quality about the resolutions of international organisations, however sharply they cut against the grain of liberalism, which makes them appear far removed from *realpolitik*. The Western countries, and the US public in particular, have tended to ignore the usefulness of these forums for the airing and co-ordinating of new policies by a newly forceful majority. The momentous gravity of the issues at stake have a tendency to be forgotten. The Thirty-third Session of the UN, coming just before the Twentieth General Conference of Unesco, was widely expected to bring together the strands of the new politics too evidently to be ignored, testing the real strength of Third World unity.

Western observers of this process, seeking means to defuse the political element of the North–South confrontation, have suggested that communications should join economic questions for consideration by the international Commission on North–South problems chaired by the former West German Chancellor, Willy Brandt – where the concept of a 'balanced flow' might, they hope, be reworked along the lines of the Helsinki formula of 'free and wider dissemination of information of all kinds'. One of the purposes would be to pre-empt Unesco's role in the international coordination of the New Order for Information, to reduce the governmental emphasis, and to bring down to concrete proposals what has been called the 'shopping-list' approach to fundamental issues of individual liberty.

To the extent that these proposals, which had not in the summer of 1978 acquired governmental support on either side, recognise the interlinked nature of Third World grievances, they had the merit of intellectual realism. But they may have discounted the momentum which had already built up in the supranational organisations. And they implicitly recognised, however, in seeking this means of defusing tension, that the battle between the advocates of an independent press, and those who see communications as an arm of national policy, had passed from the arena of purely professional concern into the centre of international politics.

The debate has reached a critical stage; what is startling is how few people – journalists, politicians or general public – in the West are aware of its existence, or of the potential consequences of continued neglect of the issues. If they continue to concern only a tiny minority, the outcome is likely to be first, that apparent Western attachment to the *status quo* will be represented, by the Soviet Union in particular, as hostility to the legitimate aspirations of the Third World. Secondly that policies will be formulated at the international level which play into the hands of authoritarian governments and increase their control over what the publics of developing countries are permitted to know. Thirdly, that frontiers will close against the exchange of information.

In international meetings, in the months before the UN and Unesco sessions, Western and Third World supporters of free expression were beginning to perceive that the cards were stacked against them far more than they had believed. Information is one piece of a new and stark jigsaw. As the pattern of the jigsaw becomes clearer, the political importance of the battle for information lies in its enormous power to determine the language in which the new world order is to be realised.

Outline Calendar

1955
April: Meeting of heads of state from the Third World, Bandung
1960
January: Meeting of experts on development of communications in Asia, (Unesco), Bangkok
1961
February: Meeting of experts on the development of communications in Latin America (Unesco) Santiago de Chile
September: Ist Non-Aligned Summit, Belgrade
1963
Organisation of African Unity founded
April: Meeting of experts on the development of communications in Africa (Unesco), Tunis
1964
IInd Non-Aligned Summit

Recent developments
1973
September: IVth Non-Aligned Summit, Algiers
1974
July: Meeting of experts on communications policies, Bogotá
October/November: Eighteenth General Conference of Unesco, Paris
1975
February–March: Conference of Arab and African press agencies, Tunis
May: Preparatory meeting on communications of the non-aligned countries, Belgrade
June: Meeting of experts on the development of news exchange in Latin America, Quito

August: Meeting of foreign ministers of the non-aligned countries, Lima

October: Centre International pour le Développement, with Foro Latino Americano, founds ILET (Latin American Institute for Transnational Studies)

1976

March: Tunis symposium on a new international information order

May: ILET symposium on the role of information in the new international order, Mexico City

July: Intergovernmental Conference on Communication Policies, San José

July: Ministerial conference of non-aligned countries on the press agencies pool; New Delhi Declaration

August: Vth Non-Aligned Summit, Colombo

October/November: Nineteenth General Conference of Unesco, Nairobi

1977

January: Meeting of the coordinating committee of the non-aligned countries' news agency pool, Cairo

February–March: Intergovernmental Council for Information of the Non-Aligned Countries meets, Tunis

November: Organisation of African Unity conference on information, Kampala

December: Meeting of experts on development of news agencies and news exchange in Asia, Colombo

December: First meeting of Unesco international commission for the study of communication problems

1978

January: Intergovernmental conference on cultural policies in Latin America and the Caribbean, Bogotá, calls for the harmonisation of policies for culture and communication

April: Second meeting of Unesco International Commission and meeting of news agencies' representatives, Stockholm

April: Meeting of the inter-governmental council for the co-ordination of information of the non-aligned countries, Havana

September: UN 23rd Assembly scheduled to debate communications policies

October–November: Twentieth General Conference of Unesco

1979

January (provisional date): Inter-Governmental meeting on communication policies for Asia, Kuala Lumpur

Bibliographical Notes

Faced with the choice of offering a bibliography which leaves some questions unanswered, or one like a pianola roll, I have opted for the former. In the interest of brevity, I have not listed all the conference papers individually, even where I have drawn on them heavily; it is clear in the text where particular speakers were, and reference to the collections of papers for these conferences will generally produce the text. It does not always exist; some of my material comes from notes made at such meetings.

The literature on communications is enormous; it is an industry which seems to grow in proportion to the shrinking of freedom to communicate. Those interested in finding out what there is on communications in Asia, for example, should refer to John Lent's 700-page bibliography (Temple University, 1975) – an admirable book which also illustrates my point. Basically, this is not a book about communications, or even the study of communications, but about their place in current political developments.

I have grouped books, pamphlets and periodicals together, and given separate sections to conferences (again, a few of them, the most relevant), and to Unesco documents and publications. The Unesco documents are in two sections: general material on communications, and documents dealing with the Draft Declaration on the Use of the Media. I have not divided the bibliographical material by chapters, because cross-reference is an essential feature of the organisation of the book and I wished to avoid duplication.

Books, pamphlets and periodicals

Asiaweek: I have not as a rule listed newspaper and weekly magazine articles, but items in the February, August and December 1976, and the April and October 1977 issues form a kind of whole, giving a consciously Third World angle on the issues. Hong Kong

Bureš, Oldrich (ed): *Towards a New World Information Order* (International Organisation of Journalists, Prague 1977)

Caribbean Quarterly: Mass Media in the Caribbean, Jamaica, December 1976

Cooper, Kent: *Barriers Down: The Story of the News Agency Epoch*, New York, 1942

Cooper, Richard N: 'A New International Economic Order for Mutual Gain', *Foreign Policy* No 26, Spring 1977

Cruise O'Brien, Rita: 'Domination and Dependence in Mass Communication', *IDS Bulletin*, March 1975

Current views on the World Information Order: collection of papers, IoJ, Prague 1977

Centre International pour le Développement: 'Mass Media and North–South Economic Relations' (Report of the Nice Seminar, October 1975). Paris, 1976

Daville, D P: *Main Basse sur Le Figaro*, Paris, 1976

Democratic Journalist, The: Monthly bulletin of the IoJ. See especially No 6, 1977: Ludovick A Ngatara, 'Tanzania forms its own News Agency', Prague

Development Dialogue: Journal of the Dag Hammarskjöld Foundation. Especially Vols 1976:2, 'Information and the new international order'; 1977:1, 'On information and the new international order', 1977:2, 'Towards a theory of rural development'; and the 1975 Dag Hammarskjöld Report: *What Now, Another Development*. Uppsala

Documentation Française, La: Afrique Contemporaine No 94, 'L'Information en Afrique', November–December 1977; *Problèmes Politiques et Sociaux*, 'Vers un "Nouvel Ordre International de L'Information"?' Paris, November 1977

Epstein, Edward J.: *Between Fact and Fiction: The problem of Journalism*, New York, 1967
News from Nowhere: Television and the News, New York, 1973

Evans, Harold: 'The Half-Free Press' in *The Freedom of the Press*, (Granada Guildhall Lectures 1974), London 1974

Fugelsang, Andreas: *The Story of a Seminar in applied communication*, (DHF), Uppsala, 1972

Government of India: White Paper on Misuse of Media During the Internal Emergency, New Delhi, 1977

Grousset, René: *The Rise and Splendour of the Chinese Empire*, London, 1952

Haley, Sir William: Introduction to *The Freedom of the Press*, London 1974

Helsinki: Conference on Security and Cooperation in Europe, Final Act pp 117–120, 1975

Hoggart, Richard: ' The Mass Media: a New Colonialism?', 1978 Standard Telephones and Cables Communications Lecture, London, 1978

L'Information dans les pays non-alignés (Report of Tunis symposium, March 1976), Tunis 1976

Intermedia: Journal of the International Broadcast Institute. Special survey on 'Communications and Research', Vol 3 No 3, London 1975

International Labour Office (ILO): *Employment, Growth and Basic Needs*, (base document for the 1976 World Employment Conference,) Geneva, 1976

IPI Report: Monthly journal of International Press Institute. Note World Press Freedom Review, January 1978. London

IPTC Newsletter No 38, (Report of the Annual Conference of the International Press Telecommunications Council), London, October 1977

International Social Science Journal: 'Towards a New International Economic and Social Order', Vol XXVIII No 4. Unesco, Paris, 1976

Irani, C.: Minute of Dissent, Report of the Committee on News Agencies, India, 1977

Lent, John A.: 'The burnt-out candle; Thailand's brief press freedom 1973–6', *Index on Censorship*, July–August 1977;

'Foreign News in American Media', *Journal of Communication* Vol 27 No 1, Winter 1977;

'Government Policies Reshape Malaysia's Diverse Media', *Journalism Quarterly* Vol 52 No 4, Winter 1975;

'The Guiding Light', *Index on Censorship* September 1977;

'Malaysian Chinese and their Mass Media' *Asian Profile*, August 1974;

'Mass Media in Laos', *Gazette*, Summer 1974;

'Press Freedom in Asia: The Quiet, but Completed, Revolution', Paper prepared for 30th International Congress of Human Sciences in Asia and North Africa, Mexico City 1976;

'The Price of Modernity: Forms of Cultural Dependency' *Journal of Communication*, Vol 25 No 2, 1975.

Masmoudi, Mustapha: 'Le nouvel ordre de l'information el le rôle de la presse dans la promotion du dialogue Euro–Arabe', speech made in Paris, 20/6/77

Ng'Weno, Hilary: 'All freedom is at stake', *The Weekly Review*, Kenya, November 1976

O'Cornesse, Dominique: 'L'Unesco, les Non-Alignés et les Politiques d'Information', *Maghreb-Machrek* No 75, Paris, Spring 1977

Pinch, Edward T.: *The Third World and the Fourth Estate: A Look at the Non-Aligned News Agencies Pool* (mimeographed study), for the 19th Session, Senior Seminar in Foreign Policy, US Department of State, 1976–77

Ploman, Edward (ed): *Vision and Hindsight: the future of Communications.* International Institute of Communications, London, 1977

Read, William H.: *America's Mass Media Merchants*, Baltimore, 1976

Riegel, O. W.: 'Satellite Communication and National Power' in George Gerbner (ed), *Mass Media Policies in Changing Cultures*, New York, 1977

Righter, Rosemary: *IPI: The Undivided Word* (twenty-five-year history of International Press Institute), Zurich, 1976

Rosenblum Mort: 'Reporting from the Third World', *Foreign Affairs*, July 1977

Satellite Communications, issue on 'Communication Satellite Systems of the World', October 1977

Schiller, Herbert I.: *Communication and Cultural Domination*, New York, 1976;
Mass Communication and American Empire, New York, 1969;
The Mind Managers, Boston, 1973;
'Transnational Media and national development', in Jim Richstad (ed): *New Perspectives in International Communication*, Hawaii, 1977;
'Now, a New International Information Order?', *Mass Media*, April 1977
'Decolonization of Information: Efforts towards a New International Order', in *Latin American Perspectives*, Winter 1978;

Smith, Anthony: *Subsidies and the Press in Europe* (Political and Economic Planning, Vol XLIII No 569), London, 1977

Sussman, Leonard R.: *Mass News Media and the Third World Challenge* (Washington Papers Series), London, 1977

Tunisia, Secretariat of State for Information: *The New World Order for Information*, Tunis, 1977

Tinbergen, Jan (ed): *Reshaping the International Order*, (Report for the Club of Rome), Netherlands, 1975

Thirty Years of the International Organisation of Journalists, 1946–76, Prague, 1976

Thomas, Harford: *Reporting on Development*, (IPI), London, 1978

Bibliographical Notes

Towards a New International Order (Report of the 7th (joint) session of the Club of Rome and of Pacem in Maribus, October 1976, Algiers, 1976

Transition towards a new international order (Journal of the Centre International pour le Développement) Vols for 1977, Paris

Tunstall, Jeremy: *The Media are American. Anglo-American Media in the World*, London, 1977. (I am particularly indebted to Professor Tunstall's book for the quotations from Charles Dickens and Alexis de Tocqueville in Chapter 3; I have, however, made a very different use of them from his.)

Whale, John: *The Politics of the Media*, London, 1977

UNESCO: Documents on communications policies

A complete and fairly frequently updated bibliography is provided by the Secretariat, running to more than 300 closely printed pages of reference and cross-reference. It gives some idea of the scale of paperwork in the field, and usefully includes reference to many works prepared outside Unesco, and available in its archives. The 'availability' varies, however, for non-members of the Secretariat; the 'limited' and 'restricted' classifications cover a large number of the documents in the archives, and the degree of cooperation from guardians of such documents also fluctuates. The catalogue (CC77/ WS/12 and COM–76/WS/20 are the references for 1977's editions) states that 'documents published by Unesco will be provided on request so far as our stocks permit'. Stocks are, however, a problem – not the least of which is the impossibility of ascertaining whether the problem is the stock, or reluctance to release the document in question. And many of the important documents for any researcher are not, of course, 'published'.

In spite of an unspoken but active policy which appears to be against the free flow of information of any kind, there are individuals within the Unesco Secretariat who clearly wish it were otherwise, and who have gone out of their way to make documents available. To a number of these individuals, I am greatly indebted; it would be encouraging to report that they were to be found in the Press Room, where even speeches made by the Director-General on his 1977 trip to India were not available. Others have made available copies of such documents – the naive would have expected them to be on general distribution – as the crucial Medium-Term Plan 1977–82, and the printed Resolutions of the Nineteenth General Conference, as well as more provisional and 'in-house' papers.

What appears below is only an outline guide to some of the

documents on which I have drawn in the chapter on Unesco, and to general assessments of the changing climate in the politics of the media business. I have taken 1970 as the starting point, because it was to the 1970 General Conference of Unesco (the Sixteenth) that the then Director General, René Maheu, presented in general terms his new strategy for communications directed at the content of information, rather than the techniques for communication. This is generally accepted within knowledgeable Unesco circles as the watershed: it also provides evidence of the extent to which Unesco has taken a lead in the formation of a 'new order for information'.

1970: 16C/4: Long-term outline plan for 1971–1976 presented by the Director-General (Paris, 11/9/1970)

1971: COM/MD/20 Proposals for an international programme of communication research (Paris, 10/9/71)

1972: COM/MD/24: Report of the Meeting of Experts on Communication Policies and Planning, Paris, July 1972 (Paris, 1/12/72)

17C/98 and annexe: Unesco General Conference, 17th Session, 1972. Report of Programme Commission IV (communication) with recommendations; general conference paper including considerations of programme and budget and medium-term plan for 1973–8 covering the communication sector.

Resolution 4.111 at this General Conference approved the Declaration of Guiding Principles on the use of Satellite Broadcasting for the Free Flow of Information, the Spread of Education and Greater Cultural Exchange. To trace the history of this Declaration in Unesco, it is necessary to go back to the 14th General Conference in 1966: but 17C/76 (Paris, 21/7/72) gives a run through the background as far back as 1962, when the General Conference first authorised the Director-General to study possible consequences of communication by satellite.

1973: COM/MD/29 Report of the meeting on Management and Planning of New Communication Systems, Paris, October 1973 (Paris, 28/3/74)

1974: COM.74/Conf. 617/4: Report of the Meeting of Experts on Communication Policies in Latin America, Bogotá, July 1974 (Paris, 4 October 1974 – this document has been totally withdrawn from the archives.)

18th General Conference:

18C/90: Suggestions to member states on measures to promote the free flow of information and international exchanges (Paris, 20/9/74)

18C/COM/3/Corr: General debate on communication programme (16/11/74)

18C/123: Report of Commission IV (communication) (20/11/74)

18C/INF.19: Closing address by Madadou Mahtar M'Bow, Director-General (29/11/74)

18C/SHC/DR.2: Resolution concerning the protection of cultural property in Jerusalem

18C/122: Report of Commission III (20/11/74)

1974: 19C/3: UNESCO 1974, Report of the Director-General, (Paris, 1975)

COM–75/CONF. 63/4: Final Report: Meeting of Experts on the Development of News Exchange in Latin America, Quito, June 1975 (Paris, 12/8/75; document withdrawn from Paris archives)

1976: SHC–76/CONF.621: Meeting of Experts on Interpretations of Experience by and through the Mass Media (Paris, March 1976)

COM–76/LACCOM/1 and 3: Provisional agenda, and Secretariat's Working Paper and Annotated Agenda, for the Inter-Governmental Conference on Communication Policies in Latin America and the Caribbean, San José, July 1976

COM/MD/38: Final Report of the Meeting, (Paris, October 1976)

COM.76/Conf.613/3: Report of the Meeting of Experts on Communication Policies and Planning in Asia, Philippines, October 1976 (Paris, 21/10/76)

Internal documents: Present programme and research studies and publications in 1977/78. 'Introduction to an New Information Order' by Gunnar Naesselund, June 1976. 'The concept of a new international information order initiated among the non-aligned countries': historical resumé, with list of non-aligned 'aims and actions' and the extent to which they link with Unesco's 1977–82 Medium Term Plan

19th General Conference, Nairobi:

19C/4 Medium-Term Plan (1977–1982) (Approved version published Paris, 1977)

19C/5: Draft Programme and Budget for 1977/8

19C/27: Draft Recommendation on Action to ensure that the people at large have free, democratic access to culture and participate actively in the cultural life of society (Paris, 6/8/76)

19C/93: Report on means of enabling active participation in the communication process and analysis of the right to communicate (Paris, 16/8/76)

19C/106: Report by the Director-General on the Inter-Governmental Conference on Communication Policies in Latin America and the Caribbean, San José, 1976

Records of the General Conference 19th Session, Nairobi, 26 October – 30 November 1976, Vol 1: *Resolutions*

1977: SS–77/Conf.201/1: Working paper for March 1978 Meeting of Government Representatives to Prepare a Draft Declaration on Race and Racial Prejudice; plus Report on April 1977 Meeting of Experts and Draft Declaration with Explanatory Report (Paris, 18/8/77)

CC/77/Conf.606: Numbered base papers for Meeting of Experts on the Development of News Agencies and News Exchanges in Asia, Colombo, 5–9 December. (The most useful for this study was Pran Chopra's 'Asian News Values').

Unpublished: Recommendations of the Meeting.

1977/8: International Commission for the Study of Communication Problems: Working Papers prepared for the Commission, Nos 1–9; includes opening statements on 14 December of the Director-General of Unesco and of the Chairman of the Commission, Sean MacBride. Other papers are:

1. Membership and biographies of Commission Members
2. Origin and Mandate
3. Methods of Work
6. A glimpse into Communications Statistics
8. From Freedom of Information to the Free Flow of Information; from the Free Flow of Information to the Free and Balanced Flow of Information
9. Communication: What do we know?
11. The World of News Agencies
12. News Agencies Multilateral Cooperation
13. Monographs I (AFP, ANSA, AP, APS, AZaP, Bernama)
14. Monographs II (CANA, DPA, GNA, INA, IPS, Kyodo, Latin)
15. Monographs III (MENA, Prensa Latina, Reuters, Tanjug, TASS, UPI)
16. Collaboration between news agencies in Nordic countries
17. A national policy for balance and freedom of information
18. An approach to the study of transnational news media in a pluralistic world

(Paris, December 77 – April 78; unpublished).

1978: Work Plans for Communications Division of Unesco, 1978–79 (unpublished provisional draft, January 1978).

CC/78/ASIOCON/1: Agenda for Kuala Lumpur Inter-Governmental Conference on Communications Policies for Asia, scheduled for 1978 (Paris, 5/1/78)

Agenda for April Stockholm meeting of International Commission for the Study of Communications Problems (unpublished).

UNITED NATIONS: resolutions etc on information

1976: 31st Session Resolution 31/139: 'Cooperation and assistance in the application and improvement of mass communications for social progress and development'. Adopted without vote (and with minimal discussion) on 16 December, this is the first official presentation of the Third World governments' evolving position on information. Presented to the Third Committee, the resolution requested the Director-General of Unesco to report to the 33rd Session of the UN (in 1978) on 'progress achieved in the development of mass communication systems'. (A preparation of a survey covering the last 15 years was set under way in Unesco as a result, for production in 1978.)

1977: 32nd Session 32/L.47: Resolution on the Application of the Declaration on the reinforcement of International Security (introduced by nine non-aligned countries); in its preamble, it refers to 'the necessity for an objective flow of information' and to 'the role and responsibility of the mass media in this respect, thus contributing to the reinforcement of confidence and friendly relations between States'. This Resolution is referred to in the Unesco Draft Declaration, in paragraph 13 of the new Preamble. 32/130: Resolution on Alternative approaches and ways and means within the United Nations system for improving the effective enjoyment of human rights and fundamental freedoms; voted (123–15) on 16 December by the Third Committee of the UN. Makes human rights 'dependent upon sound and effective national and international policies of economic and social development'.

UNESCO: Documents on the Draft Declaration on the Fundamental Principles Governing the Use of the Media in Strengthening Peace and International Understanding and in Combating War Propaganda, Racism and Apartheid

The history of this Draft Declaration, the third version of which was due to be presented to the 20th General Conference of Unesco in October/November 1978, dates in documentary form to the 1970 (16th) General Conference, under its Resolution 4.301. It is an aspect of this book which least lends itself to fleshing out with resolutions and other documentary evidence; these are very insubstantial shadows of the political pressures behind the formulation even of the first resolution. It was Resolution 4.113(3) of the 17th General Conference, in 1972, which first made a formal demand for a Declaration; subsequent meetings stem from that original request. But a reading of the published or in-house Unesco documents gives little impression of the politics of the Declaration, even where (as in March 1974) the Secretariat's hand is clearly seen in toughening reports of meetings and texts of the Draft. For a sense of the way in which this issue awakened the Western press to what was occurring in Unesco (as, perhaps, for a sense of the way in which it has subsequently been blinded to far-reaching aspects of Unesco's general communications policies by its concentration on this one issue) it is important to read the press clippings of the 1976/77 period. I have been extremely grateful to a number of persons, in Unesco and outside, who have participated in the meetings so thinly reported in officialese, and who have been willing to discuss the issue in the light of their experience.

As a result of the 1972 Conference Resolution, the following papers report subsequent events:

1974: COM–74/Conf. 616/3, 3 add, 4 and 5: Meeting of Experts Concerning the Role of the Mass Media (etc): Text of a Draft Declaration prepared for Unesco by Dr Hilding Eek; Comments on the Draft by Bogden Osolnik and J. Bourquin; Draft Report and Final Report on Meeting of Experts (Paris, papers dating from January to April 1974)

General Conference of Unesco, 18th Session:

18C/35: Text of Draft Declaration submitted by the Director-General

18C/COM (Drs. 1–11): Proposed amendments submitted to the General Conference

18C/Resolution 4.113: Proposal that the text be referred back to an Inter-governmental Meeting of Experts for consideration

18C/90: Report on Unesco's activities including the 'free flow of information' issue which was by now closely associated with the Draft Declaration

1975: After this referral back by the General Conference, there is an apparently extraordinary, but genuine, gap until the Inter-Governmental Meeting of Experts to Prepare a Draft Declaration was convened in Paris from 15–22 December 1975.

COM–75/Conf. 201/1: Provisional agenda (Paris, 16/7/75)

COM–75/Conf. 201/3: Texts of a Draft Declaration and amendments composed at the 18th General Conference

COM–75/Conf. 201/4: Background Report by Unesco Secretariat (the 'Eek Report')

COM–75/Conf. 201/Drs. 1–26: Fresh amendments, submitted to the December meeting (Paris, 16/12/75)

COM–75/Conf. 201/5: Draft report of the meeting (Paris, 16/12/75)

COM–75/Conf. 201/Inf. 4–9: Letters announcing formal withdrawal from the meeting, from Australia, Canada, Israel, the US and Italy (on behalf of the EEC countries).

(*Independent source:* Report of the US Delegation, submitted to the US Secretary of State, 2 February 1976.)

1976: 19C/91: Text of Draft Declaration as revised by the December 1975 meeting, presented to the General Conference as Item 69 of the Agenda by the Director-General.

19C/Resolution 4.143: refers the draft back to the Director-General, with instructions to hold consultations with a view to reaching the broadest possible agreement on a new text. (19C/PLEN/Dr. 20, 27/11/76).

1977: On 9 September, a proposal for a revised text was circulated, on a 'confidential' basis, to around 150 people from concerned institutions, and also to the governments which had been members of the Drafting and Negotiating Group at the 1976 General Conference. This text had in fact been arrived at during a 'technical' drafting session in Unesco in July, by consultants representing the Soviet bloc, the Western press and the Third World – and with active participation by a large corpus of Unesco staff. It is nonetheless known as the 'September Draft'. It was followed by extensive 'consultation tours', carried out by the consultants, by members of the Unesco staff, and by personal advisers to some of the top Unesco executives. Confidential reports on the reactions of those consulted were delivered by the emissaries to the Secretariat in December 1977, when a further drafting session took place from 17–22 December. The new draft was not, however, sent to the Director-General until mid-February, 1978.

UNESCO: Selected Publications

A comprehensive run through the catalogue of Unesco's formal publications, while not as formidable as the list of documents, would take up pages without being particularly helpful for a general reader. Nor have I read through the publications of the early decades of Unesco's existence, since my concern has been chiefly with current trends. The classic exposition of Unesco's approach to communications in these years is well-known through Wilbur Schramm's *Mass Media and National Development* (Unesco, 1964), and the temptations of expensive educational toys appear in his 1968 book, *Communications Satellites for Education, Science and Culture*. But although Unesco produced a certain amount of theoretical material during the 1950's and 1960's, its more typical output during this period was the statistical survey produced in its editions of *World Communications* (of which the most up-to-date, 5th, edition was published in 1975). There is also some useful material on training of journalists, technical needs and the physical problems of communications.

What follows is a highly selective list of publications, produced this decade, which are either worth reading in themselves, or because they provide clues as to the evolution of Unesco's attitude to communications as a 'total approach'.

Unesco Courier: Monthly magazine published by Unesco in sixteen languages. The relevant issues are October 1976: 'The Search for a New World Economic Order'; and April 1977: 'A world debate on information: flood-tide or balanced Flow'?

Getting the Message Across (Paris, 1975): A collection of essays arising out of meetings held in collaboration with the International Social Science Council and the International Council of Philosophy and Humanistic Sciences. It contains an excellent paper by Y. V. Lakshmana Rao on 'Information flow from advanced to developing countries'.

Moving towards change (Paris, 1976). Subtitled 'Some thoughts on the new international economic order', this book was edited under the close personal direction of the Director-General, Amadou Mahtar M'Bow, who drew on the reports of a 'panel of counsellors' which he set up soon after assuming office to consider Unesco's role in the current world situation, and on analyses independently prepared by the Unesco Secretariat. Directed towards the United Nations, and to member states, it was intended to be a key paper setting out Unesco's approach to 'action to promote development'; it is crucial evidence in assessing the Director General's strategy towards communications, and the evolution of Unesco's political stance.

Race as News (Paris, 1974). Prepared for Unesco by the Centre for Mass Communication Research, University of Leicester, this .book is an uneasy combination of theoretical essay (by Professor James D. Halloran, the Director of the Centre, it moves from a discussion of the problems of racial prejudice in reporting, to a questioning of the 'socio-economic system' under which the Western press functions), essays more closely linked to the subject of the title, and a survey of selected British newspapers' handling of race reporting. Good for the sense of the *zeitgeist*; Unesco disclaims responsibility for the content with even more than its usual caution as publisher.

Suicide ou survie? Les défis de l'an 2000 (Paris, 1977). The first in a series of publications on 'great issues of our time', inspired by a *Table Ronde* of the best and the brightest, this publication rarely descends from Olympus. It does so, however, in a contribution by Sean MacBride, which should concern all those interested in the outcome of the Unesco international commission on the problems of communication, which he heads, and which contains a strong plea for Unesco to concern itself with the right to freedom of information in the context of the pressures on the press from multinational and economic interests. An earlier Round Table, held in June 1976 and grouping many of the same participants, dealt with 'Cultural and Intellectual Cooperation on the New World Economic Order'; abbreviated transcriptions of the discussions were published in *Cultures*, Vol III No 4 (Unesco, Paris, 1976).

Communication Policies Series
A series of country reports on the present state of communications and the government's approach to them, published by Unesco and written by nationals of the countries concerned. The geographical range is enormous, and carefully representative; the books are generally informative, although not always free of an ideological approach. Intended to make comparative study of the situation in different countries (Peru and Sweden, for example) possible, the series is part of a programme of analysis of communication policies approved at the 16th General Conference of Unesco in 1970. A dozen or so were in existence at the end of 1977, with more in the pipeline.

Reports and Papers on Mass Communications
Around sixty of these booklets on communications have been published by Unesco since 1956. Their quality is uneven. Some of the earlier, most specific reports on training, experiments with educational radio and other problems are unfortunately out of print. Some, particularly among recent publications, are longer on theory than on commonsense; some are written in the impenetrable language of the communications expert. But taken together, they are basic to any understanding of Unesco's research programme and also can sometimes be a source of useful information on the subject at hand. It is undoubtedly malicious to imagine that this dividend is almost incidental to the general purpose of the series.

Among those on which I have drawn most (for different reasons) are:

No 59: Mass Media in Society: the Need of Research (1970: this was the working document for the 1969 Montreal Conference which marked a watershed in Unesco's approach to its research programme.)

No 70: Television Traffic – a one-way street? (1974: This booklet combines the results of the study by Kaarle Nordenstreng and Tapio Varis on the content and flow of television programmes, with papers from a seminar in Finland at which the study was presented.)

No 74: National Communication Systems: Some policy issues and options (1975: written by Lloyd Sommerlad, then Chief of the Communications Research and Policies Division of Unesco, and posted to Kuala Lumpur in 1977 to take charge of preparations for the 1979 Inter-Governmental Conference on Communications in Asia, the successor to the Costa Rica Conference of 1976.)

No 75: Access: Technology and Access to Communications Media (1975: by R. Webster, it contains some reflections on appropriate technology and some discussion of practical problems.)

No 77: Cross-Cultural Broadcasting (1976: prepared by researchers at the Institute of Communication Research, Stanford, it is a good resumé of what we do not know about the subject.)

No 78: Planning for Satellite Broadcasting: The Indian Instructional TV Experiment (1976: an informative, and sometimes hilarious account of the gaps between theory and practice which the experiment brought out; a well-written warning to pure theorists.)

No 81: External Radio Broadcasting and international understanding (1977: Some useful statistics, not all of them related to Yugoslavia, are provided by Tomo Martelanc and others at the Ljubljana Centre for Public Opinion and Mass Communication Research, in a study which illustrates the difficulty of trying to codify news-flow and content, and puts some of the fears about cross-cultural television broadcasting in perspective.)

Conferences and institutional papers (general)

The number of conferences on the role of the press in the new order for information, in development and in the formulation of government policy, grows steadily. Serious conference-goers can have little time for other pursuits. I have listed here some which produced papers or discussions particularly valuable for the writing of this book. I am much indebted to the Secretariat of State for Information of Tunisia, and to the Secretary of State, Mustapha Masmoudi, for a mass of documentation on ten governmental and professional non-aligned conferences which I should otherwise have had difficulty in obtaining, and which has been extremely helpful. Anong the most valuable collections of conference papers was that prepared for the Edward R. Murrow Center's conference, in May 1977, on 'The Third World and Press Freedom'. The documentation for the ILET conference held in Amsterdam in September 1977 also provides useful insights into ILET's perspectives on the situation of the media. Useful papers were also presented and discussed at the 1977 and 1978 General Assemblies of the International Press Institute and the Commonwealth Press Union's 1977 Conference.

I have listed the majority of the important non-aligned conferences in the Appendix. The reports from these meetings are important for an understanding of the evolution of the non-aligned position, and of the extent to which ideas held at first by a very small number of countries' leaders have spread since 1973, when the IVth Non-Aligned Summit first gave its attention to the politics of communications. The bibliographical guide below does not list the major political meetings, but includes some of the semi-professional seminars held at the initiative of Third World countries.

1975

February–March, Tunis: Reports and papers from the Conference of African and Arab News Agencies (Tunis, 1975)

September, Cologne: Papers from the annual conference of the International Broadcast Institute – 'The Global Context for the Formation of Domestic Communication Policy' (London, 1975)

September, New York: Seventh Special Session of the United Nations. Dag Hammarskjöld Foundation Seminar for Third World Journalists (*Development Dialogue*, Uppsala, 1976, Vol 1; Uppsala, 1976)

1976

March, Tunis: Report of the International Symposium on Developing Information in the Non-Aligned Countries (Tunis, 1976)

May, Mexico City: ILET Seminar on The Role of Information in the New International Economic Order (supported by the Dag Hammarskjöld Foundation and the Government of the Netherlands. Reports available from ILET, and major papers reprinted in *Development Dialogue*, 1976 Vol 2)

October, Nice: Report of the Seminar on World Public Information and the New International Economic Order organised by the

Centre International pour le Développement (Paris, 1976)

November, Tunis: Arabo–European Conference of New Agencies Directors; Reports and Speeches published by Tunis Afrique Presse, 1976

1977

April, Florence: Colloquium organised by the Office of Public Information of Unesco on The Free and Balanced flow of Information between Developed and Developing Countries – working papers prepared by Unesco but rejected by the conference; no official report, but unpublished resumé circulated by OPI–Unesco (Paris)

May, New York: Conference held by the Edward R. Murrow Center of the Fletcher School of Law and Diplomacy, Tufts University, on The Third World and Press Freedom: Papers prepared for the Conference to be published in 1978, New York.

June, Oslo: IPI General Conference. Unpublished papers on session on Cultural Imperialism and the Media, plus reports in *IPI Report*, July/August and September issues, (London, 1977)

July, Manila: OPI–Unesco Asian Seminar for Journalists: No report published, but material drawn from private reports and from the speech of the Philippines Secretary of Public Information, Francisco S. Tatad and from the papers given by Lloyd Sommerlad of Unesco and by other officials and participants

September, Amsterdam: Papers (unpublished) prepared for the ILET Conference on International Communications and Third World Participation; A Conceptual and Practical Framework. Report under preparation for circulation in 1978, (Mexico City)

October, Tunis: United Nations (Office of Public Information) Colloqium to mark World Information Day, on Public Attitudes in the Developed Countries towards the New International Economic Order. No official report, but papers prepared for the conference available on request (New York, United Nations)

October, Sarajevo: Papers and working documents from the Conference of Representatives of Radio and TV of the Non-Aligned Countries (International Press Centre, Belgrade)

November, Venice: Unpublished conference papers prepared for the Cini Foundation's IVth International Conference on Information Problems – on New Perspectives in North–South Communication

1978

January–February, West Berlin: Aspen Institute Conference on A New Look at International Communication Policy – no written papers, but report of meeting in *IPI Report*, February 1978

March, Canberra: International Press Institute General Assembly: reports in April and May issues of *IPI Report*, including major conference papers. Particularly important is Sean MacBride's keynote address on The Right to Information.

April, Cairo: Second Edward R. Murrow Center conference (co-sponsored by the Faculty of Mass Communications, Cairo University, and the Middle East News Agency); reports prepared for the conference include Bert Cowlan and Lee M. Love, 'A Look at the World's Radio News', and Wilbur Schramm *et al.*, 'International News Wires and Third World News in Asia'.

April, Stockholm: International Seminar on the Infrastructure of News Collection and Dissemination, organized by the Swedish government and Unesco for the benefit of the MacBride Commission. Unpublished summaries available in Unesco Secretariat. For papers, see above.

I have drawn on a number of individual unpublished papers, sent to me by their authors or by colleagues. They include the speech of the Prime Minister of India, Morarji Desai, to the November 1977 IPI Seminar in New Delhi, and the paper given by Amithaba Chowdhury to the Salk conference on the future held in the US in September 1977, on 'Media Values: Some Thoughts on the News Scene in Asia' (unpublished). Interviews with journalists and politicians, particularly in the Third World, have also produced much of the material in the book.

In addition, the major international news agencies – Reuters, the AP, UPI and the AFP – have provided information, some of it on a confidential and 'background' basis, some of it more formal. In New York, I talked to a wide range of staff in both the American agencies, both at executive and at reporting levels, and was able to observe the treatment of copy in the news rooms. The directors of the Middle East News Agency and the Agence Tunis Afrique Presse have both given their time to talk about the professional and political problems of national agencies in the Third World, and the difficulties and opportunities which cooperation with other national agencies presents.

Index